LANDRY'S LAST STAND
A Fading Dynasty, A Miracle Season & Tom Landry's Last Chance To Save America's Team

Ryan Bush

Copyright © 2018 Ryan Bush

Ryan Bush Publishing

First Edition - All rights reserved.

ISBN-10: **0-9979823-2-2** ISBN-13: **978-0-9979823-2-9**

Ryan Bush Publishing

490 E. Cougar Lane

China Spring, Texas 76633

Web Site - Dallas Cowboys Vault at RyanBush.biz
Facebook Pages:
Dallas Cowboys Vault
Decade of Futility
Dallas Cowboys Dirty Dozen
Dallas Cowboys Landry's Last Stand
Twitter - @rcbushCowboys

CONTENTS

	Acknowledgments	vii
	Introduction	9
	Part One / THE SALE	
1	THE MEETING	17
2	THE VALLEY OF THE SOUL	24
3	TEX'S DILEMMA	39
4	THE BAD GUY	50
5	THE FINAL COUP	63
6	IN THE CROSSHAIRS	79
	Part Two / THE SEASON	
7	THE LONG ROAD TO BUFFALO	94
8	THE HOPEFUL & NEEDY	118
9	DALLIANCE WITH DUTY	128
10	MAKING AN IMPRESSION	139
11	THE LONGSHOT	147
12	THE FIRST MILE	155
13	THE HOLDOUT	162
14	HELLO AGAIN, GOODBYE FOREVER	172
15	THE GREAT BIRTHDAY BASH	180
16	THE GREAT UNEXPECTED	195

17	HOME COOKING	222
18	THE BATTLE OF TEXAS	235
19	TEST OF ENDURANCE	252
20	SLAYING THE STEEL DRAGON	266
21	WINDS OF OPPORTUNITY	275
22	THE GREAT FALLOUT	287
23	SHOW OF CHARACTER	301
24	THE GAME OF THE YEAR	311
25	THE PERFECT REBOUND	324
26	THE NO-SHOWS	337
27	THE UNEXPLAINABLE	345
28	HEROES	357

Part Three / THE TAKEOVER

29	A SHIFT IN TACTICS	372
30	THE END	379
	EPILOGUE - A FINAL WORD	390
	BIBLIOGRAPHY	394
	ABOUT THE AUTHOR	398

ACKNOWLEDGMENTS

Some projects need a helping hand. Others need two or three. *Landry's Last Stand*, I like to think, required a whole army of helpers to see it through to the end. There's no use denying the fact that I've been blessed to have many positive influences aid me throughout the long writing process of this book. To them I will always be grateful.

Thanks to the Lord for a calming spirit of patience.

Thanks to Daddy for believing when I couldn't.

Thanks to Mama for caring when I didn't.

Thanks to Sterling for putting up with me on the long, hard days.

Thanks to Brent Bankston for coming through with more research material than I could have asked for.

Thanks to the staff at the Baylor library for putting up with my countless questions about one obscure topic after another.

And it would be grossly remiss of me to not say a word of thanks to the many writers whose work I came across while researching this book. Long before I ever became a writer, I was a reader. You all constantly remind me why: Randy Galloway, Blackie Sherrod, Frank Luksa, Skip Bayless, Steve Perkins, Mike Rabun, Carlton Stowers, David Casstevens, Denne Freeman, Paul Domowitch, Jarrett Bell, Verne Lundquist, Steve Pate, Ron Spain, Dave Klein, Tom Uhler, Ron Durham, Patsy Leftwich, John Anders, Dan Barreiro, Cathy Harasta, Tim Cowlishaw, Sam Blair, Mark McDonald, Bob St. John, Barry Horn, Gary Myers, Brad Sham, Harless Wade, Jane Wolfe, John Madden, Joseph Grant, Paul Zimmerman, Hubert Mizell, Rick Telander, and Joel Buchsbaum.

INTRODUCTION

The footfall of a national monument sounded down the long sloping corridor, a nearly indistinguishable echo reviving with each step taken, until finally this walking pillar of football sophistication made his way out of the shadows of the hallway and onto an artificially manicured stage. The lights were still dimmed, the cameras yet unmanned, and a seating capacity of more than 60,000 remained spare of nearly all patrons. It was a moment of welcome that could be comprehended only by shared experience.

Hot to the touch, dripping with the sweat of a thousand summers, venerable Texas Stadium closed its ever-loving arms around Thomas Wade Landry in an unforgivably humid embrace. It was the evening of September 9, 1985 within a quaint open-air arena in Irving, Texas, a time and a place intermixed with the peculiar combination of sultriness and anticipation. The only head coach the Dallas Cowboys had ever known had just walked out of the tunnel and was now pacing the green carpeted field in a slow, ponderous stroll in and among the dozens of Cowboy players who were lined up in neat rows performing their routine stretching.

Landry's eyes told of an intense focus, moving impassively over the group of faces with a steely and almost impersonal gaze. In his chiseled chin and set jaw were all the indications of strength, confidence, and determination. Landry's brow told of the unforgiving terror of a Texas summer sun, as the 60-year old coach could be intermittently seen wiping beads of sweat from it with the palm of his hand.

Yes, it was hot. Hot enough to fry an egg on a seat, hot enough even for Landry to shed his customary suit jacket in favor of a short-sleeved white shirt. Even with the sun preparing to set in the western sky, the temperature outside was still an uncomfortably warm 101-degrees. Down on the playing surface, underneath the hole in the stadium's half-finished roof, it felt more like 120-degrees, giving the stadium the feel of a well-tended furnace.

Back and forth he roamed, arms folded, a monument adorned with the graceful crown of endurance. In a profession that chewed up and spit out coaches with brutal precision, Landry was less than two hours away from beginning his twenty-sixth season on the Dallas sideline in riveting style – a primetime showdown on national television against the Washington Redskins. The rivalry was an old one, but the hour in Landry's football life was decidedly new, providing him with an unusual backdrop for what had become a very familiar occasion.

For so long the leader and captain of a thriving NFL dynasty, Landry now found himself caught in the midst of a complicated rebuilding process that demanded his team remain simultaneously competitive. Whether it was in the bleachers or in the press, the expectations inherent with ten NFC Championship Game appearances in thirteen seasons from 1970-82 had officially been severed, making Landry – for the first time during his tenure - the head coach of an aging, fading roster. No longer did the city dream of another push to the Super Bowl, or point to a group of up-and-coming rookies as franchise saviors. Instead, they murmured about lackluster performances, uninspiring holdouts, and suspicious decisions by the Cowboys' sideline general.

Landry had been in the business far too long to be more than momentarily bothered by the moods of sportswriters or fans. It had been established long before by some wise prophet of old that the majority of the bleacher bums and the press pens cared only about wins and losses, and comprehended but little of the inner-workings of a football team. Consequently, the many magazine articles and the incessant water-cooler talk indicating his imminent demise Landry could brush off with an indifferent tribute to the emotions of the misinformed and the unintelligible.

Of a far more serious nature than any of these common displays of discontent were the dark clouds of misgiving emanating from the Cowboys' front-office. Though imperceptible to the public eye, Landry's long-standing position of autonomy in Dallas was now under attack from the office of none other than Texas E. Schramm, the Cowboys' general manager, whose operational tactics in recent months had been guided by a newfound principle of impatience. A franchise fixture since its inception in 1960, Schramm's dogged determination to turn the team's fortunes around had revealed a meddlesome side that witnessed him encroaching upon Landry's own turf. Several weeks after the Cowboys had concluded their 1984 campaign by losing consecutive games that left them on the outside of the postseason for the first time in a decade, Schramm had attempted an uncharacteristic power move by venturing to force Landry to alter his coaching staff. Only a well-timed excuse from the head coach prevented Schramm's efforts from being rendered a success.

It had been but a small victory for Landry, his analytical mind perceiving a much more imposing figure in the background that made Schramm's intrusion far less of a personal affront than it at first appeared. Landry had but stalled the wheels of organizational adjustment that was surely to come, provoked by the caustic perspective of the Cowboys' new owner, H.R. "Bum" Bright.

Bright's purchase of the team from a dying Clint Murchison Jr. during the spring of 1984 had been received with all the pomp and ceremony identifiable with a passing of the torch. But the honeymoon period didn't last very long, as Bright's sharp business mind was soon overshadowed by a tempestuous personality and an inflexible demand for results on the football field.

Despite what many newspaper clippings indicated, Bright's very presence as owner had changed the working dynamics of the Cowboys establishment, putting members of a long-standing hierarchy in an uncomfortable position that only grew more so as the pressure to succeed increased. That Schramm should so boldly poke and prod in the area of Landry's own coaching staff was a testament to the change that was sweeping throughout the organization. Schramm was not the same because the Cowboys were no longer the same. The Cowboys were not the same because their new owner spoke a far different language than the one that had pervaded the team's office for the better part of a quarter-century.

Caught in the middle of this behind-the-scenes drama was

Landry, a man trying to hold onto the controls of the franchise's most visible aspect – the team itself. By staving off Schramm's advancement, Landry had managed to maintain control for the time being. But how long would it last?

Were the world aware then of the many shadows that hung suspended over Landry's sweat-streaked figure as he roamed the grounds of Texas Stadium in contemplation of yet another season and another meeting with the Redskins, they would have emphatically declared him a beaten man and on the fast track to unemployment. His team, they said, was too old. His intellect, they feared, was failing him. Without support from the top, Landry was as good as finished.

In retrospect, such a judgment would have been deemed foolhardy, because there was to be no whimper from Landry or the Cowboys on that night against the Washington Redskins. Instead of an ending, the Cowboys shocked a national television audience by assembling the pieces for one final beginning. It was a prelude not of Super Bowl destiny, but of a season that would be forever distinguished by Landry's finest coaching job and his final playoff team in Dallas.

It was the beginning of Tom Landry's last stand.

Landry's Last Stand

Ryan Bush

PART I

THE SALE

CHAPTER 1

THE MEETING

"Sooner or later everyone sits down to a banquet of consequences."
Robert Louis Stevenson

    Far from the warmth of memories dear and the bright sunlight of public adulation, a valley conveniently shielded by the passing years lies in the shadows of a monument-crested ridge. As deep as the wound of false hope, as barren as the branch of failure, as far-reaching as a decade that knew no end to disappointment, this valley houses the unwhispered, unwanted secrets that first plagued, then buried one of America's iconic football empires.

    The common soul of man finds no comfort in the heartless whistling wind that blows cold upon this land, rustling restless branches with a sharp, heedless tongue. For beneath the soft-laying sand that is ever shifting with the winds can be found particles of this bygone age, relics from a brief moment in time when Clinkscale, Downs, and Rafferty were household names. A faded, weather-worn sign here reads "Thurman's Thieves." A little digging over there reveals a fedora. And nestled under the protective arms of an aging, drooping pine can be found a half-filled bottle of Scotch keeping company with a shattered trophy case.

Even today, eerie echoes can still be heard walking the pathways of this gorge, unaccountable reverberations that haunt these dormant surroundings which have long been forsaken in the pursuit of happiness. Within this land of regret, there is no ear to hear the many tales which the Dallas Cowboys of the 1980s told, nor eye to see the inner workings that led to their eventual demise. The fan in the stands, the sportswriters, and the committed historians all disappeared when the walls of the Dallas dynasty at last came crumbling down, ashamed at such an exhibition of mortality.

Were the curious traveler of today to steal an upward glance toward the ridge, he would find three monuments in radiant sunlight, gazing back over their most brilliant years of work when the Cowboys rose from the dust of an expansion project to win Super Bowls in 1971 and 1977. Each one, Tom Landry, Tex Schramm, and Gil Brandt, played an integral part in creating the mystique of a franchise that eventually became dubbed "America's Team," and stands tall even today as the three front-office figureheads who gracefully and innovatively made the blue-and-white star into an international brand.

But upon further inspection, there is evidence of a fourth pillar having once stood alongside these football giants, the remains of which can be found piled loosely in a scattered litter of rubble in a lonely corner of the valley below, near a voluminous - but now empty - cash vault. Many an old-timer has pondered the uncertain demise of this once-great man named Clint, who abruptly disappeared from society in the early 1980s and died in seeming ignominy. And though they may have offered guesses that brushed close to the truth of what went down in Dallas, nothing could have ever prepared them for the earth-shaking end that it truly was.

To understand this scene is to pull up a chair of contemplation and pay heed to a wind that whispers a winding tale of individually-crafted misfortune, intermixed with the deflective forces of corporate consequence. It's an eerie discourse of long forgotten facts which narrates the climax of a brilliant business career, the resulting demise of his most treasured asset, and the creation of a deep, dark valley that Cowboy fans could never quite forgive, nor forget.

The mechanical gate that swung inward to admit entrance offered a scene of warm, pleasant memories within. Cold with concern, the man behind the wheel noted the ethereal canvas now before him, yet could not bring himself to crack even the faintest of smiles. His foot pressed on the accelerator with anxious aplomb, propelling the car slowly down the driveway, his 62-year old face as impassively sorrowful as an empty woodbox on a white winter's morning.

The month was March of the year 1983, and all around Texas E. Schramm were bold indications that spring, in all its glory, had arrived in north Texas. And yet, to cast even a cursory glance upon this 25-acre estate, Schramm would have to wonder if it had ever left in the first place. Yes, even after all these years, the grounds of 6200 Forest Lane looked exactly as Schramm had remembered them. Plush green lawns. Artistically-trimmed hedges. Strategically-positioned oak trees. And lining the long private drive were thousands of tulips, with a two-mile row of azaleas dancing in attendance.

At another time, on another day, Schramm might have gleaned a sense of comfort from these picture-perfect surroundings. But, if the feeling in his gut proved to be accurate, this was not to be a day for toasts or sentimental reminiscing. Schramm's forehead was creased with foreboding, his jowls drooping from a burdensome anticipation of unpleasant business ahead.

As the president and general manager of the National Football League's Dallas Cowboys franchise, "Tex," as he was known around town, was well acquainted with difficult decisions. He was also in a position privy to every move there was to be made. And, at the moment, Schramm knew better than most that the Cowboys were staring at unforeseen crossroads.

The sting of a third consecutive NFC Championship Game defeat was just beginning to subside around the city of Dallas, and Schramm was looking forward to the challenge of getting his team over the proverbial hump and back into the Big Game.

There had been a time when playing in the Super Bowl was a commonplace event for the Cowboys, a franchise that participated in pro football's ultimate championship game on five separate occasions during the 1970s, winning twice. But with the turning of the decade came a turning of their luck, as the Cowboys stumbled on the doorstep time and again, their cause for defeat deep-rooted in a rolling ball of misfortune and distrust that grew larger and larger with each disappointment.

The 1982 season had not been a pleasant one for the Cowboys, despite the fact that they enjoyed so much success on the playing field. The players strike in September had led to a lot of finger-pointing on the team, something that lasted all the way through the final playoff game versus the Washington Redskins, a 31-17 loss that left the Dallas locker room conspicuously divided.

So while pundits and fans were engrossed with spring training box scores and a looming pennant chase, Schramm and head coach Tom Landry were busy working on a plan that would not only change the tenor of the locker room, but dramatically alter the direction and outlook of the franchise. The Cowboys, he hoped, were about to be exciting and dominant again, all at the same time.

Not that Schramm was really expecting any of these topics to come up in conversation on this particular morning. It was not often that Schramm received an invitation to his employer's mansion for a weekend meeting. The fact that one had been suddenly dropped upon him earlier in the week had made Schramm wary of some unknown doom awaiting him around the next bend.

The winding trail led him to a conspicuous clearing, where Schramm pulled up in front of a massive limestone structure. To be completely accurate, the sprawling mansion did not glisten as it once had, but was nevertheless an impressive structure, if for no other reason than its gargantuan size. The 43,500 square-foot horseshoe-shaped castle belonged to the boss. And when the boss called, Tex was a man who jumped.

The house's interior was everything that an average person wouldn't have expected it to be. Large-screen television sets, stereo components, and dozens of electronic gadgets peeked at visitors from behind hand-finished walnut paneling. There was a mammoth swimming pool for friends and guests to cool off in, and another smaller private pool just off the master bedroom. The bar looked to be an ordinary one, but was distinguished by an electronic drink machine operated by a button near a shining row of spigots.

Tex was ushered past all of this and into an office, a spacious, orderly sanctum with confines that could easily house a family of four. It was there Tex met Clint. For Tex, Clint Murchison Jr. was a man of comparable age and incomparable wealth. For decades, his family name had been revered throughout American business circles for being full of money-making schemes. For today, though, Clint was just full of bad news.

A conspicuously short man with a personality often suspected of being sheltered behind an owlish expression and an omnipresent pair of black-rimmed spectacles, Murchison was prone to use humor when delivering messages among friends and close acquaintances. But not today. Today, he was somber, his beady eyes burning into Schramm's, earnestly, emotionally, sincerely. After months of putting it off with one excuse after another, Murchison was now confronting the hardest decision that he had ever been forced to make. It was tearing him apart on the inside. He only hoped it wouldn't tear the Cowboys apart with him.

The gravity of the situation was not lost upon either of the men in the room. It had only been a few months since Murchison had moved his corporate headquarters into the same office building as the Cowboys. Had he wanted to deliver an everyday directive to Schramm he could have availed himself of the opportunity on any weekday. There could be only one reason that Murchison required a private weekend conference inside the walls of his secluded castle.

Not one for making small talk, Murchison immediately got down to the business at hand, inviting Schramm to take a seat and turn an ear. With Schramm comfortably ensconced, Murchison was, at last, free to state his peace. Beginning with his failing health, which had recently been rendered terminal by doctors, Murchison detailed the physical descent which would soon leave him first inarticulate, and ultimately speechless. He was already becoming increasingly reliant upon a wheelchair to get around. Soon, he would not even be able to travel with the team to away games. Due to this degenerate condition, Clint was adamant in his belief that it would be in the best interest of everyone associated with the Cowboys for Tex to find a buyer for the team as soon as possible.

Whatever news Tex was expecting, this certainly wasn't it. Of course, Tex had heard rumblings through the grapevine about Clint's health issues. Who around Dallas had not? Tex had even experienced these firsthand on a recent return flight after a Cowboys victory, when Clint's speech was noticeably slurred. Many had thought this was due to a drinking problem. Come to find out, it was something far more serious. But to sell the team? This was something that Schramm could not have anticipated in a million years. Schramm had never given it a thought that anybody other than Murchison would own the Cowboys. Why would he, when Murchison was one of the wealthiest men in America?

The thought may have occurred to Schramm that Murchison was overreacting to what was certainly an emotionally disturbing infirmity. Murchison had never been a very active owner as it was, choosing always to hang back and remain invisible in the shadows. He didn't make speeches. He didn't have a radio show. He didn't seek interview time in the postgame locker room. Clint didn't burn the midnight oil with the Cowboys coaching staff, or pore over scouting printouts in lieu of the draft. Why, he didn't even attend the owners meetings, having delegated that duty – and inherent authority – to Schramm. If not for his preference to ride first-class on the team charter to all road games, it is doubtful whether his own players would have been able to pick out the Cowboys' owner from a crowd.

But any ideas Schramm may have been entertaining of attempting to talk him out of such a momentous decision were effectively squashed under the weight of the next disturbing revelation. Murchison, who for so long had played the role of king and caretaker to one of America's largest financial empires, was now a walking piece of dead meat that creditors chased like starving vultures. After a lifetime of wealth, Murchison was officially and undoubtedly broke, his pool of money having finally evaporated under the glare of numerous bad investments. Like the cagey businessman that he was, Schramm could clearly see that his boss's mind was made up. And nobody in their right mind tried to talk Clint Murchison Jr. out of something he felt convicted of.

So with simple understanding and sympathy Schramm shook hands, walked back to his car, and drove away back down the long driveway and through the gate, his mind intent on the new mission which had been unexpectedly laid in his lap. Left behind, hunched over at the desk, Clint Murchison Jr. pondered what was left of his own life. He did not smile at the thought.

Clint, you see, knew better than even Schramm the momentous impact selling the Cowboys would have upon his own life. More than merely a sad goodbye, Clint Murchison Jr. was saying forever and ever farewell. To friends. To a team. And to every dream that had ever come true.

CHAPTER 2

THE VALLEY OF THE SOUL

"Men like Murchison don't come along too often."
Dallas Morning News **columnist John Anders**

A fly on the wall would have sworn that Clint Murchison Jr. was having second thoughts about this professional football business. For a fleeting moment in time, George Halas would have likely concurred with such a sentiment. Murchison was but a simple step away from finding himself at his long-awaited destination; inside the prestigious ring of NFL ownership. Yet the look on his face clearly indicated grave concern, if not complete discomfiture. Might the wheels of his mind be suddenly running in reverse, searching for an escape?

The year was 1959, and Clint had already been assured behind closed doors that he would be awarded the National Football League's new Dallas franchise, which would begin operations the following season. But this conversation with George Halas was certainly an eye-opener for the prospective owner.

Murchison had flown to Chicago to visit with the

owner/head coach of the Bears, who was only too willing to inform Murchison of what to expect in the coming months. Having watched Murchison's desperate, yet futile, attempts to purchase an NFL franchise over the last couple of years, Halas knew the man across from him to be in earnest. Yet, Clint Jr. was like all newcomers to professional sports; eager and idealistic. Halas was there to bring him down to earth with a strong dose of reality.

The discussion was long, serious, and covered a variety of topics, before Halas finally got around to mentioning the price Murchison would possibly pay for the new franchise.

"He asked me what I had in mind and I told him something in the neighborhood of $50,000," recalled Murchison. "He leaned back in his chair and said the league was thinking more in terms of two and one-half million dollars."

Murchison's face grew grave for a moment or two. He pursed his lips, as he was wont to do when faced with a dour situation. What happened next caught Halas completely off guard.

"I sat there for a second or two," Murchison said, "then stood up, grabbed my heart like I was having a heart attack, and fell to the floor."

Halas remained speechless for just a moment, uncertain of what to do next. Should he phone for a team of paramedics? Should he give first-aid?

Only when Murchison rose from the floor wearing a devilish grin did Halas finally relax. Smiling in spite of himself, Halas knew in that same instant that getting to know Clint Murchison Jr. was going to be quite the experience, even if it was to be a journey steeped in abrupt complexity.

The blood of a Texas family is thicker than branch water, flowing toward a destination as staid as the sweat of tradition. Rolling, chuckling, trickling indifferently over the common stones of age, gender and status, this most sacred tie that binds a clan together will inevitably find its way into a pool of ultimate pronouncement that weighs the actions of each individual life with all the merciless authority of a courtroom gavel. Though striving high, though going far, there is no avoiding this final feast of consequences. Blood, they do say, will always tell in the end. This truth acknowledged the world 'round is especially applicable in the Lone Star State, where ambitious dreamers are prone to push, prod, and brag their way into wealth, caring not a penny's worth for what lays trampled behind them.

For Clint Murchison Jr., a man born to a pedestal of financial prominence, it was just such an unexpected confrontation with an invisible lambasting menace during the autumn of life that transformed him from an aging wheeler-and-dealer to a broken, dying derelict. After decades of chasing business deals into the darkest corners of the globe and basking in the carefree creativity of self-indulgence, the specter of repercussions finally came home to roost, laying waste to an empire and haunting Murchison's last years with a perpetual scene of destruction.

This fall of the Murchison Brothers' kingdom into bankruptcy during the early 1980s was a familiar tune to countless other Texas businessmen who endured a similar fate under the weight of a lifeless economy. Yet it strikes a distinct note within the annals of American history for its direct link to the equally devastating collapse of Clint's most celebrated invention.

Clint was a second-generation businessman with a chip on his shoulder so burdensome as to make it imperative that he be remembered differently than as a mere chip off the old block. But this was easier said than done. For Clint Jr. to distinguish himself apart from his father would take some doing.

More than just another cagey millionaire at the top of the corporate chain, Clint Sr. was a perfect example of the proverbial Texan pulling himself up by his own bootstraps to scale the highest mountain. A veteran of World War I, Clint Sr. returned to his hometown of Athens, Texas after serving as a lieutenant in the Army to begin working as a bank teller. A few years and more than a few investments later saw Murchison making millions in the Texas oil fields. By the late fifties, his was recognized as one of the seventy richest families in America.

To be a Murchison was to be a gambler, and nobody rolled the dice in quite the manner of Big Clint. As befitting his position as patriarch of the family empire, Clint Sr. knew how to play the game both ways. He could be a careful planner one minute, while the next an insouciant plunger. This latter trait was something that Clint Sr. was especially proud of. From the very beginning, the Murchison blueprint for success was founded on the premise of borrowing to the maximum.

"The only time I ever lost in a deal was when I used my own money," Clint Sr. once quipped. "When you start using your own money, you start thinking you can do anything. Cash makes a man careless."

This renegade approach would have been impractical for the multi-million-dollar undertakings that he specialized in were it not for an uncanny eye for opportunity. Whether it was in the field of energy, real estate or construction, Clint Sr. had an instinct for making money that was the stuff of legends. Consequently, he was allowed to think, dream, and plan outside normal business parameters without the worry of being denied the required financing.

A reputation for striking it big preceded Clint Sr. wherever he went, allowing him to extend his plans and ventures to the borders of the limitless. In the business marketplace of America, the name of Murchison was as good as gold, a simple handshake serving as an invaluable promise and assurance for hesitant creditors. It moved deals through doors that, to others, would have been closed or – at the very least – slow in opening. A wink, a nod, and the dotted line was signed. This was the way of the Murchison family for over fifty years. It worked on the prairies of Texas. It worked on the busy streets of New York City. It worked all over the world.

But a bag of money can be a harsh taskmaster, especially when pride becomes intermixed. For all of the big strikes and notable success stories following them, all was not cozy at the

Murchison office. Profits were pouring in by the millions, and Clint Jr. was suffering from a severe case of professional discomfiture.

Clint Jr. had harbored such high hopes for the business his father had given him and his brother John to run. Murchison Brothers was supposed to be, not only a part of his inheritance, but a means to establish himself in economic forums throughout the nation. You see, Clint Jr. thought a lot of his name. He thought a lot of himself too.

And why not? Clint Jr. had achieved the highest grade-point average ever at Lawrenceville prep school in New Jersey. He was the head of his class at MIT, and graduated from Duke University Phi Betta Kappa with a degree in electrical engineering. Clint Jr. was, practically speaking, a genius. Being smart, though, wasn't enough to nurture a sense of accomplishment or inner stability. Clint Jr. had never been forced to pinch pennies like millions of other children coming out of the Depression. He was always the smartest and the richest kid in his class, with plenty of food on the dinner table each night. From an outsider's view, Clint Jr. had everything that one could desire.

But inwardly, Clint Jr. always felt like he was missing out on something. His mother, Anne, and brother, Burk, both died when he was young, leaving him longing for attention from a father who was nearby, yet constantly busy with friends, associates and business dealings. The scars that tragedy and circumstance left him healed slowly over time, yet not quickly enough to prevent Clint Jr. from turning inward when dealing with future disappointment.

Clint Jr. always felt slighted by the fact that John Dabney flew more than fifty missions as a pilot in World War II, while he was turned away from the combat field due to his superior intelligence and wound up enrolling in the V-12 program at Duke University. John was lauded afterwards for being something of a hero, while Clint lurked and listened in the shadows, inwardly chafing at the hand fate had dealt him. Being brainy had cost him the chance to be named among the nation's bold.

The business world proved to be equally unfair to him, as

Clint Jr. found himself in a perpetual shadow that he could not outrun. No matter how hard he tried, no matter how many business deals he pushed through, he always felt as if he was being treated like the junior partner in the firm. Wherever he traveled, Clint Jr. found his father's name to be preceding him. To outdo his wheeling-and-dealing father became Clint Jr's guiding principle of existence. He never paused long enough to consider if such a motivation was unnatural, if not simply unnecessary. He had a dream, and that was the important thing.

To dream upon a star is a way of life in Texas that transcends age, gender and status. As long as the heavens are high and there is room to reach upwards toward the clouds, the Texan will strive forward toward accomplishment, even if, as in the case of Clint Jr., it was toward his own demise.

The longer he carried this burden, the more daring and reckless Clint Jr. became, sinking millions into deals in a desperate attempt to, not only prove himself an equal to his father, but as his unquestioned superior. Along the way he became careless about investment risks and details, and equally indifferent toward his own company's board of advisors, establishing himself instead as an uncontrollable maverick.

"The more you told him something couldn't work," recalled one of Clint Jr's close friends, "the more he was going to prove to you that it could."

Sometimes this strategy worked. There were other times when it did not. Once, Clint Jr. plunged into a residential deal that his father thought a smart operator could make a million dollars on. When the final card was played, Clint Jr. was discovered to have lost half a million.

Another time, after Clint Jr. had lost a large amount of money on a deal, Clint Sr. gave his son a noisy lecture in the office:

"There's nothing wrong with losing money. You expect that to happen at times when you're investing, but we've got experts on all these subjects all over the country." Then raising his voice, "The trouble with you is that you don't check with any of them."

Clint Jr. could console himself after such a scolding because he was only emulating the style that Clint Sr. had employed for so long. Clint Sr. was well known around the Murchison's offices for going rogue and completely ignoring whatever alternative plans his advisors may have offered him. But the critical difference between father and son was in their ability to decipher between human relationships and business.

For decades it had been family custom to hand off the management duties of a new business to a trustworthy someone. Occasionally, Clint Sr's good faith came back to bite him, but very infrequently. And when a business venture appeared to be turning sour, Clint Sr. wasn't one to waste time bemoaning his misfortune – he would get out of a deal or sell his stock without stopping to give it a second thought.

Conversely, Clint Jr. would often pick friends or acquaintances to run his companies, many of whom didn't even have the necessary qualifications to do so. In the common event that profits were minimal or altogether non-existent for these companies, Clint Jr. would then cling to the hope that a run of good luck was just around the next corner. His loyalty and a stubborn belief in himself would not allow him to fire anyone, or even to simply cut his losses on the project.

As a result, Clint's side of Murchison Brothers struggled far more than it should have, though John's frugal and more conservative investments continued to prevent the company from living in the red as the 1970's neared a close. But by then, Clint Jr. had ascended to that untouchable pedestal in the public limelight. He had found the destiny his heart had so longed for. Ironically, it was in this particular venture that Clint Jr. surrounded himself with the right people.

Clint Jr. first met Tex Schramm in the fall of 1959. Clint Jr. was on the lookout for a general manager to run the professional football franchise the NFL had promised would be his in the city of Dallas.

Clint Jr. had been actively trying to purchase an NFL team for several years, but after being left at the altar on more than one occasion, he decided that buying an expansion team was probably going to be his best chance to get a chunk of the action.

Clint Sr. had often chided his son for trying to get his hooks into pro football, citing it as little more than a high-powered cash-vacuum. It was true that professional football was not exactly a money-making industry during the 1950s, but Clint Jr. had a hunch that television was the perfect tool to change all of that. And even if it didn't, Clint Jr. didn't see the harm in having a little fun. It wasn't like the expenses of a football team were going to break the Murchison budget.

It wasn't very long before he was awarded a team for Dallas and his search for a hands-on front-office figurehead then began. Schramm had been suggested as a likely candidate, and a meeting was soon arranged.

It was during this first sit-down that Schramm laid out his philosophy on how a football organization should operate, stressing the necessity of a clear line of authority. Said Schramm:

"The only person the players should be responsible to is the coach and the only person the coach should be responsible to is the general manager, and so on up and down the line."

Schramm was obviously anxious to avoid the drama of a meddlesome owner, something he had experienced a few years before when he was the general manager of the Los Angeles Rams.

Clint couldn't have been more enthused at gleaning a portion of Schramm's vision for the new team. This mode of operation was, Clint assured him, the exact same philosophy which the entire Murchison family used back at their empire headquarters. Explained Clint: "Get the best men for the job and let them run the show."

A man who allegedly took advice from no one not only listened to every word from Schramm, but eventually agreed to abide by them. Ten days after their first meeting, Clint shook hands with Tex. The deal was sealed.

It wasn't long after that when Clint got goose bumps upon hearing Schramm's choice to become the head coach for the new Dallas franchise. Tom Landry was someone who Clint could appreciate, in some ways even relate to. Indeed, Landry was a rare specimen.

After ten seasons as a player and assistant coach with the New York Giants, Landry was renowned up and down the eastern seaboard as a certified football intellectual of 36 years, often guilty of being the smartest coach in the room and on the field. A wizard while at the blackboard with a piece of chalk, Landry was only a few years removed from having invented his own defensive formation, the 4-3 defense, which was quickly copied by the rest of the NFL. A stickler for detail and a faithful servant to the complex fundamentals of the game, Landry was so prepared and so knowledgeable of his craft that he was rumored to be able to anticipate an offensive play even while blindfolded.

While in New York, Landry and the Giants had participated in three of the previous four league championship games, winning in 1956 in a 47-7 rout of Chicago. Along the way, Landry's unit had attained a standard of dominance that made defense the trendy thing in the Big Apple, where Giants fans were regularly seen giving a standing ovation following a defensive stop.

In Landry, Clint Jr. thought he detected a bit of an Einstein, a genius whose intellect had been restricted in New York as a mere defensive coordinator. Everyone he talked to on the matter – whether it was Chicago Bears head coach George Halas or NFL commissioner Bert Bell - had no doubts about the fact that Landry had a complete grasp about both offense and defense, and was more than qualified to be an NFL head coach. Signing off on the hiring of Landry was one of the easiest decisions that Clint Jr. would ever make as owner. It would also qualify as one of his most important.

Clint Jr. didn't realize it at the time, but Tom and Tex were a match made in football heaven, their individual strengths and idiosyncrasies perfectly suited for their new roles with the newly-christened Dallas Cowboys. Landry was a coach with exacting principles and ideology relating to the construction of a roster. He could spell out for Schramm exactly the type of players he was looking for, no matter the position.

Schramm, in turn, had enough imagination to take Landry's detailed information and do something with it. In an age when teams weren't able to spend an abundance of money on scouting, Schramm turned the Cowboys offices into a hub for oddball ad campaigns, birthday wishes and other forms of gimmickry, all with the intent of obtaining information on college players. Height. Weight. 40-yard dash time. Individual statistics. All of it.

When not running the personnel department, Schramm's genius for marketing was on vivid display. His invention of the blue-bellied star was the perfect touch for a team striving for respect, a can't-miss symbol of authority that would one day be recognized as the most popular logo in the league. The addition of silver helmets and pants a few years later proved to be the finishing touches for the suddenly sleek Dallas Cowboys.

There was an unspoken acknowledgment from near and afar of the many built-in challenges that awaited the new franchise. Landry would be working with what amounted to a short-handed roster for several years before he and Schramm would be able to fill the many holes with adequate draft selections. Their home stadium – the famed Cotton Bowl – would be practically empty for some time as well, as fans were either disgusted with the product on the field or more interested in supporting the efforts of Dallas' other pro football team, the AFL's Texans who also played at the Cotton Bowl.

Without a doubt, it was destined to be an uphill battle to get the Cowboys even to the realm of respectability. But football insiders also realized that Schramm and Landry working together had the potential to take an expansion doormat such as the Cowboys and transform them into an NFL giant. All they needed was some time.

Clint gave them that time, and was rewarded with something he had never imagined obtaining for himself in the realm of professional football. In buying the Cowboys and then allowing them to grow from dust to dynasty, Clint had inadvertently accomplished in the sports arena what he had originally set out to do in the business world. Clint's association as majority owner of the world-famous world champion Cowboys franchise afforded him a position in the world spotlight as the model businessman of his time.

He not only had more than enough cash to carry his team through the lean years, but also the perfect temperament to allow the experts to do their job. For a what-have-you-done-for-me-lately world looking on, Clint Jr's resume was suddenly more impressive than not only all of those snooty Rockefellers from the northeast, but even his elder namesake from Texas, Clint Sr.

A destiny that would have emotionally overwhelmed a

lesser man was treated much like an inevitability by Clint Jr. After all, why shouldn't America's marquee businessman be the owner of America's marquee football franchise? This, surely, was an unavoidable fate for Clint Jr.

And suddenly, football had become more than just a game. Football had become more than just fun. Football was allowing Clint Jr. to enjoy a privileged existence that the corporate arena never afforded him.

It was the Cowboys that distinguished Clint Jr. from his dad. It was the Cowboys that allowed him to come out from Clint Sr's long shadow.

Without the Cowboys, Clint Jr. was just a stuffy second-generation businessman who rode the coat-tails of his father's genius. Because of the Cowboys, Clint Jr. was a celebrity and a mystical front-office figure with America's Team. This was one wave of fortune and popularity that Clint Jr. envisioned himself riding for many years to come.

It was through this curious combination of genius, cash and luck with the Cowboys that he had finally alighted upon his precious pot of gold at the end of the rainbow. His demise, as it turned out, was not nearly as complicated.

The sorrows of tomorrow are fashioned by the mistakes of today. After so long doing things his own way, Clint Jr. was of the opinion that he was above even this axiom. Come to find out, his tomorrow had simply been years in the making. Even while on top of the world, he was a reckless man destined for a head-on collision with a wrecking-ball.

Some men don't know how to hold onto their woman. Clint Jr. was like that with money, though it took several decades – and a family death - for this to become apparent. He never knew that the dollar had a limit, nor understood the mystical sciences that made the post-depression American economy hum, leaving the Murchison empire vulnerable to collapse with the economic crash of the early-1980s.

Clint Jr. was self-aware enough to realize that he had been born into a dynasty. But it would have been a severe blow to his ego to discover that a family member, John Dabney, had been protecting that position all these years.

When the two brothers joined forces with Murchison

Brothers in 1949, "they shared some similarities," wrote Jane Wolfe in her No. 1 best-selling book *The Murchisons*. "Both had been educated in eastern prep schools and Ivy League colleges. Both married Texas girls, and each had two young children. Together, they had come home to work.

"But the two brothers had grown apart during their years away at school and the war. John, who was twenty-eight in 1949, enrolled at Hotchkiss when he was sixteen and had been away from Dallas for twelve years. The camaraderie or closeness the brothers felt in the odd, isolated, all-male household in which they grew up had almost disappeared. Their personalities, which were never very similar, became markedly more different when they started in business. Clint Jr. was even more shy and more introverted than he had been before. He was abrupt to the point of being impolite.

"John Dabney, on the other hand, while still far from gregarious, was warm, kind, and pleasant. Clint Jr. hated social events and spent most of his time in the office making deals, and when he was away from the office, in an endless series of adulterous affairs...

"...Despite their personality differences, from the very start in business, the brothers were a team. Everything they owned, they owned equally, right down to the last million."

At their father's advice, the two brothers opted to specialize in areas of personal interest. John Dabney chose financing, and Clint Jr. opted for real estate and construction. Clint Jr. was the gambler, always trying to hit the big home-run, while John preferred to play it safe, finding solace in the mundane bloop single. John wasn't against taking a chance, but he preferred to line all his ducks up in a row before doing so. It wasn't long before Clint Sr. started referring to his sons as Vice and Versa.

Like his father before him, John had learned the value of looking before leaping by counting pennies as a bank-teller. He knew how to use a table of statistics, figures and charts to predict the likelihood of a project's success. His was an analytical approach to turning a profit.

To his younger brother, reliance on such fancy sets of hieroglyphics were the guttural sounds of a foreign language.

Business, by golly, was supposed to be an avenue of grand opportunity, not a byway of endless restrictions. Prudence was for the poor, the big strike awaiting the bold. Shuffling your feet was a sure way to get left behind.

To Clint Jr. making money was a game to live by, a bank-vault merely a glistening cavern with limitless depths to test and explore. With a never-ending pot of riches in his lap, inflation was but a word to him, a term used by the financially-strapped or the warped and frustrated businessman. He seemed to care even less about the marriage between inflation and interest rates.

But this was a slippery slope to play on where a fluctuating value system was concerned. Clint Sr. had made philosophical changes to Murchison Brothers in an effort to combat post-war inflation during the 1950s, but daddy wasn't always going to be around to help his boys avoid hardship. Clint Sr's involvement with Murchison Brothers changed dramatically after he suffered a stroke in the late fifties, convincing him to step back and spend more time on his ranch. Nearly twenty years later, when the economy's trajectory began to slide downward, Clint Sr. had already passed on, with John Dabney soon to follow, leaving the youngest Murchison alone in the corporate world to fend for himself. Not that Clint Jr. hadn't been acting on his own for some time already.

"Many years earlier Clint Sr. had asked John to keep an eye on his younger brother in business, to make sure there were limits on how much of the partnership the brothers would risk," wrote Wolfe. "Clint Sr. often repeated this request, and John promised to do so. But by the mid-seventies it was evident that John was having virtually no success restraining Clint, and consequently that there was trouble ahead."

Beginning in 1973, Clint Jr. began surrounding himself with a handful of like-minded personal advisors, a group of daring mavericks interested only in gargantuan deals. It didn't take very long for Murchison Brothers to be affected, as Clint Jr. sunk millions into one bad deal after another. With his brother spending more and more time away from the office while traveling, Clint Jr. took on a larger role in choosing the company's investments, often ignoring the staff of advisors which John trusted so much, heeding instead the suggestions of his new "partners". Loyalty, unlike with Schramm and Landry, did not pay.

"Clint Jr. just threw money at people he perceived to be his friends," said Henry Gilchrist, a longtime family attorney. "He was doing this out of sight of his family and family advisers and there was no way of stopping him."

"He was pledging everything in sight with no plan for when or how he was going to pay it off," Clint Jr's nephew, John, said in *The Murchisons*. "This huge debt was growing by the day."

By 1975, Clint Jr's side of the Murchison Brothers was a complete mess, his success rate on high-risk gambles down to around twenty-percent. Only the prudence exhibited from John's team prevented the company from reporting a loss. But John wouldn't always be around to protect his younger brother, as Clint Jr. discovered in 1978 when John divided the company into separate halves, severing his business relations with Clint Jr.

And when John suddenly died in 1979, the handwriting was on the wall, promising a quick and devastating end to the Murchison empire.

"Credit and inflation were the twin spurs that propelled the Murchison empire for decades," explained Wolfe. "Clint Sr. had taught his sons that as long as they invested other people's money in Murchison properties, and the purchasing value of the dollar continued to fall, they would get richer and richer. But Clint Sr. built the bulk of his fortune when interest rates were 2 percent or 3 percent and inflation was rampant. By 1978 interest rates had hit 18 percent, a much higher rate than inflation. Houses stopped selling because potential buyers could not afford the mortgages' interest, and land values plummeted."

For a company that invested so much into non cash-flow real estate and Clint's risky long-term deals, this spelled trouble. Bank notes kept arriving, but Murchison Brothers didn't have any cash on hand to pay them off.

Yet, Clint Jr. continued to borrow, stubbornly forging ahead, indifferent to possible consequences down the road, determined to continue the family tradition of borrowing big and waiting on an even bigger payoff. Pretty soon, the walls began to close in around him. With the economy in a freefall, financial restrictions became a reality. For the first time in Clint Jr's long business career, requests for loans were succinctly and emphatically denied. The debt had overwhelmed him.

With his company unable to make its $80 million annual interest payments, let alone its principal payments, Clint Jr. was forced into making the most difficult decision of his business career. There was no way to avoid it. He would have to sell his crown jewel football franchise. Clint Murchison Jr. would have to endure without the Dallas Cowboys.

But could the Cowboys endure without him?

CHAPTER 3

TEX'S DILEMMA

"Regardless of who buys the Cowboys, it won't be the same. It won't be as good."
Dallas Times Herald columnist Blackie Sherrod

The heart of a dying man is often a reflective force of confusion. Prone to being tangled up in the seductive web of sentiment, it often wanders through a dithering mist of memories in an attempt to gain perspective of the past years. Psychologists and parsons alike have long marveled at this phenomenon which has graced the ending of many an existence, often brushing it off resignedly as an indelible characteristic of a mortal search for meaning.

Shadowed and darkened by the specter of an unavoidable end, the last mile of the full road of life is the natural landmark that invites one and all to look back and find peace with God and all that is earthly dear. Confronted by such a reality, it can be natural for anyone to misevaluate their own lifetime contributions to family, friends, or business associates. Many can't help but overrate their worth. Some manage to undersell theirs.

Consider then the irony of Clint Murchison Jr., long renowned by business associates for having, not only an unshakeable confidence, but also a giant-sized ego, mistakenly assuming that Tex Schramm could find another owner for the Dallas Cowboys in the same mold as he had been for nearly a quarter-century. A man who had withheld nothing of pleasure from himself as an adult was now selling himself at a discount value, refusing to allow a scarred psyche to acknowledge what was undoubtedly an uncommon worth.

Low-balling his own value to the franchise was Murchison's one mistake during his ownership tenure. Ironically, it proved to be fatal for everything the Cowboys symbolized. Had Murchison been aware of the fact that his enormous wealth was absolutely critical to the Cowboys' standing among the NFL's elite, then Clint Jr. might have been more diligent with his affairs at Murchison Brothers. Because when the Murchison empire fell, the bubble that Landry and Schramm had been operating in for nearly a quarter-century was set to burst, exposing them suddenly to the commonplace hazards of the profession, where trust and job-security were all but non-existent. Without Murchison's presence, the effectiveness of the combined genius of Schramm and Landry were greatly neutralized.

"Murchison most probably would have found another Schramm who could have done the same imaginative construction – given the same backing and freedom. He could have hired another Landry, another capable coach who could have accomplished the same goals under the same conditions. Certainly Murchison could have employed other scouts who, with that budget, could have set up the same spy system as Gil Brandt," wrote Dallas Times Herald columnist Blackie Sherrod in November 1983.

"The point being, Murchison could have found another general manager who could have done as well, another coach who could have reached the same heights, another scout who could have garnered the same data. But Schramm, Landry, and Brandt could not have found another Murchison."

Considering his habit of maintaining a low profile around the Cowboys, it was easy to dismiss Murchison's impact upon America's preeminently transparent football franchise. Dallas was like all Texas towns in that they preferred their people to use accomplishment and notoriety as a means to gloat. The fact that Murchison consistently refused to make himself a part of the Cowboys' ongoing success story was treated as evidence that he, in fact, was not.

His wealth was well-noted in public circles but, when discussions of football matters surfaced, Murchison was treated as little more than a convenient background fixture, an inconsequential front-office figure alongside the three leading musketeers – Schramm, Tom Landry, and Gil Brandt – who were glorified daily with glowing public accounts of nerve and daring.

Only behind the walls of team headquarters could whispers of Murchison's far-reaching impact be distinguished above the din of the crowd. For Cowboy staffers, Clint Murchison Jr. was indeed the perfect owner.

Deep pockets and social indifference made him immune to the pressures of public opinion, allowing Murchison to be his own unique man and the Cowboys his own unique team. Loyalty was important to Murchison, who grew up under the old-school impression that a man's word was a solemn oath, and a handshake an unmistakable gesture of goodwill, understanding, and trust.

Murchison had learned to trust Schramm's word from the very beginning of their relationship. At their very first meeting at the Dallas City Club in 1959, a discussion broke out of the dubious prospect of financial losses the franchise was sure to absorb during its initial season in the NFL. Murchison suggested a figure of $100,000. Schramm wasn't nearly so optimistic.

Recalled Schramm: "I told him that with a new franchise he was going to lose something like two and a half million before ever getting a football team that would draw. He looked at me and said, 'That's ridiculous. The most we can lose is two or three hundred thousand.' I said, 'No, that's not true. The most you're going to lose is eight or nine hundred thousand, maybe a million…a year.' We had a pretty good disagreement on the subject, but I was hired after that one conversation."

Looking back upon it, Murchison admitted that Schramm's projections were closer to being accurate. "As things turned out, we lost somewhere between $500,000 and $750,000 that first year," Murchison said.

At the very beginning when he was awarded the Cowboys franchise in 1959, Murchison promised Schramm a free hand to run the team as he saw fit, only asking that Schramm keep him informed of the Cowboys' happenings and plans. Though the deal was reached while Murchison was caught up in the excitement of starting a new franchise, there was never any doubt on Schramm's part that his new boss meant business.

Despite circumstance offering numerous opportunities to renege on that understanding over the next twenty years, Murchison proved as good as his word. He refused to fire Landry when the press and fan-base begged him to during those lean years in the early-1960s, instead awarding his embattled head coach with a ten-year contract extension. Unlike many other NFL owners, Murchison refused to get involved in contract negotiations with star players, allowing Schramm to maintain a firm grasp of the Cowboys' scepter. And, other than a witty quip or two on rare occasions, Murchison faithfully avoided reporters, choosing instead to allow coaches and players to bask in the spotlight and project the image of the franchise.

With their owner often standoffish and aloof, many Cowboy players weren't even aware of who Clint was, other than some guy who occasionally entered the locker room and shook their hand after a big win. This ignorance parlayed itself into more than one humorous scene.

Golden Richards played wide receiver in Dallas for five seasons during the 1970s, and tells a story about his first encounter with the Cowboys' boss.

"We were on the plane returning from a game my rookie year," said Richards, "and this little guy with a flat-top and one of those awful thin ties came back into the players' area. I thought he was a sportswriter and began to give him a really hard time. I was popping off my best one-liners; things like, 'I bet that tie was really something back when it was in style,' and 'Does your personal barber travel with you?' The guy laughed about it and proceeded down the aisle.

"When he was out of earshot, (backup quarterback) Craig Morton, who was seated next to me, says, 'Golden, do you have any idea who that guy is?' He quickly informed me that it was Clint Murchison. I can't tell you how badly I wished for a parachute.

"It was over a year later when we happened to be at the same party at (linebacker) Lee Roy Jordan's house," Richards continued, "Clint was mingling with the players, not really saying much. After a while he went over to Lee Roy's gun cabinet and got this rifle out and came over to where I was sitting and pointed it at me. 'I just wanted you to know,' he said, 'that I haven't forgotten what you said about my tie.' That's the kind of sense of humor the man has."

No matter how distant Murchison was from his players, Schramm made sure to make his boss feel a part of the team, providing him with regular reports of roster changes, ticket sales, contract disputes, and any travel needs that may have arisen. Even though he was not an active participant in the ongoing drama of a football team's operation, Murchison loved to hear what was going on with the Cowboys, and was always ready to lend a helping hand.

"If you need anything," he often told Schramm, "don't hesitate to ask."

And when Schramm asked, Murchison was always there to answer the bell, no questions asked. Money was never an issue. During the twenty-four years of his ownership, not once did Murchison ask to see the Cowboys' books, nor did he ever collect a check as majority owner of the team.

"Clint always plowed all the profits back into the club," said Schramm.

This was the fashion of the Cowboys for nearly a quarter-century, with the owner playing the role of a rich, proud papa quietly cheering his sons on from the sideline in whatever endeavor they attempted. Win or lose, Murchison was always there with an encouraging word.

"When you try to second-guess your associates, they'll quit," Murchison explained. "I don't see myself as a football genius. I have people who I think are. The wisest thing for me to do is to let them perform to the best of their abilities without hindrances from me."

Perhaps even more rare for someone in his position as owner was the trust he demonstrated to general manager and head coach. Shortly after Dallas captured its second world championship in January of 1978, Murchison rewarded the Cowboys' two prominent figureheads by giving each of them lifetime contracts. More than merely highly-respected employees, Schramm and Landry were now business partners of the owner himself, providing them a stability that every other front-office duo in the NFL could only dream about. With unmatched job security, Schramm and Landry were able to maintain their long-term vision for the franchise even while the Cowboys endured a mild roster transformation surrounding the retirement of All-Pro quarterback Roger Staubach at the turn of the decade.

In June of 1982, after sixteen consecutive winning seasons in Dallas, Landry was asked to explain how the Cowboys had stayed on top of the NFL mountain for so long. It didn't take him very long to credit the invisible man at the top of the organization.

"It's got to be the people you have playing for you, and the people you have working for you," said Landry. "I think we've been constant and more consistent than others. It starts at the top of management. If you have someone who owns the club like Clint Murchison, with a great deal of confidence in the people who work for him, who will back them, and won't panic when you're up or down – that's the reason we've been successful.

"It's the people who work for us and the players playing on our football team. They know that they're pretty much going to be here next year and there's not going to be any drastic changes like you see in so many professional teams. So I think that gives them a sense of security and they're very loyal."

In Clint's case as it pertained to his role with the Cowboys, the truth was as he had intimated so flippantly to business partners during hundreds of board meetings in past years: There really was only one Clint Murchison Jr.

Murchison's greatest endowment to the Cowboys had been his hands-off style of ownership, which allowed the front-office intellectuals to build and sustain a winning program. Ironically, with his empire crumbling and his financial backside pinned to the wall, Murchison had extended one final request that Schramm was almost certain to fail in.

With worldwide contacts at his fingertips, Schramm could locate wealthy businessmen easily enough. It wouldn't be too hard to find a few with a passable interest in owning the Cowboys either. *Who in America didn't want to own the Cowboys?* But nowhere behind a corporate desk was a clone of Clint's capabilities to be found. This unavoidable fact was one which Schramm was confronted with numerous times throughout the calendar year of 1983, as he sought to find Murchison's replacement as owner of the Cowboys.

"I wish I felt there was another Clint Murchison out there somewhere," Schramm said in December 1983. Schramm's plan of campaign promised to be a thorough one, as well as clandestine. For some, optimum performance is achieved through separation, where ultimate concentration is possible. All Schramm asked for in this instance was to be in control of the situation.

To immediately publicize the news that the Cowboys were on the market would only complicate matters by increasing the variables and opening up the vacuum of public opinion. The last thing Schramm wanted was for his office to be turned into an auction house where his secretaries would be working feverishly to procure the highest bidder from callers, and for news reporters tramping around muddying the hallways while searching for scoops.

Though certainly wanting to do good by his cash-strapped employer, Schramm also would have told you he couldn't have cared less about the highest bidder. It wasn't going to be just any old rich galoot who would buy the Dallas Cowboys. Not on Schramm's watch.

Initial telephone queries designed to gauge possible interest in buying the Cowboys were covertly administered, as

Schramm privately compiled a list of names which were then placed under the glare of painstaking background checks. Through the studying of financial spreadsheets and detailed reports on business investments, Schramm added a series of pros and cons next to each name, stacking information against the intensive negotiating sessions ahead.

The preliminary efforts continued behind closed doors, yet the list failed to grow as Schramm might have hoped it would. One of Murchison's stipulations had been for Schramm to try his very best to pass the torch of ownership over to someone with deep business ties in the city of Dallas. In this way, Murchison hoped the Cowboys would retain their relatability to local fans and business owners.

If nobody suitable from Dallas emerged onto the scene, Schramm had been encouraged to seek out a Texan instead. Nobody understands the tradition of the Cowboys better than a Texan, right?

The execution of this plan proved to be a stop-and-go affair for Schramm, whose path was littered with circumstantial debris at every turn. There had been a time not very long before when wealthy Texas businessmen were growing on trees, but that wasn't the case by the time Schramm started his search in the spring of 1983.

The story, as is so often the case in the Lone Star State, began over a cup of tea. Texas Tea, to be exact. As the year 1973 dawned in Texas, the average price of oil was $3.50 per barrel. Business was good. But when Saudi Arabia decided later that year to cut off their flow of oil to the consuming nations, the Texas economy was set for a boom of epic proportions. Less than a decade later, in 1981, the price of oil had skyrocketed to an average of $35 per barrel, while Texas led the nation in petroleum production, having produced more than twice as much as second-place Alaska.

This frenetic pace of business activity in the field of energy created a tidal wave that rolled over nearly every segment of the Texas economy. In the 1970s and early 1980s, Texas was the second fastest-growing state in the nation behind only Florida. Texas was also the third-most populous state behind

California and New York, and was projected to surpass New York in the early 1990s.

This growth produced more growth, as increases in population created demands for goods, services and housing, producing even more jobs and further stimulating the economy. Prompted by such a dizzying pace of prosperity, prices followed at a proportionate trajectory, making Texas the envy of the on looking world. As a consequence, a flood of money from both domestic and foreign sources poured into the state, from large commercial banks, investment banking houses, insurance companies, pension funds, and wealthy individuals.

But the cold winds of change started blowing through the Lone Star State in late 1981when oil prices began suddenly dropping, continuing on a steady descent that reached $27 per barrel by the end of 1983. This unforeseen occurrence caused a transparent ripple effect throughout the state and nation which crippled some businessmen, while striking the fear of God in others.

The first domino fell in Oklahoma City on July 5, 1982, with the failure of the Penn Square Bank, one of America's largest and most aggressive oil and gas lenders. The failure was disappointing but of little shock for those in the industry, who were familiar with its gross mismanagement in recent years. Yet the fallout was catastrophic.

Later that month, Continental Illinois National Bank and Trust in Chicago meekly revealed that it had purchased approximately $1 billion in energy loans from Penn Square. Continental was rewarded for this disclosure by numerous rumors of insolvency, which led to repeated runs by domestic and foreign investors. Nearly two years to the day after going public with the news, the government engineered a convenient bailout.

The scene was just as dispiriting back in Texas. Less than two weeks after Penn Square officially went under, the *Dallas Morning News* spurred on the growing feeling of uncertainty with an article alleging that many of the loans handed out by the National Bank in Abilene, Texas were bad, causing a three-day run shortly after in which the bank handed over about 12 percent of its deposits. On August 6, Abilene National, a bank with

$450 million in assets, officially merged with Mercantile Texas Corporation, the predecessor of MCorp of Dallas, the second-largest banking organization in Texas.

If anyone was gullible enough to deem it but an unfortunate coincidence that the two largest banks to fail in 1982 (Penn Square and Abilene National) had both grown rapidly by lending to the oil and gas industry, they were brought out of their state of denial the very next year. During 1983, only three banks failed in Texas, and all three were located in Midland and Odessa, the very heart of oil country.

The most significant of the three failures reached Schramm's ears on October 14, 1983, when the First National Bank of Midland went under. With $1.4 billion in assets, the collapse of First National was the second-largest bank failure in U.S. history, causing Schramm to wonder who would be next to succumb to the thumb of financial misfortune. Clearly, the growing itinerary was fast becoming a thing of the past in Texas, as businessmen across the state were found to be tightening their belts against an uncertain future.

Due to the confusing fiscal whirlwind the region was enveloped in, Schramm found the search for the next owner of the Dallas Cowboys to be growing more tedious than even a veteran businessman like himself could have anticipated. Not only was he double-and-triple-checking investments and securities, but Schramm also received hours upon hours of technical counsel from financial advisors who tried to project the future growth – or lack thereof – of each potential suitor. Schramm was a good listener, knowing full well that all of this detailed information and technical jargon was necessary, yet hardly bulletproof. After all, if the Texas economy wasn't invincible, then what was?

During the majority of the Cowboys' long, thrilling, and ultimately exasperating 1983 regular season, Schramm kept busy in his office inspecting portfolios and assessing personalities. One by one, prospective buyers were crossed off the list, until the day came in late autumn when Schramm closed his notebook with noticeable relief, having whittled the possibilities down to a mere handful.

The time had come to let the rest of the world in on the secret. America's Team was for sale. The mighty Dallas Cowboys were there for the taking - just so long as you could convince Tex Schramm to give them away.

CHAPTER 4

THE BAD GUY

"In the middle of difficulty lies opportunity."
Albert Einstein

There were days in his life when, had the opportunity afforded itself, Tex Schramm would have easily traded places with a rat. Or even a Redskin. November 13, 1983 was definitely one of those days.

Between the inherent demands on his time by the football season currently in progress and his own clandestine search for a new owner, Schramm had been afforded hardly a moment's peace for roughly three months running. Phone calls. Media requirements. Late nights. These were his constant companions during the early days of autumn, omnipresent reminders of the dark clouds of change beginning to slowly gather over the franchise.

Being the competitive man that he was, Schramm refused to give in to circumstances, choosing instead to shake his fist at the growing stack of papers on his desk by burning the midnight oil with unhealthy regularity. Consequently, his workplace charm and professional mannerisms were fast disappearing. Tex was turning into a grouch.

As his secretary was well aware of, these last few weeks had been more of a drudgery than anything else for the Cowboys' president and general manager, as Schramm went about his work in a sour mood, his temper short and the dark lines under his eyes deepening noticeably. If not for the surprising success of the Cowboys on Sundays, Schramm would have likely been rendered an unbearable associate by everyone at team headquarters.

It was at the suggestion of his secretary that he take advantage of the Cowboys' next road trip by taking time out for a bit of relaxation. Schramm smiled at the thought. It now seemed ages since his six-week stay in Thousand Oaks during the Cowboys' summer training camp period. It would be good to get back to the coast, Schramm figured, both for his complexion and his good humor.

But, as Schramm might have expected, his troubles followed him all the way to sunny San Diego. Intent on catching some rays and catching a break from the daily headaches of his Dallas office, Schramm traveled with the team on the westbound flight on Saturday afternoon. A quick check into his hotel room enabled him plenty of time to dip his toes in the sand and surf before enjoying a late dinner. He slept well, awaking refreshed and ready to face a new day filled with familiar problems.

The Sunday morning sun was barely above the distant blue horizon and Schramm was already on edge, his thoughts, hopes, and worries engrossed with a Cowboys team on the brink of a franchise-best 10-1 start. Forgotten for the moment was the paper work and the burdens that awaited him back in Dallas, an afternoon matinee against a struggling 3-7 Chargers squad looming large. *10-1!! Wouldn't that be grand!! And where were all the sportswriters who had so gleefully written off the Cowboys before the season?* No doubt about it, this was a big day in Schramm's world, an exciting moment in time to be a member of the Cowboys' organization.

And then the phone rang.

Schramm walked across the room, yet hesitated while hovering over the nightstand. He wanted nothing more than to leave the receiver on the hook. But, being a man of responsibility compelled him to answer, and thereby ruin his weekend getaway.

The voice on the other end was clear, a fact Schramm noted with a scowl. (He had been sincerely hoping for a bad connection.) The voice was polite. Schramm listened. To conclude, the voice projected tones of inquiry. Schramm cursed. *Why now, of all days? Wouldn't tomorrow have done just as well? Would football never be fun again?*

An early-morning telephone call from a reporter was the last thing Schramm wanted. Especially from one who was prepared to go to press with a story claiming that the Dallas Cowboys were on the public market. Oh, Schramm had to give this writer due credit. He had all his facts in order, facts which Schramm knew could only have circulated into the hands of the news media through one of two avenues. And since Schramm knew he himself hadn't been leaking stories, that left only the Murchisons to consider.

But Schramm didn't want to consider the Murchisons. Not at this hour of the morning, anyway. Having served as a calming influence and a source of stability for nearly a quarter-century, the Murchison name was fast turning into a boil on Schramm's flabby neck, sapping his creativity and his planning with parasitic acumen. He couldn't make a move without their consent. He couldn't find a buyer lest they approved. In short, the Murchisons were in the position of telling Schramm how to go about his own business.

Like the stubborn, trail-wise veteran that he was, Schramm refused to have terms dictated to him on any account, spawning a silent, secret struggle for power and money that lay masked and protected behind the veneer of an exciting Cowboys football season. A chore that had been laid out by Clint Murchison Jr. originally as a simple plan of selling a football team now pitted Tex against one of Texas's most influential families.

Had this behind-the-scenes drama been unfolding at a different time of year or on a different part of the globe, the media might very well have ferreted this story out for public consumption. But with the Cowboys pulling out one miracle after another during the 1983 season, news minds in Dallas were more than occupied with the prospects of America's Team making their long-awaited return to the Super Bowl, leaving Schramm alone to play a witty game of politics in an attempt to maintain control of a sensitive situation.

Now this telephone call from a reporter threatened to strip Schramm of a certain amount of that control. Schramm rolled his eyes while contemplating a proper response, the irony of the moment failing to elude him. *Did it really require him flying all the way out west to California for someone in the Dallas grapevine to spill the beans about that rich dude from Florida preparing a bid to buy America's Team? What a life! Oh, well. Like they say, when the cat's away...*

But back to business. Should he admit the Cowboys were for sale, or invent some crafty excuse yet again to discourage inquiries from the press?

Though many months had passed since their private meeting, Schramm was still uncertain as to the proper time to make public the news that Clint Jr. had placed the team on the auction block, making him the caretaker for one of America's best kept secrets of the time. Schramm's initial plan had been to keep it under wraps until sometime during the 1983 regular season. Doing so would provide him with more than six months in which to gauge the market and compile a list of potential suitors, while also allowing time for the one-in-a-million chance that Clint Jr's fortunes would suddenly take a turn for the better. (Not that Tex actually believed that they would. But hoping for a miracle still possessed an intrinsic value for him, if only to deflect the brunt of what awaited Tex and the Cowboys in the future days.) It didn't take very long for that plan to be accompanied by a list of qualifying factors.

Behind closed doors, Schramm made no bones about the fact that he was not looking forward to this sale. For obvious reasons, yes, and for some not so obvious. He hadn't gone very deep into the process of searching out a new owner before Schramm came to grips with the slimy, distasteful complications accompanying the sale of the Cowboys. Not only would he have to deal with the fallout of a struggling economy, but also the uncertain tides of a family squabble.

The hour of internal bitterness first came to the Murchison castle in the aftermath of John Dabney's 1979 death, when his son, John Jr., took on the role of the proverbial bull in the family's china shop, running over everything and everybody in sight. John Jr. was 31 years old, and for years had been pleading with his father and uncle to take the debt off the grandchildren's trust. Now, in his newly-appointed position as a co-executor of the estate, he was bent on getting his hands on his own money, cost and prestige notwithstanding.

Like his father before him, John Jr. recognized that Clint Jr. was destined to run the family fortune into the ground. So before bankruptcy should drag both sides of the family down, John Jr. sought to have the partnership dissolved and immediate access to his trust fund granted.

Within two weeks of John Dabney's death, John Jr. moved into his father's corner office and fired off a memo to Clint Jr.: "I want Murchison Brothers dissolved quickly, and I want the trusts delivered."

Clint scanned the letter with amused interest before immediately tossing it into the trash. But John Jr. was not to be put off so lightly. He fired back at his uncle by seeking out an attorney to guide him through the tangled webs of a lawsuit. And so, one by one, the dominoes of discontent began to fall.

From out of left field, his mother, Lupe, then filed a lawsuit against John Jr., moving to have her son removed as co-executor. The pressure was so intense and the scene so toxic that John Jr. resigned his position before the case came to trial.

John Jr., though, was not done with his uncle. Not by a long shot. In February of 1981, he filed suit against Clint Jr. and his four children. The suit claimed that Clint Jr. had used funds from John Jr's $30 million trust fund, and it demanded $30 million in exemplary damages and a temporary injunction forcing Clint Jr. to separate John Jr's assets from the family trust. The following October, Clint Jr. paid over $6 million to his nephew, while the remaining $24 million was still encumbered with debt.

John Jr. continued to press the issue, threatening to expose his uncle's tenuous financial position, and thereby provoke an angry flock of creditors to swoop down on the reigning king of the Murchisons. With both sides of the family now turned against him and rumblings of discontent emanating from local banks, Clint Jr. came to the realization that he would have to start liquidating Murchison Brothers assets in an attempt to fend off his fast-growing debts. Inevitably, the sale of the Cowboys was soon broached, a topic of interest and concern, ironically, for the entire family.

For years, the public had assumed they knew all the relevant details about the Murchison boys. It was generally assumed that the two brothers were equal partners in almost everything. The rumor was that John was the sole owner of a big resort in Colorado. And Clint Jr. owned the Cowboys by himself. John owned a ranch south of the border. Clint owned an island in the Bahamas. Everything else was believed to be split down the middle.

But in the process of settling John's estate, the fact that John was actually an equal partner with his brother in the Cowboys came to light. Clint Jr. owned 45-percent. So did John. *So much for the theory that Clint Jr. was the only low-profile owner in the NFL.*

For the sportswriter and fan, this little tidbit about John served as an intriguing fact of history about the franchise. It would serve as water-cooler talk for a day or so, before fading into the background to be likely forgotten. For Tex Schramm, it was the unavoidable link which made him a key player – if for only a short time - in the ongoing feud on Forest Lane.

Aside from the glaring misdeed of misusing his family's trust funds for more than two decades, Clint Jr. had also drawn the ire of the Murchison clan with his initial strategy of settling his brother's estate. Under Texas law in the early 1980s, at the time of a partner's death, the remaining partner was required to pay off all debts and collect the assets, yet there was no time limit on dividing the property. Clint Jr. could take as long as he wanted to divide the assets of the partnership, a convenience which he made full use of in the first two years after his brother's death. So while Clint Jr. kept stalling the process with one excuse after another, John Jr. and Lupe were left in the lurch, a fact which, at the end of the day, didn't sit well with any of the Murchisons. By the time Clint Jr. agreed to a settlement with his family a couple of years later, his credibility rating among the rest of the Murchisons was non-existent. They trusted him with not an inch of their life, nor a penny of their money. In so many ways, his own family now treated him like an outlander.

This was the reality that swept up Schramm in a convoluted melodrama in 1983, making his earnest attempts to find a good and proper buyer for the Cowboys far more of a hassle than they would have ordinarily been. Schramm was like any American diplomat. He hated interference from those he deemed to be outsiders. Even worse, he hated the sights and sounds of disloyalty, on a corporate level, yes, but especially on a familial level. For Schramm to feel the effect of the Murchison feud was to watch his hair stand on end and his stomach turn inside out, not to mention watch his life at the office become suddenly rolled up into a gigantic ball of conflict.

Tex was no dummy as to his status in this poker game. To family members determined to get what they considered to be a fair shake out of the sale of the Cowboys, Tex was viewed little differently from Clint Jr. Tex was a bad guy. Tex could not be trusted. Ok, well, maybe a little bit. But he would definitely bear watching in this matter. He had associated for too long with Clint Jr. to be anything more than a snake in the grass.

Schramm wanted to take the process slowly, so as to be sure the Cowboys were in safe, secure hands for the future. The Murchisons were only out for a big payday and, having seen enough of Clint Jr's habit of stalling the wheels of progress in matters that required the doling out of cash, weren't inclined to wait for it either. They wanted the money, and they wanted it now.

Furthermore, some of the family were inclined to drag Clint Jr. though the mud to get it. If, say, they were to reveal his cash-strapped financial status to the public, that would (a) accelerate the process of selling the team and (b) ruin Clint Jr. for good, two mutually desirable options for the family.

But at what cost? asked Tex. And on whose watch? Not on mine, he told them. Schramm, through the voice of Clint Jr., assured the rest of the Murchison family it was in their best interests to keep the family's precarious financial situation under wraps. Were that unsavory secret to be revealed at this juncture, the likely selling price for the team could very well come down drastically, costing everyone involved millions of dollars. A recent *Forbes* article estimating Clint Jr's worth to be in the neighborhood of $350 million may have technically given the public the wrong impression about the stability of the Murchison empire, but it could work to the family's advantage as long as everyone kept their shirts on and their lips buttoned.

Schramm requested they keep even the fact that the Cowboys were for sale a secret while he tested the market for Clint Jr's replacement. The economy was in a weakened state, Schramm reminded them, so he needed to do some homework to ensure the financial stability of the possible suitors. It was to everyone's benefit that Schramm have all his ducks lined up in a row before breaking the news.

Reluctantly, the Murchisons agreed to give Schramm some time to do some checking up. Just how much time, apparently, differed among certain family members. In June, while Schramm worked behind the scenes sorting through names and compiling a list, the rumor was floated among the Dallas-area media that the Cowboys were on the market. Somebody, so the story went, had been calling around town seeking tentative bids for the team. That rumor, Schramm later discovered, came from someone in the Murchison camp. Someone not named Clint Jr.

Schramm stoutly denied the rumor when pressed by reporters on the issue, maintaining control of the situation by offering the convenient excuse that the Cowboys' franchise was being evaluated not for a sale, but for the purpose of settling the late John Murchison's estate. Pete Rozelle, he explained, had simply done what an NFL commissioner was supposed to do in cases like this, by appointing a committee of three NFL owners to study the situation and arrive at an estimated value of the property.

Schramm's account accomplished exactly what he knew it would; quiet the clamors of concern from the outside world while putting a few disgruntled Murchisons back in their place. Around Dallas, unless your name was Tom Landry or Billy

Graham, it was going to be an uphill battle to discredit the word of Tex Schramm.

Try as they might over the next few months, the Murchison family could not get the media to accept the fact that the Cowboys franchise was actually preparing to change hands. The rumor continued to bounce around Metroplex newsrooms during the summer months, a rumor that nobody with credentials knew quite what to do with. To go to press with a story claiming the rumor as fact would be to go squarely against the testimony of Schramm, a practice considered taboo by local reporters for years. So it just sat there simmering, until the arrival of a new football season finally pushed it to the backburner altogether. October came, and still no announcement from Schramm's office, making for an anxious bunch of Murchisons roaming the streets of Dallas. *Was Tex ever going to come out with it? What kind of brew was the old devil cooking up now? Was he planning on pulling a fast one over on the family, trying to get Clint Jr. a few extra dollars while leaving the rest of his kin hanging out to dry?*

Truth be told, by this date on the calendar, Schramm didn't know exactly which strategy to employ. He wasn't asking for any opinions, but he wasn't confident of his next course of action either. Had a concerned group of Murchisons known then that the temptation to delay the announcement until after the 1983 season climaxed was being strongly considered by Schramm, they would have likely phoned for a lawyer and brought a suit against Clint, Tex, and the Cowboys right away.

You see, Schramm wanted the best deal possible for his longtime employer, and the Cowboys' fast start to the regular season had set the wheels of Schramm's brain in motion. Clint Jr. was concerned that he would only be able to get a combined $60 million for the team and the Texas Stadium lease, which ran all the way through the 2008 season. Schramm thought it more probable to get a higher bid, something in the range of $75 million. That number would jump closer to $100 million if the 1983 Cowboys were to parlay their run of early season success into, say, a Super Bowl championship. The odds of doing so probably weren't in their favor, but it was a thought to hold onto, for a while anyway.

What seemed a wild fantasy for Schramm to ponder back in October seemed slightly less so by mid-November, with the Cowboys sitting on top of the conference standings having notched nine victories through their first ten games. Schramm's experienced eye told him that this Cowboys team didn't dominate games in the fashion that past championship teams from Dallas had. But he also recognized the fact that 9-1 was no accident. The 1983 Cowboys were a good team. If their late-game fortunes continued, they could very easily be remembered as a great team, a turn of events that would allow Murchison to forever walk away from the team with an extra pep in his step, not to mention a few extra dollars in his pocket.

Nothing would have pleased Schramm more than that. But when he answered the phone on the morning of November 13 to find another inquisitive reporter on the line, he knew his own luck would never hold for that long. January was too far off with so much money concerned. The Murchison family, short-sighted on a business level at this point due to a desperation for their fair cut, wanted the story that the Cowboys were for sale to become public knowledge. They wanted to get the bidding process under way as soon as possible, with as wide a range of bidders as possible.

And, all frustration aside, Schramm realized that was their prerogative in the matter. The money from John's share was rightfully to be theirs. So, why not get on with it, and start the ball rolling now? After all, the last thing Schramm needed was to have the family run to the courts or – even worse – to the NFL commissioner with some wild tale about Schramm conspiring with Clint Jr. to defraud John Murchison's relatives of their rightful share from the team's sale. Schramm was already involved with the Murchisons far more than he cared to be.

So when the reporter asked Tex to verify his story, the team's weary president admitted it, and promised to address the situation publicly after the Cowboys' game with the San Diego Chargers later that afternoon. Pragmatism had finally given way to resignation. The news was to finally go public, ready or not.

Schramm had done the best he could in the preliminary rounds of this drama to secure the Cowboys a chance at a bright future and Clint Jr. at walking away with a nice wad of money.

His actions during the ensuing bidding process were of an even more exemplary nature, as Schramm's tight-fisted hand squeezed the clamoring crowd of cash-hungry Murchisons into ultimate submission, fostering a sale of the Dallas Cowboys that was both sad and stunning.

A new year had dawned in America, and Tex Schramm was still in a sour mood. Not since the day he had announced the Dallas Cowboys were for sale had anything gone as planned. Not with his team, and certainly not with the negotiating process with prospective buyers.

Not only had the Cowboys lost that November afternoon in San Diego to an underwhelming Chargers squad, but then had crashed and burned at the end of December, limping into the playoffs on a two-game skid before being bounced in the Wild-Card round at Texas Stadium by the Los Angeles Rams. And as for Tex's luck in finding a satisfactory replacement for Clint Murchison Jr., well, that depended on whom you asked.

The first hat tossed into the ring came from Boca Raton, where George Barbar and family, including wife and five adult children, had parlayed a handful of provident real estate ventures into a financial empire. They were a family of substance. Most importantly, though, they were people to be trusted.

"Pick up the phone in Pompano and call anyone in business there, or anywhere else around here, and ask them about the Barbars. Ask them about our reputation. The answer you'll hear is what I'm proud of," stated the Barbar patriarch in March of 1984.

In one sense, the Barbars were just the kind of salt-of-the-earth people that Schramm had been looking for all along. Much like in the case of Clint Jr., their word was their badge of honor, and a deal was a deal right to the end. Clinging to such principles for so long while climbing the corporate ladder made it hard to believe that they would be corrupted by the bright spotlight that awaited them in Dallas.

"When you're big time in Boca Raton, you're big time anywhere," noted Randy Galloway in the *Dallas Morning News*.

But, in this high-stakes search for Clint's Clone, there was no getting around the fact that George Barbar's business locale was a strike against him. From the very beginning, Clint Jr. had been steadfast in his preference for the next owner of the Cowboys to hail from Dallas or, at the very least, somewhere within the bounds of the Lone Star State.

Thus, Barbar's $91 million bid from an office in Florida, while certainly impressive and well above the bar that Clint and Tex had agreed upon as an acceptable price, did not guarantee that he would be the Chosen One. Fair or not, Barbar's ultimate fate in the matter would depend upon the credentials of the candidates who came after him. That fate, to the understanding of the local news media, was effectively sealed several weeks after with the arrival of the next group of high rollers upon the scene.

Vance Miller, 50, and W. O. Bankston, 71, had taken different paths to achieve success and had different fields of expertise in the business world. Miller was a third-generation real estate giant with a degree from Southern Methodist University. Bankston – once an embalmer's assistant, a truck driver, and a construction worker – quit school after the seventh-grade before ultimately getting rich by selling cars.

Yet, soon after Tex Schramm let it be known that America's Team was on the market, the entire world became aware that the two local businessman shared quite a lot in common – specifically, their love for Dallas and their love for the Cowboys. And if any group of prospective investors possessed an inside edge at the negotiating table, this Miller-Bankston duo certainly did.

Since the late seventies, each had been business partners with Clint Murchison Jr. in a banking & trust venture. Bankston, a season-ticket holder since the franchise's inception in 1960, had attended all but two of the Cowboys' home games in their 24-year history, and was a longtime friend of Schramm's. They knew the Cowboys. The Cowboys knew them. From the vantage point of locals and sportswriters, this was a match made in football heaven. Yes, surely even God himself was smiling down on this turn of events.

But just when it looked like this perfect union would become a joyous reality in Dallas, Tex Schramm put his foot on the rubber and offered up a curveball for the ages, leaving his audience baffled in the head, buckling at the knees, and marveling at the machinations of his unmatched mind.

CHAPTER 5

THE FINAL COUP

"If Clint makes the decision without anyone else's input, then the odds lean back to Miller-Bankston. But the word is that Tex will have a large say."
Dallas Morning News **columnist Randy Galloway**

His office calendar displayed a since-forgotten date in the middle of January, and Tex Schramm, that alleged professor of all things conniving, was plotting yet another scheme while navigating the winding roadway of reflection. Clint & Tex. Twenty-four years. It had been a good run together. A fun run. At times, even a bit of a crazy run.

It didn't require a panoramic perspective of the past for Tex to acknowledge that he and Clint – while turning the Cowboys around from can't-win to can't-lose – had attempted some brazen and daring maneuvers during their long-standing association. Even all these years later, Tex had to shake his head and wonder just how they had managed to pull off as many deals as they did. Why, they had to be crazy! Come to think of it, maybe they were crazy. Just crazy enough to make it work, presumably.

Only Murchison would even ponder the prospects of stealing a fight song from under George Preston Marshall's nose with the intent of selling it back to the Washington Redskins' owner in exchange for the key vote that assured Clint Jr. of owning an NFL franchise in Dallas. Only Murchison would dare to stick his nose up at Dallas city officials and build the Cowboys a world-class stadium in suburban Irving.

Schramm wasn't afraid of going out on a limb to achieve a goal either. A secret meeting between Schramm and Kansas City Chiefs owner Lamar Hunt in 1966 spelled the end to the costly feuding across the landscape of professional football, resulting in the merger of the American Football League with the NFL. And Schramm was the one man in America possessing the intestinal fortitude necessary to stare down Cowboys' hard-nosed All-Pro middle linebacker Lee Roy "Killer" Jordan in a contract dispute during the early 1970s, before ultimately agreeing to a bitter truce. It didn't bother Schramm in the least that he never forgave Jordan, just so long as he proved to every other player in the Dallas locker room that Tex, though aging and the owner of a drooping waistline, was still one tough son-of-a-gun at the negotiating table. Nobody was going to run over Tex Schramm. Not for money. Not for anything.

While sifting through these many memories of what was soon to be a bygone era, it may have shocked Schramm to realize that he and Murchison had never been fortunate enough to tackle a landmark problem together during their time with the franchise. This was due, in large part, to the strictly regimented chain of command that everyone in the Cowboys' front-office adhered to, of which Murchison's stand-offish attitude was essential.

It also helped to have competent people such as Schramm, Tom Landry, and Gil Brandt running the show, three men who were seemingly born to leadership roles. Nobody within the Cowboys' hierarchy needed to babysit the other. Nobody needed to tell the other how to do his own business. Each was perfectly capable of executing his own duties without calling for reinforcements from down the hallway.

Schramm and Murchison had moved mountains in their

own way, on their own turf. But now, an unforeseen set of circumstances promised to change all of that. If Schramm was reading this situation correctly, for the Cowboys to move into the future with the best ownership group possible supporting them, he and Clint would need a whole lot of luck in the coming days. More importantly, they would need each other.

Nearly three months since the bids started pouring in from the outside world, the owner and general manager had, as yet, been unable to come to a mutual agreement about the two prospective ownership groups. If forced to pick one, Murchison sided with the Miller-Bankston group. Murchison had to admit that having a pair of longtime business associates assume control of the team would be as fitting an end to his tenure as he could hope for. It would be almost like the team was staying in the family, only, come to think of it, Murchison was glad that it was not.

Schramm was leaning toward the Barbar's, or was it simply away from Miller-Bankston? There was some feeling he couldn't seem to rid himself of concerning the two Dallas businessmen, too many red flags popping up in his head about them.

Personally, Schramm was less than enthused with certain terms of their offer. While Miller and Bankston planned to give Schramm and Landry a small portion of the team and allow Schramm to be the team's representative at NFL meetings, Schramm was not going to be allowed to have the voting trust.

After so many years of acting the part of a dictator, Schramm wasn't exactly receptive to the idea of being a mere ambassador at a round table of kings. This was football, not world politics. If Miller and Bankston didn't have the confidence or wherewithal to personally represent the Cowboys' interests to the rest of the league, what made them so sure they were capable of competently running the team from afar? Did they really think themselves better equipped than Schramm to call the shots for America's Team?

At least Barbar, though unwilling to provide the Cowboys' general manager with a small share of the team, was insistent that Schramm run things as he always had. Clint Jr's relatives seemed partial to Barbar too, their eyes lighting up like golden saucepans at the $90 million offer that came across the family desk back in mid-November. They wanted to sign the papers and divvy up the money right away.

However, Clint Jr. was there to stall the wheels of progress immediately, promptly telling the Murchison clan where to get off and sit down. The bidding process, which was only days old at that point, would play itself out before a final decision was made and a new owner selected. Clint Jr. was going to be picky, and he was in a position to be so.

And, speaking of being picky, there was that one strike on Barbar's resume sticking out like a sore thumb. Perhaps it was the ripple effect of the bloody Reconstructionist movement in the aftermath of the Civil War, but Texans like Murchison were automatically suspicious when any outsider picked up stakes and tried to enter the fold. Whether they were aware of it or not, following behind every stranger on Texas soil was the shadow of a carpetbag.

Aside from the warm weather factor, Murchison considered the comparable elements between the Lone Star State and the Sunshine State to be few and far between. Texas was agriculture and oil. Florida was palm trees and surf. Texas was hard work and sweat. Florida was beach chairs and vacations. (Besides, Florida had a fatal attraction to hurricanes.) About the only thing Texans and Floridians shared in common was their stance on personal income tax.

There was no way around it. These were slim pickings that Schramm and Murchison were dealing with. Of the two parties being considered, there was no perfect candidate to choose from. The longer Schramm and Murchison waited for another bidder to arrive on the scene, the more apparent their precarious position became. If nothing changed on that front within the next few weeks, if another high-roller didn't step up to the plate with cash in hand, someone – either Schramm or Murchison – was bound to be unhappy when this was all over.

Schramm claimed the decision was ultimately Murchison's. According to those close to Clint Jr, the decision was understood to be equally Schramm's. Sooner or later, something had to give.

Feeling more and more like a prisoner of circumstances,

Schramm could sense the walls closing in around him. Time was short. But, upon checking a notepad for a list of names, Schramm discovered that he still had one phone call to make. True, it was likely a shot in the dark, but what was there to lose at this point?

The number Schramm dialed on that day in mid-January was local, a call to a businessman owning a nickname so descriptive as to suggest he was a yokel. Legally, it was a Harvey on the other end of the line. Technically, it was a Bum, and no ordinary one at that. This Bum was Bright and just the man Schramm was looking for to save the day, and save the Cowboys in the process.

Born the son of a pharmaceutical representative, the legend of Harvey Roberts Bright was decidedly a short one. While still a baby, his father happened to glance over at him and was so struck by something in young Harvey's appearance that he instantly rechristened his son. Forevermore, Harvey was known as Bum.

He always said he was lucky to have been raised in a well-to-do home, but the fact remains that Bum Bright was born to bigger and better things in life. He was decidedly not born to be average. By 1982, at age 61, the assets of his corporate creation, Bright Banc, were valued by Texas Monthly Magazine at $500 million. One year later, *Forbes* ranked Bright as one of the 400 wealthiest Americans, with personal holdings estimated at $125 million.

From Schramm's perspective, Bright's deep roots in the Dallas business market made him a logical candidate for the Cowboys' ownership role. Having once served with him as a member of the board of trustees of a Dallas bank, Schramm could personally vouch for Bright's character. First, though, Schramm needed to know if Bright was even interested in becoming an owner. Based upon their first conversation which took place just after Christmas, Schramm's hopes that Bright would come to the rescue appeared to be misplaced.

Bright was listening. He even asked to look over the books. But when he realized that a majority ownership interest in an NFL franchise required a 51-percent share, Bright balked. With high-capital ventures in banking and savings and loans industries already in the works for his company, Bright couldn't afford to tie up that amount of cash in an investment like the Cowboys that would yield minimal returns. Bright said thanks, but no thanks.

Schramm couldn't give up on Bright at this juncture of the game. The names of the Miller-Bankston team and those of Barbar's group had just been sent to the league office for the traditional security check, a process of intensive screening by an independent firm that would take about six weeks to complete. From the perspective of Schramm's office chair, it was imperative that he locate another interested party during that time frame, before the pressure for Murchison to finally make a selection became intensified. He needed Bright. Schramm's response to Bright's refusal was to telephone the commissioner's office. He knew Pete Rozelle to be a friend. Schramm also knew that Rozelle had every intricacy of the complicated NFL rulebook perfectly memorized, and there was one clause that Schramm needed to have clarified at this time.

Was it a hard and fast rule that a majority owner have at least a 51-percent share, or was it simply a policy? Rozelle claimed the latter, reminding Schramm that four other NFL franchises were being currently operated by a "managing partner." Rozelle told Schramm a partnership could be formed as long as someone had the voting trust in league matters. Schramm was skeptical that league owners would vote to approve any limited partnership group that followed Bright into the deal. Rozelle told him not to worry about it. If it was Schramm that was to be the managing partner, the deal stood a good chance to be approved.

With that cleared up, Schramm contacted Bright and told him the news. Bright's assistant, George Bayoud, was then ordered to round up a group of Texas businessmen for the purchase. Negotiations began in earnest, and in private.

The three sides involved in signing off on a new owner now each had a candidate to support. The family wanted Barbar and his superior cash offering. Clint Jr. preferred the Miller-Bankston partnership. And Tex was now siding with the Bum.

Of course, it goes without saying that the family really didn't have a say in the matter. No tail was going to wag this dog. Not that Tex was going to waste time trying to convince them of that. But he did feel confident that, in time, once the details of the offer were put down on paper, he would be able to convince Clint Jr. to throw his support behind Bum.

Of a much more public variety was the article that appeared in the *Dallas Times Herald* on Super Bowl Sunday, quoting Vance Miller as saying he had reached a deal in principle with Murchison to become the next owner of the Cowboys. It also said Miller and Bankston were in Tampa Bay to watch the much-anticipated clash between the Raiders and Redskins as guests of Schramm's. Miller allowed himself to be quoted. He later claimed his words were taken out of context.

"Tex got us the tickets, but we didn't sit with him. We just wanted to go to the game," Miller said. "The story made it look like Tex was taking me to the Super Bowl and that we had an agreement. It scared the other people they were negotiating with. Tex was upset."

One week later, Schramm was upset again when he sat down at breakfast and unfolded his Sunday edition of the *Dallas Morning News* to find Miller and Bankston prominently featured, posing in Bankston's office with Cowboys memorabilia in the background. The cover story also disturbed other members of the Cowboys' front-office.

Schramm, however, had too much legitimate business to transact to fly into any kind of a noteworthy rage. Bright had his hands full too, as he discovered on Wednesday when a reporter approached him with a query about Bum's possible interest in buying the Cowboys. "How do rumors like this get started anyway?" was Bright's response, before promptly disappearing behind a door.

The next few days at Schramm's office were spent with Bright and Bayoud serving as company, the three businessmen whittling a list of 100 prospective investors down to 10. The requirements were strict. Candidates needed to have "good, moral character," in the words of Bright, deep pockets, and "didn't need to be on an ego trip." With that accomplished, the group adjourned for the weekend, promising to get down to brass tacks on Monday.

Little did Schramm know what would go down that

Sunday night, with Miller and Bankston continuing their own ego trip by appearing on Dale Hansen's *Sports Special* program on Channel 8 television in Dallas. With Schramm rolling his eyes at the screen in disbelief, Miller and Bankston told the entire city how excited they were about their efforts to buy the Cowboys. Schramm flipped the channel in disgust. This was getting ridiculous.

Schramm had been up front at the negotiating table that he was looking for an owner to carry on the hands-off laid-back style of Clint Murchison Jr. He couldn't have made himself any clearer on that point. Yet, here were Miller and Bankston practically flinging themselves at every reporter they came across. If they were so outspoken before buying the team, what was to be expected afterwards? A radio show? A Broadway show? Where would it stop?

According to Schramm, it stopped during the first week in March when, unknown to the outside world, he and Murchison came to an understanding with Bright. Finally, all those weeks of tedious discussions were over. A deal had been reached, an agreement made. The new king of the Cowboys was to be a Bum.

How Schramm expected to turn this secret into a reality became something of an uncertainty when the announcement was made to the rest of the Murchison family, thus provoking Clint Jr's relatives into an unholy rage. They cursed Clint Jr with impressive alacrity, threatened Schramm with everything short of an ax murder, and spit upon the name of Bright. Of superior importance and possessing an equally dramatic quality, they phoned their lawyers. Another squabble was set to ensue.

But Schramm never blinked. He took the verbal abuse in stride, knowing full well the mountains that could be moved with the proper employment of time, chance, and opportunity. So it was that with the aid and support of his longtime partner, Schramm was able to approach this blockade the Murchisons promised to build, and destroy it with all the flair of an indifferent magician.

Wednesday, March 7, 1984 dawned upon north Texas a cold and clear companion of good tidings. In rural areas, the ground was covered by a thin layer of frost. The experienced farmer, eager after the bitterness of a cruel winter, knew better than to worry about his early crop. Winds from the southwest promised the coming of warmer days ahead.

Back in the suburbs, newsstands were already experiencing a heat wave of their own, melting fast from an inordinate amount of curious early-morning readers. No sir, it didn't take big news very long to spread in Big D. And Gary Myers' article in the *Dallas Morning News* certainly qualified as big news.

The headline in the sports section said it all: "Cowboys Sale Coming Down To Two Groups." The text explained the rest, how the Miller-Bankston outfit and Barbar family were each confident of ultimate success for their team in this long, weary matter, yet anxiously awaiting the final decision by Clint Murchison Jr., which was expected to be reached at any moment.

The months and weeks of negotiation had now come down to mere days of deliberation. The end of the Dallas Cowboys Ownership Sweepstakes was finally within sight. Meanwhile, at just that moment inside a first-class Honolulu hotel, Tex Schramm rolled over in bed in an attempt to catch a few extra winks before sunrise. Prior to falling back asleep, though, Schramm afforded himself a deep, throaty chuckle, which soon – provoked by some source of secret devious mirth – transformed itself into a devilish cackle. For the first time in a long time, Schramm was enjoying himself. He closed his eyes and slept like a man without a care in the world, content in knowing what others did not.

John Murchison Jr. had a bee in his bonnet. Based upon the buzz in the room, there might very well have been two bees up there. He was sure that his uncle, along with that no-good tramp-like friend of his called Tex, had fallen off the straight and narrow way and were busy once again with some dishonest dealing or other. What's more, John Jr., in front of the entire Murchison family, claimed he had the evidence to prove it.

John Jr. called everyone's attention to certain particulars of Bum Bright's offer to buy the Dallas Cowboys. Why, he asked, was Clint Jr. and Tex Schramm so supportive of the Bright group? According to John Jr., the answer had to do with the Texas Stadium Corporation, the company that owned the lease to operate the stadium through the year 2008.

Several years before, the corporation had been removed from the Murchison Brothers' partnership, and was now owned exclusively by Clint Jr. The franchise itself remained jointly owned by Clint Jr. and John Sr's estate, each with 45-percent. (Two other investors owned the remaining 10-percent.)

Lupe, now the sole executor of her late-husband's estate, was being warned by John Jr. to be aware that Clint Jr. was attempting to negotiate a higher price for the Texas Stadium Corporation, which lowered the price that could be asked for the team. The offer from Miller and Bankston for the stadium lease was believed to be in the neighborhood of $15 million. There could be only one reason, John Jr. insisted, why Bright was offering at least $20 million; Clint Jr., that old fox in a wheelchair, was trying to stick some extra gold in his own poke. (It is uncertain as to the particulars of Barbar's offer.)

Lupe, who was a big fan of the Cowboys and a few months earlier had even pondered the prospect of buying the team herself, didn't know who or what to believe in this matter, finding herself caught once again between her son and brother-in-law. It was, after all, a subjective interpretation about the fair value of two different assets.

Other relatives were only too willing to believe the worst about Clint Jr., and quickly threw their support behind John Jr., who was busy threatening lawsuits and all kinds of legal action against his cash-strapped physically-impaired uncle. As if to dispel any notion that Clint Jr. may have been entertaining that his hot-headed nephew was only running a bluff, John Jr. called in the family lawyers to see what could be done about such an obvious money-grab.

At his employer's prodding, Murchison's business advisor, Jack O'Connell, contacted Schramm, who was in Hawaii for the NFL's Competition Committee meeting, and made him aware of what was transpiring back on Forest Lane. Schramm was not amused at hearing the news.

Only a couple of days before, Bright had demanded that Murchison and Schramm cut off all negotiations with the other two groups, as a show of good faith. Bright had given them everything they had asked for in the agreement (a fair price, a free hand for Schramm as the general manager, and a group of local, conservative-minded investors, etc.). Now, he wanted their promise in return not to use his offer to drive up the price with Barbar or the Miller-Bankston group. "A deal is a deal," Bright reminded them. "Done is done."

Both Schramm and Murchison assured Bright that he was the man they wanted to fill the role of Cowboys' owner, but were quick to point out it would be bad business on their part to send the other two groups packing at this juncture. In the unlikely event that the NFL rejected Bright's bid, Murchison needed to have a second option at hand. He couldn't afford to destroy those relationships, not when he still might need them.

After much talking around the point, an understanding of solidarity was finally established between the parties. Bright was The Man. And while the lines of communication would still be open, Barbar, along with Miller and Bankston, were, in fact, being shut out. A deal was a deal…just so long as it wasn't.

With the understanding that they were not to overplay their hand, the first step was to make the family aware of Bright's offer. No mention was made of the fact that Clint Jr. had already selected Bright's bid in private. As far as the family was concerned, Bright's $80 million offer ($60 million for the team and $20 million for the stadium lease) was merely under consideration.

Schramm expected some discussion on the matter, just not the kind of argument that ensued. And when John Jr. called in a group of attorneys, Schramm became worried. Not worried that a legal mind would discover anything crooked about the deal. As was par for this course, the Murchison's threats had more bark than bite to them.

No lawyer was going to be able to prove that he and Clint Jr. were somehow robbing the family of any rightful compensation, not after negotiating the terms of the richest sale of a team in the history of professional sports. If anything, they were likely to be applauded. The Cowboys franchise was set to bring ($60 million) nearly twice what the Denver Broncos did ($34 million) a couple of years before.

At this stage of the game, Schramm was more concerned with the time factor. He needed the family's stamp of approval. Without it, he couldn't submit Bright's offer to the league office, not with the possibility of a long, drawn out lawsuit hovering over it.

If Schramm hadn't been stranded on an island, he might have deemed it suitable to blow his top. *These people are incredible! They were of a completely understanding nature when Clint Jr. was prepared to select a bid $35 million cheaper than what he could have had, yet find cause to threaten a day or three in court the moment that Uncle Clint and Big Tex negotiate a deal $25 million richer. Seriously?!?!*

Evidently, at least one member of the Murchison clan – whether it was John Jr. or someone else Schramm did not know – had read enough of Bright's offer to realize that it stood a fair chance of being accepted by Clint Jr. They had been following the story in the newspapers, and knew all about Clint Jr's reluctance to hand over the franchise to a Florida businessman, and recognized the fact that Bright's financial offering ($80 million) was significantly higher than the one submitted by Miller and Bankston ($55 million).

All this blustery talk of contesting the legality of the offer may have simply been a case of pure spite against Clint Jr. Then again, maybe there was a legal loophole they planned on taking advantage of. Schramm didn't care either way. He didn't need this case going to court. If that happened, there was no telling when it would get resolved. Any lawyer, provided with enough incentive, could leave a legal trail of smoke so thick and winding as to clog the paths of progress for months.

Schramm had been secretly planning on having Bright's offer voted on at the NFL's owners meeting in Hawaii, which was still almost two weeks away. He wanted the next owner of the Cowboys to be well established before the NFL draft took place in April, and the ensuing contract negotiating period. For that to happen, Schramm had to somehow convince the Murchisons that Bright, a suspiciously late entry into the Ownership Sweepstakes, wasn't as important a figure as they thought him to be. Schramm, in a manner of speaking, had to get the dogs to call off the hunt. The only way to do that was to lead a false trail, and hope the family took the bait.

A former editor himself once upon a time, down in the state's capital city for the *Austin American-Statesman*, Schramm knew a little bit about the power of the Texas press. He also knew that the Murchisons, though flaring up in anticipation of a knock-down drag-out legal argument with Clint Jr., were actually ready for the whole thing to come to an end. They were no different than any other greedy bunch. They wanted to get their money and get out. A few convenient "news leaks" to local reporters from the offices of the Cowboys' general manager and Clint Jr. would, Schramm thought, be just the recipe to bring that about.

The Murchisons wanted a quick way out. Schramm was prepared to give them what appeared to be just that. Yet, who would have suspected it to arrive in the innocuous form of Gary Myers' *Dallas Morning News* article on March 7, a source far above suspicion if there ever was one. Therein, Schramm provided every piece of information the family needed to hang themselves on. Led by the impulsive John Jr., the Murchisons fooled themselves into thinking they understood the situation, but made the critical mistake of underestimating Schramm in the matter.

Yes, Tex could be a devil when it came to details, a devious man ever aware of the desires, tendencies and personalities of those around him, and how best to turn them to his advantage. Schramm knew the Murchisons had grown impatient during the six-week period that the Barbar's and the Miller-Bankston team were being screened. He also knew impatience to be a cousin to haste, and only one step away from carelessness.

It had all seemed so simple to them when the family gave their nod of approval to both groups. They kept expecting Clint Jr. to make a decision, to pick one or the other, but he never did. It was in this situation that Clint Jr's reliability really paid off for Schramm. Because Clint Jr. could keep a secret, his family was never able to glean any sense or even a hint that a game-changing deal was being worked out behind their very backs.

Had Clint Jr. suffered a slip of the tongue during this time, there's no telling what the reaction of the rest of the Murchisons would have been. But, for all they knew, Bum Bright had dropped out of the race weeks before.

Clint Jr., through the voice of O'Connell, simply explained that, by waiting it out, he was only trying to protect himself. Before picking either one of the two groups, he wanted to be sure they cleared NFL's security measures. It wouldn't do anyone a bit of good to have to publicly renege on an ownership announcement.

At the end of February, both the Barbar group and the Miller-Bankston group were declared to be in the clear. Still, no announcement came from Clint Jr's office. The introduction of Bright's bid into the mix a few days later explained why. According to the instant understanding of his relatives, Clint Jr. was trying to use Bright's offer to stick a few extra million dollars in his own pocket by taking advantage of his exclusive ownership of the Texas Stadium Corporation. Or so they thought.

According to Myers' report, Schramm, from his sun-drenched outpost in Hawaii, had just made public his desire that a decision on a new owner be made on, or before, the eighteenth of March, in order for the other twenty-seven NFL owners to vote on Murchison's choice of a replacement during the owners meetings. And, if that was the case, then Bright couldn't be Clint Jr's choice to succeed him, not since Bright and his group of investors had yet to be even submitted to the same screening process that the Barbar's and the Miller-Bankston had just passed through. Per league rules, no ownership group could be approved without first passing all of the qualifying stages of the NFL's intensive security guidelines.

So what then was preventing Clint Jr. from making his choice? Could it be Clint Jr's strong sense of loyalty holding him back, his insistence on dealing with Bright in good faith? Had he promised Bright that he would only make his selection sometime after the rest of the family signed off on the deal? Was that Clint Jr's way of letting Bright know he was going to get a fair shake? Considering what happened next, it is just barely possible these were a few of the deliberations bouncing off the walls of the Murchison camp for the better part of March 7.

Later that afternoon, the mood of the Murchisons – for some unexplained reason – officially changed. A family which had spent the previous few days threatening to invoke seemingly every form of government-sanctioned judgment upon the debilitated form of Clint Jr. suddenly found cause to backtrack with all the meekness of a Turkish monk. Quietly, reverently, they offered their approval of Bright's offer, fully trusting in the set of circumstances which made it appear to have already been eliminated from consideration.

Now, with that obstacle having been removed from the field of play, Schramm was free to spring the trap. The following day, March 8, Bright's team of investors were officially submitted to the required screening process. The Murchisons likely smiled at the report, knowing it was too little and too late to do the Bum any good. *Six weeks? Ha! He barely has six days to work with!*

But that's where they were wrong. Schramm, likely with complementary encouragement coming from Pete Rozelle's office, convinced the Dallas investigative firm of Dale Simpson and Associates to complete in 10 days what usually took six weeks. And when Simpson's firm held up their end of the bargain, the Murchison fat was in the fire. Schramm had conned them all. On March 19, 1984, Bum Bright was chosen to be the second owner of the Dallas Cowboys.

Back in Dallas, Clint Murchison Jr. was smiling from his wheelchair. And, as readers discovered in the following morning's edition of the *Dallas Morning News* where he was pictured standing next to the new owner, so was Tex Schramm.

Against what, at times, seemed to be great odds, their last ride together as business partners turned out to be one grand coup. Clint and Tex, at long last, had pulled it off…together. It was a bittersweet memory of firsts and lasts to be cherished for their remaining years.

CHAPTER 6

IN THE CROSSHAIRS

"Coaching is the only profession that, as you get older, most people think you get dumber."
George Young, New York Giants General Manager

The spirits of promise and assurance danced across the warm sand that day on the island of Hawaii where Tex Schramm and Bum Bright collaborated for what, to attentive ears back in Dallas, proved to be a heartwarming keynote address.

Brandishing smiles so wide as to make Barbie blush, these two Cowboy confidants spilled all of the essential beans to reporters, providing hope that the NFL's newest high-profile partnership would yield old results in time.

Though the search to find a new owner had taken longer than expected, Schramm played the part of a jubilant politician while standing in front of a microphone, assuring his supporters that the battle had been won, with no quarter afforded to compromise.

"The No. 1 priority was to find ownership to continue whatever success the Cowboys have had through the years and to continue the image and reputation of the team," Schramm said. "I think we've found our man in Bum Bright."

Bum, to his credit, said all that was expected of him, swearing to a verbal affidavit which guaranteed him transforming from an affluent businessman into a shadowy recluse, just as soon as his plane landed back in Texas a few hours later. "If you thought Clint Murchison was an invisible owner, you will be shocked at me," said Bright. "My group that I represent and I will be more invisible than he was. It is not our intent of getting involved in running the ball club...

"So far as operation of the club goes and what the Dallas Cowboys stand for, you will not notice a blip in the operation. Tex will have absolute authority to hire and fire players, coaches, administrative people, secretaries – to do everything that is necessary for the Cowboys to continue to be a strong organization...

"I can't consider any time when I would step in," continued Bright. "Look at Tex's record. It would be ludicrous for anyone to think they could add to Tex's direction. There will be none of that. It was a condition of the limited partners."

The news sounded almost too good to be true. Schramm would manage the team without any outside interference from the owner while continuing to represent the Cowboys at league meetings, and Tom Landry as the head coach would answer only to Schramm. The Cowboys were back in business, operating just like they always had when a man named Murchison owned the team. Super Bowl, here we come!

A long, complex chase now over, Schramm looked more relieved than anything else. His front-office role had been preserved, his former boss awarded a good price for the sale of the team, and the Cowboys were still owned by a prominent Dallas businessman. Tex Schramm, three months before, would never have predicted such a desirable outcome.

"I'm just glad it's over," Schramm said. "Hopefully, things can get back to normal."

But only Schramm was aware of the long odds of normalcy remaining in Dallas for very long. Despite the many words from Schramm and Bright exultantly claiming the contrary, the superstructure of America's Team had in fact changed drastically overnight, making this hiring of a Bum to be one of Tex's greatest and riskiest gambles.

The perception of Bright now being painted in the public square was not anywhere close to the reality facing Schramm behind closed doors. Bum was not Clint's Clone, nor would he ever be. And Schramm wasn't moaning over the fact. Schramm had read the handwriting on the wall before ever embarking on a search for a new owner. He would never, ever find another Clint Murchison Jr. to bankroll the Cowboys. That was just the way it was, an inevitable reality when – after years of dealing with a perfect boss – being suddenly faced with the task of trying to decide the lesser of three evils.

Schramm didn't apologize for going out of his way to ensure that Bright became the new owner of the Cowboys because he saw absolutely no reason why he should. Of the three cards Schramm could have chosen to play, Bright was still the man who gave the Cowboy tradition the best chance of enduring.

Bright knew how to hold his tongue, as evidenced by his secretive habits during contract negotiations. He also had the respect of his fellow Texans. And with the Bright empire having experienced exponential growth over the past decade, it was hard to imagine the Cowboys going onto the market again anytime soon.

Bright, very clearly and very authoritatively, provided a stability for the organization which Schramm perceived to be lacking in the ownership groups he bypassed. Vance Miller and W.O. Bankston, based upon their behavior during the bidding process, would have provided Schramm with one public relations headache after another. George Barbar's presence would have required Schramm to be constantly defending the credibility of the "imported" owner to skeptical local business owners. Neither option happened to pique Schramm's interest.

Schramm's list of daily duties was a long one. He liked to think he had better things to do than worry himself at every turn about the movements of his boss. If Schramm had wanted to play nanny, he would have become a sports agent long before deciding to settle down to the grind of a general manager in the NFL. (Come to think of it, Tex Schramm would have made an ideal agent. He always did enjoy levying a threat or two across a desk.)

According to Schramm's way of thinking, Bright's flaws were on a much more manageable level. At home he was known as a warm, compassionate man, but at the office Bum was a cut and dry businessman with an acid tongue. Of a two-sided coin, Schramm was definitely dealing with the rougher half. But at least Bright was honest, even if brutally so.

For Bright, money was the highest form of status symbol. Living in the red was socially unacceptable, even morally so. Bright's stance would have been a breath of fresh air in the political realm, but it placed Schramm, and ultimately Landry, in an uncomfortable position at Cowboy headquarters. The art of winning football games in Dallas had never before gotten tangled up in the web of finance. That was all about to change. Bright had seen the company books and knew that the Cowboys made a $600,000 profit in 1983. Before the ink had even dried on the dotted line, Bright's team of investors said they saw no reason why the Cowboys couldn't make an even larger annual profit in the future.

Already in the planning stages was more than 100 suites to be added near the top level of Texas Stadium, where fans could entertain friends and business clients in style at the big game. The price for one of these "Crown Suites" varied from $300,000 to $1.5 million, giving Bright – the sole owner of Texas Stadium Corporation – the prospects of an even larger windfall, in due time.

Despite his public posturing in Hawaii after the news broke about his purchase of the team, Bright wasn't interested in preserving the structure of America's Team. He wasn't interested in saving the Cowboys, per se. Lofty ideals of upholding an impeccable tradition did not appeal to him. Bright admired Schramm's business savvy, and respected Landry's calm demeanor on the sideline. But buying an iconic institution such as the Dallas Cowboys was purely a business investment that he hoped would lead into other business opportunities. For Bright to cash in on his financial expectations, the Cowboys would have to continue to perform at a high level. With times being what they were, fans weren't going to spend their precious few dollars on a ticket to watch a mediocre team. Not that Bright was particularly worried on this front. He had watched the Cowboys for too many years to be concerned with any dip in performance.

The new owner still considered the Cowboys to be one of the NFL's elite franchises. Bright made it very clear he was looking forward to Dallas being an annual participant in the postseason, with an occasional berth in the Super Bowl. And why not? Dallas was only a year removed from a third consecutive appearance in the conference championship game.

Though the 1983 squad had been bounced from postseason play in the Wild-Card round by the Los Angeles Rams, the Cowboys would surely regroup and rebound. They always had. But Schramm had his doubts on this issue. The nucleus of talent – Bob Lilly, Roger Staubach, Drew Pearson, Charlie Waters, Mel Renfro, Cliff Harris, among others - anchoring the great

Cowboy teams of the 1970s had largely disappeared. To further compromise matters, the draft classes being brought in weren't as strong as they once had been. The Cowboys' strength was being slowly sapped through the clutches of time, revealing an aging roster that achieved peak performance only in uncertain, spasmodic stretches during a season.

For the emotionally attached fan, it could be hard to recognize this fading pattern. The Cowboys, after all, still had the No. 2 ranked scoring offense for 1983, averaging nearly 30 points per contest. The defense wasn't too shabby either, based upon the statistical chart, ranking ninth in points yielded per game.

But Schramm knew better than to trust a chart of complicated numbers when his eyes told him something very different. Against the best teams in recent years, the Cowboys were constantly seen struggling to maintain pace. Often, by game's end, their remains resembled road-kill far more than the battle-scarred frame of a valiant contender.

Schramm, you see, had his own chart of recent printing to chew on. By the end of the 1983 season, Dallas had lost three consecutive games to San Francisco. They had dropped their most recent encounter versus the AFC behemoth Los Angeles Raiders at Texas Stadium. And only a 20-point second-half rally on the opening Monday night of the 1983 campaign separated the Cowboys from a three-game slide versus their archrival, the Washington Redskins. (The 49ers, Raiders, and Redskins had combined to win the previous four Super Bowls.)

For Bright to have agreed to allow Landry and Schramm to run the show like always was easy enough to do because the Cowboys had done nothing but win during the previous twenty years. But if what Schramm was smelling in the wind actually came to pass, Dallas could very easily be closer to the middle of the NFL pack than the top in 1984.

In that case, a cut-and-dry businessman like Bright, wearing exacting principles on his heart and equally clear demands on his sleeves, was bound to be faced with disappointment. For Schramm – or any other member of the front-office – to make an attempt at verbally illustrating to Bright the many nuances of the Cowboys' complex position would have been a futile endeavor indeed. All that philosophical mumbo-jumbo about ebbs, flows, and the common laws of parity didn't align with his skills of reasoning.

Bright's perception of the action on a gridiron was steeped in simplicity. He couldn't help but see the game of football as a ledger with parts moving over a neatly-spaced field of green. The rule of measurement was very simple. His team had either won or lost. They had either succeeded or failed. There was no middle ground. The proof was not in the pudding, but on the scoreboard. And Bright, mind you, hated to be associated with a loser.

Even more pertinent to Schramm's immediate plan of campaign was the fact that Bright wasn't someone to sit around and wallow in a mire of mediocrity. If things weren't going well, Bright didn't have to be prodded to make changes. Action, in such a case, was to be considered his calling card.

In 1981 Bright was appointed to the board of regents of Texas A&M University by governor Bill Clements. (Bright was a 1943 graduate of A&M and an ardent supporter of the school.) Later that same year his fellow regents appointed him chairman.

After watching the Aggie football team finish in fifth-place in the Southwestern Conference that fall, Chairman Bright did the unthinkable by removing head coach Tom Wilson and luring Pittsburgh Panthers sideline general Jackie Sherill to College Station with a 10-year $3 million contract. The "Big Aggie," as Dallas Morning News columnist Randy Galloway soon began referring to Bright, made a lot of little Aggies mad that day. Bright couldn't have cared less. Bringing Sherill to the Brazos Valley accomplished his goal of making Texas A&M relevant once again on the college football landscape. In Bright's world, winning was the only name of the game.

It didn't require supernatural powers for Schramm to peer into his crystal ball and perceive trouble brewing on the near horizon. An activist in the owner's box would not only complicate Schramm's position, but also threaten that of Landry's. Schramm would never cast a vote in favor of firing Landry but, if push came to shove, who knew if he would even have a say in the matter? If Bright was bent on bulldozing over officials like he was back in Aggieland, then Landry would be barbecued on the public spit with or without Schramm's consent.

During the spring of 1984 Bright was quick to sense the spirit of discontent that the city of Dallas harbored for its football team. He read the papers and watched the nightly newscasts. The mood was palpable, if not contagious. All that fans around town could talk about was that December loss to Washington which had cost the Cowboys the NFC East crown and a first-round bye in the postseason. Washington had shamed Dallas. Washington had played in the last two Super Bowls. Washington, Washington, Washington.

Bright believed he knew of a remedy. Just weeks after promising to be an innocent, invisible bystander in all football matters, the new owner went on record suggesting that the Cowboys might need to try a new approach in their method of player training. According to Bright, if Dallas expected to supplant Washington at the top of the conference pecking order, moving their annual training camp site from balmy Thousand Oaks to the steamy conditions in Brownwood, Texas just might be in order. The move not only would save money, but also enable Cowboy players to train in grueling conditions such as the Redskins were accustomed to during August along the Susquehanna River. Sunshine and flip-flops were nice, but a little sweat never hurt anyone either. If it worked for the Redskins, it could work for the Cowboys too.

Schramm stomped out that grassfire before it had time to inflict any significant damage, assuring California business owners and local newsmen that the Cowboys had no intention of changing their summer training headquarters. Landry still believed that the optimum weather conditions in southern California afforded Cowboy players the best opportunity to work themselves into playing shape for the season ahead. The Cowboys, to be terse, were not the Redskins. Which was exactly Bright's point.

By this time, Schramm had realized that he would have to be proactive in order to nurture the owner-general manager relationship. He couldn't allow Bright to get the feeling that the Cowboys would settle for anything less than the very best. Bright was a man who needed to be pleased. In order to do that, Schramm would have to anticipate his every move, and give the appearance that he was leaning in the same direction as the owner.

First on the agenda, though, was a goodwill gesture. Going into the 1984 NFL Draft, the Cowboys were in need of a young, fast tackling-machine. Dallas' aging linebacking corps came under heavy scrutiny in the aftermath of its Wild-Card playoff loss at Texas Stadium to the Rams. Only Schramm could have recognized an opportunity to kill two birds with one stone with strategic use of the Cowboys' No. 1 selection. In retrospect, it was a nice touch, not that anyone in the audience could have misinterpreted its intentions.

Bright wasn't fooled by the selection of Aggie do-it-all linebacker Billy Cannon Jr. The Cowboys had never, in 23 years of hand-picking college talent, selected a football player from Texas A&M. For them to pick one barely a month after Bright had bought the team with their very first selection was too much to be a coincidence.

Still, Schramm's gesture had its desired effect. Bright was pleased, so much so that he disappeared behind his office door to be virtually unseen or unheard of for the next handful of months. And in contented silence he watched a very eventful first season as owner unfold before him, while Schramm led the chorus of local hand-wringers.

The decision to promote Gary Hogeboom to the starting quarterback role to begin the 1984 regular season was one that pleased Schramm because it showed Bright that the Cowboys were still a franchise dedicated to living by the bold and daring move. It was only after Hogeboom struggled, and the Cowboys consequently missed the playoffs, that Schramm admitted what he had already known in his secret heart; the Cowboys were fading faster than anyone at team headquarters cared to admit.

The sportswriters seemed to know this too, which meant that Bright was reading all about it by now. Schramm's position had now become one of delicacy. He was caught between tradition and necessity.

When Murchison had been the owner, Schramm and Landry were able to be painstaking in their approach to business, whether it be through the draft, in the film-room, on the field, or in marketing. The Cowboys were a franchise built to last, a setting of corporate confluence and stability that all others envied.

Furthermore, Landry and Schramm were not only established, they were secure in their roles, lifetime members of the Cowboys if they so wanted. This was their reward for their success and faithfulness to the organization over the years. Schramm and Landry, in essence, were family members, linked to an unbreakable chain of command.

The only loyalty that Bum Bright understood was that of success. Which put Schramm in the unenviable position of having to please two masters; Bum and Tradition. Schramm had promised Clint Murchison Jr. that the Cowboys would operate on the same foundation of delineated authority as they always had, with him and Landry out front running the show.

Schramm and Landry had always been tied at the hip, their relationship established through a mutual respect and trust seasoned by years of success. For so long, one had relied upon the other with such a harmonic synergy as to become an interchangeable part of the Cowboys' functioning body. Bright's expectations had changed all of that, provoking a discordant song of conflict to break out within the front-office. For the first time in franchise annals, Schramm and Landry were singing different tunes.

Schramm needed to convince Bright, with some tangible evidence, that the Cowboys were taking steps to turn the ship back in the right direction. But how to do so without trampling over Landry?

Landry's turf had always been considered sacred ground in Dallas. The head coach was responsible for the roster, coaching staff, and weekly game-plan. Outside interference was not to be tolerated, violators rumored to be exiled for life on a remote island. Or something like that.

But with pressure coming up from behind in the form of Bright, it was Schramm who decided upon a compromise to this longtime understanding between Cowboy associates. He was now living like never before, dangerously and with almost criminal intent. Schramm was seeking to alter Landry's staff.

General manager and head coach sat down in a private meeting shortly after the conclusion of the 1984 season. Schramm rolled out his idea, generally that the coaching staff was due for an overhaul. Landry was quick to protect the credibility of his assistants, reminding Schramm that all of these coaches were well respected in their fields, and that many of them had been with the team during the Super Bowl days of the previous decade.

"Schramm told him he didn't want to fire anybody, but, perhaps they could be moved to other jobs in the organization and replaced by some younger people who might make more of an impact," wrote Bob St. John in his 1989 book *The Landry Legend*.

(There is no record of the specific assistant coach Schramm sought to displace at this meeting, but it is not difficult to formulate an educated presumption. Around the city of Dallas, 1984 will always be remembered as the Year of the Quarterback. Sometimes for better, oftentimes for worse, the Cowboys quarterback inevitably found his way into the forefront of Monday's headlines, fueling a weekly drama that finally ended on the final night of the regular season when Dallas was officially eliminated from the playoff race. Nine wins and seven losses had nurtured the unanimous sentiment that the Cowboys needed more from their quarterback.

Hogeboom and veteran Danny White had combined to attempt 604 passes during the 1984 season, a franchise record for a single season. Among 15 NFC quarterbacks, White ranked eleventh and Hogeboom thirteenth in passing efficiency. They combined to throw for 18 touchdown passes and 25 interceptions.

In 8 of 16 games during the season, Dallas quarterbacks had more interceptions than touchdowns. As an additional stamp certifying the struggles of the position, Dallas finished the 1984 campaign ranked No. 20 in the league in yards-per-pass completion.

For Schramm to try to replace Jim Shofner as quarterbacks coach after such a season wouldn't be out of the question at all. Shofner had all the qualifications Schramm needed to warrant a strong-handed dismissal that would satisfy the owner. Not only could the quarterback struggles in Dallas be traced back to his arrival on the scene in 1983, but Shofner's name would also ring a bell of recognition with Bright.

Shofner, once upon a time, was the head coach at Texas Christian University when the Horned Frogs were the unquestioned doormats of the Southwestern Conference, losing twenty consecutive games over the course of the 1974-75 seasons. Bright was in attendance at Kyle Field in November 1976 for Shofner's final away game as head coach, where the Aggies rolled to a 59-10 victory, cementing TCU's eighth defeat of the season by at least 20 points. Oh, yes. Firing Shofner would be one sacrifice that Bright could not only understand, but also appreciate.)

The Cowboys' on-the-field product had always been a free-flowing extension of Landry's football genius. The multiple offense and all its moving parts was his. He had invented the Flex defense, a scheme too complex for outsiders to copy. Landry even fancied himself the team's unofficial kicking instructor. Wherever someone looked on game-day at Texas Stadium, Landry's philosophical imprint was very apparent.

It only made sense that Landry be very particular about filling out his own staff. Tom wanted assistants who were loyal and willing to put aside their own ego and ideas in order to teach the rudiments of Landry's system. In Dallas, the Landry way was the only way.

Since the turn of the decade, Landry had watched numerous trusted assistants get away from him. Dan Reeves (Denver), Mike Ditka (Chicago), and John Mackovic (Kansas City) all left the Cowboys to accept head coaching appointments with other teams. Finding adequate replacements would be tough, no doubt, but it was Landry's job to do. Until Schramm came calling with the idea that he had a say in the matter.

Indeed, Schramm can thank his lucky blue stars that Landry was a practicing Christian. A lesser man would have left the paint peeling off the walls at such a brazen encroachment. But flying off the rails wasn't Landry's way, nor within his job description. Landry knew better than to consider this a personal battle. This wasn't Tom versus Tex. Nevertheless, the head coach knew that the walls of a new reality were closing in around him. Though of an ultra-competitive disposition, Schramm had never crossed over the bounds of Landry's authority before. There could be only one explanation for why he was doing so now; Bright.

Landry was now backed into a corner, with no apparent way out. At the provocation of the owner, Schramm was seeking to reshuffle Landry's own deck of coaching cards. But this was about more than just finding a younger assistant who could more easily relate to players in the locker room. Schramm wasn't after a new man so much as he was new ideas.

Landry understood the situation. Schramm was battling perception, not the head coach. And the perception was that Landry had been employing the same offensive and defensive schemes in Dallas for the better part of a quarter-century. After so long on top, the league had finally bypassed the archaic Cowboys.

Where would this leave Landry in the whole grand scheme of things? If he were to lose control over coaching staff personnel, the very foundational philosophy the Cowboys had operated upon since 1960 would be effectively dissolved. And in that case, Landry would begin the inevitable transformation from a head coaching icon to a sideline figurehead whose word was acknowledged by staff members, but ultimately, ignored.

With the intent of avoiding such an undesirable fate, Tom tried to meet Tex halfway. He agreed with Schramm that changes needed to be made, but claimed that, at this time in his career, he didn't have the time to fully train a new coach and wanted to keep the same staff intact for the 1985 season.

Landry's strategic volley had placed the ball back in Schramm's court. It was up to him to agree or offer yet another compromise. Ordinarily, he would have pushed back. But Schramm had come to the table unprepared to fully execute his plan of takeover. There was no young coach waiting in the wings to sign a contract, nor had Schramm even made a list of available assistants. Schramm cursed himself for not doing his homework.

Landry got off the hook, only to land on another. Schramm reluctantly agreed to allow Landry to keep the same staff for the upcoming season, but not before coming to a mutual understanding that the topic would be re-opened between the two front-office figures the following year. Meanwhile, Schramm promised to be scouring the league for the brightest young assistants the game had to offer. He would have all his ducks lined up in a row next time.

Landry had one season to prove to Schramm and to Bright that bringing in outside help was not necessary. For so long the beneficiary of a foolproof support system surrounding him, Landry was about to learn what life was like for every other head coach in the NFL who found their employment rating unequivocally tied to the previous game's outcome. One season. It wasn't much, but it was all he had.

The following July in Thousand Oaks, Landry chatted with Bob St. John in his office early one morning before practice. St. John was a fair-minded man with a pen of discretion, a member of the working press who Landry didn't mind sharing some insight with. During this particular interview, Landry dropped a few hints as to the conditions he was then working under.

"Bum Bright didn't get where he is by taking care of everybody along the way," said Landry. "He's a tough cookie, and I don't know what pressures might be exerted on somebody like Tex if, say, we ended up going 6-10 this year. I don't think it'll happen, but it seems almost inevitable that it will sooner or later, because of all the winning seasons we've had."

Landry even went so far as to say that his job might not be safe. "You're not serious," argued St. John. "You don't really think anybody would fire you after what you've done all these years?"

"Well," Landry said, smiling, "if you have some losing seasons you never know what will happen."

A new hour had arrived. The time was now right. For the Cowboys. Yes, even for Landry himself.

For the first time in the star-spangled history of America's Team, the head coaching hot-seat had landed in Dallas, isolating Tom Landry on an island with a silence so deafening as to be broken only by the ominous tick-tick-ticking of an invisible clock.

PART II
THE SEASON

CHAPTER 7

THE LONG ROAD TO BUFFALO

"Staubach the player and Staubach the person spoiled a city, because he gave it 11 years of perfection, on the field and off. When you've seen one-of-a-kind, it's difficult to be satisfied with anything less."
Dallas Morning News columnist Randy Galloway

"Somehow, leadership hasn't come naturally for Danny White."
Skip Bayless, Dallas Times Herald columnist

The football news cycle could often be found at a complete standstill during the dead of winter. But on January 22, 1985, the Doubletree Inn in Dallas was buzzing from the scratching of busy pens. Newsmen by the dozen were standing at attention, making each jot and tittle count, ears tuned to every word coming from the guest of honor. Even after all these years, when

Roger Staubach spoke, the world listened.

Staubach was being his normally gracious self in acknowledging what, in the minds of every socially aware American, was considered an inevitable election into the Pro Football Hall of Fame. He reminisced, he avoided self-glorification, and he gave credit to teammates and coaches. Then the legendary quarterback had a bright idea.

"Wouldn't it be something," joked Staubach, "to make a comeback after being elected to the Hall of Fame?"

That gave the crowd of reporters cause for pause. *Wouldn't it though! That would be the biggest news to come out of Dallas since...since...why, since Roger retired!*

Everyone in the room commenced laughing at the thought, while harboring in the back of their minds the painful knowledge that Danny White – God bless him - was not.

Whether in politics or sports, bad news is like a disease. It spreads fast. And when that news happens to revolve around the well-being of America's Team, it spreads doubly-fast. The news that broke concerning the Dallas Cowboys in the spring of 1985 had – to be perfectly accurate – been suspected for several months. But, like every good reporter knows, before writing a story, first check with Vegas. The betting line sees all, tells all. What it told about the Cowboys' prospects for the coming autumn was not pretty at all.

The odds for the Cowboys making it to Super Bowl XX were 9-1, according to Culver and Glantz. Harrah's in Reno had them at 10-1, and Barbary Coast at 15-1.

The parlor patrons having obviously given up on the Cowboys as an NFL force, it only made sense that the press soon follow suit. So out came the preseason football magazine publications, complete with forecasts of doom and gloom for Tom Landry's fading squad.

Inside Sports tagged Dallas as one of the four teams "likely to decline in 1985...These guys look like the Green Bay Packers going into the 1969 season." *Pro Football Illustrated* magazine picked the Cowboys to finish fourth in the NFC East, behind St. Louis, Washington, and New York. *Street & Smith* magazine had Dallas finishing fourth in the division, as did the *Sporting News' Pro Football Yearbook*, in which Dave Klein wrote, "Landry is the dean of NFL coaches but it will take one of his best coaching jobs ever to get this crew into the playoffs."

Ever the diplomat, Landry took all of this doubt and criticism in stride, even daring to agree with where the Cowboys allegedly stacked up within the NFC East. "I pick us fourth. I like that position. I like to come from behind," he said matter-of-factly.

Not that anyone in the media was holding their breath on the Cowboys being any sort of sleeping giant in 1985. The team had lost too many players in recent years for that to happen.

After the 1983 season, the Cowboys waved goodbye to nine veterans. Offensive tackle Pat Donovan, defensive end Harvey Martin, wide receiver Drew Pearson, fullback Robert Newhouse, and tight end Billy Joe Dupree all retired. Quarterback Glenn Carano opted for the USFL, as did linebacker Bruce Huther and defensive end Larry Bethea. Also, wide receiver Butch Johnson was traded to the Houston Oilers for Mike Renfro.

The fallout after the 1984 season was just as alarming. Veteran middle linebacker Bob Breunig and offensive guard Herbert Scott retired. Wide receiver Doug Donley and second-year starting outside linebacker Billy Cannon Jr. joined them shortly.

None of which seemed to bother Landry in the least. Landry had a noticeable bounce in his step during the spring months while preparing for his twenty-sixth season as head coach of the Cowboys. He knew something that the outside world did not.

His Cowboys may have been lacking in outstanding talent overall, but he still believed in them and in the possibilities for success in 1985. It didn't matter that the public was all set to bury the 'Boys as a hopeless cause. He saw a light at the end of the tunnel, a bright ray of hope shining forth from one of the darkest days and lowest points he had ever experienced during his tenure. That snowy, wind-bitten day would be forever sealed in his mind under a most simple heading: Buffalo.

Buffalo was more than just a destination. It was the end of a long, weary journey of waste. It was a landing spot for a team spinning wildly out of control, stuck on a downward spiral of selfishness and discontent. In Buffalo, of all places, the world-renowned Dallas Cowboys had hit rock bottom.

Tom Landry had been to Buffalo, and was better for it. What's more, the same could be said for each and every one of his battle-scarred players.

It was the American comedian Jackie Gleason who once credited the Almighty with possessing a sense of humor, based strictly on the existence of the human race. The quip engendered a few laughs from the audience then, as it still does today. Had Gleason paused long enough from working a crowd to also search for proof of God's timing in life, he would have only needed to glance at the career timeline of Tom Landry.

A veteran of more than thirty NFL seasons, Landry was as accomplished a sideline general as the game of professional football had ever seen, with a reputation seasoned through the golden rays of grace, competitiveness, conquest, and higher thought. But all along the path of his long football journey, he had been rewarded for being in the right place at the right time. The fatalist might call that a strong run of luck. A Christian like Landry deemed it to be more blessings than any one man rightly deserved.

Landry could lay claim to having a brilliant football mind. He could not, however, have personally invoked the opening of the many doors of opportunity which he was so fortunate to have walked through on his way to becoming a coaching legend in Dallas.

Only a war could have delayed his college career at the University of Texas long enough for Landry to meet his future wife as a 23-year old junior. Only plans of marriage could have led to the impulsive decision to sign with the New York Yankees of the AAFC for $7,500 while walking off the field after his final college game.

Landry's pro career could have easily gone up in smoke when the Yankees were bought out by the NFL's New York Giants one year later. But head coach Steve Owen liked Landry's booming punts so much that he decided to place him on the Giants' roster. Little did Owen realize that Landry would soon develop into a defensive specialist for the Giants, first as a defensive back, then as a coordinator.

In 1958, a simple case of soul-searching led Landry to profess a newfound faith in Jesus Christ, changing his outlook on life and football. Weary with being away from his home state of Texas for six months out of every year, Landry began making plans to leave coaching and the Big Apple permanently behind.

So when Tex Schramm offered him the head coaching position of the Dallas Cowboys in December of 1959, Landry agreed to join the fledgling franchise thinking it would be the last phase of his transition back into the real world. In Landry's mind, he would coach for a few years before being fired, and then settle down behind a corporate desk for the next twenty years. And it might have turned out just that way, had it not been for the unmatched faith of the Cowboys' owner.

Landry's Cowboys were an exciting team in those early years, but managed to win just 13 of 52 games from 1960-63, a fact which didn't sit well among local fans. As a part of any other organization, he would have likely been unceremoniously dismissed. But with an owner like Clint Murchison Jr., who enjoyed filling the role of a contrarian, Landry was instead awarded a 10-year contract, convincing Landry to commit himself to being a full-time NFL head coach.

During his days as a defensive coordinator for the Giants, he had invented the 4-3 defense, a scheme opponents quickly copied and began using for themselves. Upon arriving in Dallas,

Landry promptly created a complicated style of motion offense as a counter attack, designed specifically to defeat the strengths of the 4-3 defense which he had created.

But Landry didn't stop there. As complicated as the Cowboys' motion-offense was and as difficult as it was for opponents to stop, Landry realized that, were his team to ever ascend to the top of the NFL summit, they would have to learn to defend Green Bay's devastating power sweep. So Landry went to the blackboard and came up with the Flex defense, which called for the four defensive linemen to position themselves in an offset manner along the line of scrimmage, based upon recognition of certain "keys" before the snap of the ball.

The odd alignment proved to be an extension of Landry's far-reaching genius. Not only did the Flex give the Green Bay offense fits in consecutive NFL Championship Game meetings in 1966 and 1967, but also became a staple of the Cowboys franchise, a scheme too complicated for outsiders to borrow.

In 1975 Landry unveiled another gadget. In an attempt to provide Dallas quarterback Roger Staubach an extra second or two in the pocket, Landry installed the fabled Shotgun formation into the Cowboy playbook. What was used as a means of trickery by San Francisco for a short time during the early 1960s, before a rash of injuries to 49er quarterbacks convinced head coach Red Hickey to put the formation on the shelf, quickly became a fixture of the Dallas offense, as Landry proved to a skeptical league that the Shotgun could also be used to execute even the simplest of plays.

The Shotgun, according to Landry, called for Staubach to line up about five yards behind the center, where he would then receive the snap before scanning the field for an open receiver. If a target didn't present itself, Staubach was free to use his legs to escape the pocket and ad-lib from there. The Cowboys also surprised their opponents by running draw plays and throwing screen passes from the new formation.

Los Angeles Rams linebacker Isiah Robertson, still steaming from an 18-7 Week 1 loss to the "new-look" Cowboys at Texas Stadium, referred to the Shotgun as "rinky-dink." Robertson, however, never dared to question the effectiveness of the formation.

One year after missing the playoffs with a sub-par 8-6 record, the 1975 Cowboys used the Shotgun to become the first Wild-Card team to make it all the way to the Super Bowl. And though they eventually lost Super Bowl X to Pittsburgh in valiant fashion, the Cowboys and the Shotgun made believers out of everybody. By the turn of the decade, nearly every NFL team had incorporated the Shotgun into its offensive playbook.

But Landry's innovative mind could not carry the Cowboys on its own. Even Landry needed the benefit of an on-the-field support system to make it all work. To get the job done on Sundays, the coach had to have players.

The presence of veteran quarterback Eddie Lebaron was essential to the installation of Landry's wide-open multiple offense, as was the willingness of defensive tackle Bob Lilly to the success of the Flex defense. Lebaron had a tiny frame and a patient soul, and was more than willing to listen and adapt to the ultra-complex style of offense Landry proposed. Lebaron's example was enough to convince headstrong rookie Don Meredith to buy into the system too.

And Lilly, after a couple of years as an above-average defensive end, saw his career change overnight when Landry moved him closer to the ball. Without Lilly's dominance in the middle of the Dallas line proving to skeptical teammates that the funky formation could work if given a chance, Landry's Flex would, in all likelihood, have never lasted in Dallas, and would have disappeared from the NFL landscape altogether.

Lebaron and Lilly can be credited with helping to establish Landry's peculiar philosophy in the Dallas locker room. It was through the insertion of a young, confident quarterback into the starting lineup a few years later that the Cowboys established themselves as one of the NFL's elite franchises.

Within the hallowed Bible Belt, that expansive Southern region in North America noted for its sanctimonious Sundays, there has long been an inherent reluctance of using the profane. But in the early 1970's, a phenomenon so revolutionary in character had even the highest-ranking priests swearing by the name of Roger Staubach. Staubach, a mere mortal with Catholic upbringing and Naval education, had the powers to turn to gold the dust of a broken play, using only his feet and competitive ingenuity. Legend has it that he could alter the final outcome of a game on the strength of his sheer will.

With Staubach manning the controls of the Cowboy offense, Landry's innovative brilliance shone like never before. When Dallas struggled to get over the hump in big games with Meredith and Craig Morton at quarterback during the late-1960s, Staubach – fresh off a four-year term of service in the Navy – was there to step up and provide the difference. In Staubach's first season as the unquestioned starting quarterback in Dallas, the Cowboys reeled off 10 consecutive victories on their way to a 24-3 conquest of Miami in Super Bowl VI for their first world championship title.

Staubach, the quintessential quarterback for Landry's offensive system, guided the Cowboys to three more Super Bowl appearances over the next seven seasons. Not only was he an affluent passer, but "Roger The Dodger" could also escape from a backfield scrum and scramble for yardage. His competitive spirit rubbed off on fellow teammates, providing the Cowboys hope of engineering a late-game rally even when the odds were clearly set against it. This positive attitude enabled Staubach to guide no fewer than 23 game-winning drives in the fourth quarter during his days in Dallas, earning him the additional moniker of "Captain Comeback."

No comeback looms larger on his list than the one he sparked coming off the bench in relief of Morton during the 1972 Divisional playoff game in San Francisco. Trailing 28-16 to the 49ers, Staubach fired two touchdown passes in the final 1:18 to make the Cowboys 30-28 winners.

His "Hail Mary" touchdown heave to wide receiver Drew Pearson in the waning seconds of a 1975 Divisional playoff game against Minnesota serves as one more example of Staubach's magical ability to pull an unlikely victory from the jaws of certain defeat.

Staubach's enchanted dance was an autumn weekend spectacle in Dallas through the 1979 season, when he then shocked the entire fan base by coming face-to-face with his own mortality. Due to recurring concussions and concerns over his long-term health, Staubach announced his retirement in March of 1980 before a crowd of reporters at Texas Stadium. His goodbye was short, sweet, and surprisingly permanent, causing many to wander the streets of Dallas that day in shock and disbelief. In football terms, mortality was little more than a fancy word for imperfection. The fact that Staubach was something less than supernatural was news to many. *Roger retire? I thought he was supposed to have hailed from Utopia?*

The accompanying fact that Staubach would not be quarterbacking the Cowboys into the 1980s meant that Landry was due for a stark readjustment as the head coach. There had been a time in his career when Landry struggled with the dichotomy of exacting preparation from the coaching staff during the week and slipshod execution from the players on Sunday. Watching Staubach perform his dramatic act from the sideline had eased the pain of more than one Monday morning film session for Landry, who could more easily forgive shortcomings from his troops in the aftermath of victory. Staubach's time had also given Landry time to mature, both as a coach and as a person.

Landry was never the fastest or the quickest guy on the field during his playing days. So he had to study film to gain an advantage. Perhaps that is why he believed there was never an excuse for a player not to be completely mentally prepared when he stepped onto the field on Sundays.

Landry was, in so many ways, the perfect coach. His dress code was impeccable, his speech unsoiled by cursing. His game-plan was flawless. Seeing his own players perform in a less than exemplary manner left Landry puzzled and often frustrated during his early days in Dallas.

But as he studied the Bible more and his faith in Jesus grew, Landry realized more and more that God was in the business of dealing with imperfect people. Why then should he chafe at dealing with imperfect athletes?

Landry had struggled to deal with the personality of Meredith, a handsome fun-loving quarterback who cherished his fair share of good jokes and stiff drinks. But he was better prepared to handle the shortcomings of Staubach's successor, and was in a better position to balance public expectations and overall fairness.

The media could be cruel, and they could affect a player's psyche. They also could poison a locker room against a quarterback. Sportswriters had been merciless in their criticism of Meredith during the 1960s. But the negativity failed to undermine his support in the locker room, in part because "Dandy Don" was part of a less-than-dandy team that had never won a lot of games.

But the situation in the early 1980s was completely different. Staubach was the standard that every other Cowboys quarterback after him would be compared to. Because of him, success in Dallas went by an entirely different definition than it did in other football towns. Anything less than an annual trip to the Super Bowl was now deemed to be a failure, by both the press and the local fans.

The city of Dallas has always been run by a group of elitists. Bankers. Stuffed stooges. Desk pigeons. It is an industrious air that blows between the towers of downtown, tinged with the unquenchable thirst for success and notoriety. The rich of the earth congregate freely there, with standards as lofty as the blue heavens above. It is a place where days are counted in dollars, the breadth of the city related to a bank vault. Clocks are tuned to the sound of safes. The well-to-do of the region lead the morning commute, with aims, some dare say, as high as their noses.

At the beginning, back when the Cowboys played their games at the old Cotton Bowl, expectations for the pro football team of local origin consisted of a deep winter run and maybe a trophy of tiffany at the end. By the conclusion of Staubach's tenure at quarterback, the city had designs on every Super Bowl trophy of future production. Nay, not merely designs, these were nothing short of demands.

Citizens prided themselves on being members and contributors to the state's leading banking center. The smell of newly-printed cash nearby was a source of comfort, not to mention the highest-ranking of all status symbols. Yet there was also the pervasive idea in this concrete jungle that the three-piece brigade from the office understood the nuances of the rough-and-tumble battle over a pigskin as well as any other farmer with dirty fingernails from a rural Texas town, or even better.

This notion manifested itself through the common insistence that the Cowboys enjoy postseason success on an annual basis. In the game of football, heroes were often born out of sweat and ingenuity. Always after Thanksgiving, never before Christmas. The playoffs were reserved for moments of a hero's making. The playoffs could make or break you as a player. But be sure of this; they surely would define you. Especially if you were the Cowboys' quarterback.

Surrounded by a community that was founded on the philosophical bedrock of high-class production and business flair, it was easy to understand how "Captain Comeback" could eventually become widely regarded as the one and only "Captain America." Somehow, someway, Staubach managed to live up to many – if not all – of the impossible expectations attached to his team and his position. Staubach was the starting quarterback for eight seasons in Dallas. The Cowboys qualified for the playoffs in seven of those seasons, reaching the Super Bowl in four.

And even on the rare occasions when the team failed to advance that far, Staubach was somehow exonerated from all blame. Staubach played poorly in Dallas' 27-10 loss to Minnesota at Texas Stadium in the 1973 NFC Championship Game, but all fans could remember was the absence of Lilly and All-Pro running back Calvin Hill from the lineup due to injury.

In 1976, the Cowboys were bounced from the Divisional playoffs by the Los Angeles Rams by a 14-12 score, a disheartening outcome that was rationalized through the knowledge that Staubach was dealing with a broken finger on his throwing hand.

The conclusion to Staubach's final season was chalked up as a case of rotten luck. Already down three starters – defensive end Ed "Too Tall" Jones, free safety Cliff Harris, and strongside linebacker Thomas Henderson – and with two starters – wide receiver Drew Pearson and running back Tony Dorsett – noticeably ailing, the Cowboys lost another nail-biter to Los Angeles in the Divisional round, this time on the merits of a deflected game-winning touchdown pass of 50 yards from Rams quarterback Vince Ferragomo, off the fingertips of Dallas linebacker Mike Hegman, and ultimately to Rams receiver Billy Waddy with 2:06 remaining in the fourth quarter. That this 21-

19 defeat should have come on the heels of Staubach's most improbable comeback to nip Washington 35-34 and capture the NFC East division crown a week before only made the news of his retirement more difficult to swallow.

Inevitably, somebody had to take the torch from Staubach and carry it into 1980 and beyond. It's always been a cause of wonder as to why it had to be Danny White. White never experienced the glory commonly associated with a passing of the torch. He only felt the burden of expectations attached to his position.

There were moments that White was tantalizingly clutch, picking up the trailing Cowboys and carrying them across the finish line on his back to victory. But when the weather turned cold and the Cowboys were in a tight spot, White's golden arm turned to rust. At least, that's the way many choose to remember it.

The vine of frustration flourished with each passing failure. The frustration was not only in the stands, but in the locker room as well. White's own teammates questioned his competitiveness, his toughness, even his intellect, all the while harboring the greatest disappointment that Danny White was in fact anything but Roger Staubach.

White admittedly felt the pressure of living up to his quarterbacking predecessor in Dallas. He couldn't run from it. But he couldn't live up to it either.

Athletically speaking, Danny was not Roger. He could have been forgiven this physical shortcoming if he had found a way to get his team into the Super Bowl. White was a pocket quarterback in the mold that Meredith and Morton were before his time. White was a better passer than Morton, but he was less fun than Meredith.

Before being handed the starter's keys, White had been the backup to Staubach for four seasons, in which he filled in during some critical moments. He played briefly in Super Bowl XII against Denver, and a year later led the Cowboys from behind after Staubach had been knocked out to beat Atlanta in the NFC Divisional playoffs at Texas Stadium.

In White's first full season as the Dallas starter, there was a thought that he was taking right up where Staubach had left off. After guiding the Cowboys to 12 victories and a rout of Los Angeles in the Wild-Card playoff game, White engineered a postseason comeback for the ages, nipping Atlanta with a last-minute touchdown strike to Pearson. But the next week, White was shockingly proven mortal in a listless 20-7 loss to Philadelphia in the NFC Championship Game.

One year later, White and the Cowboys came up short on the doorstep of the Super Bowl once again, falling to the upstart 49ers 28-27 at rowdy Candlestick Park in a classic battle that went down to the wire. In the final minute, just moments after Dwight Clark made "The Catch" to put San Francisco ahead, White had the Dallas offense on the march. Already across midfield, the Cowboys were one simple play away from being within kicking range of their Pro Bowl place-kicker, Rafael Septien. But then White, caught in a crowded pocket, was raked across the arms by a defender, and fumbled the ball and the 1981 season away forever, inking another what-might-have been moment into the history books for the Dallas fan base to make sense of.

White's troubles were small compared to what they would become. Behind the scenes, frustration was beginning to grow concerning White the quarterback. But his behavior the following summer had more than a few in the Cowboy locker room questioning his ethics as a team leader.

The strike of 1982 appeared to be the beginning of the end for White in Dallas. White went for a bold and daring move, and wound up nearly bringing himself down in the process. The strike began with White hanging well back in the shadows, which was to be expected. He wasn't the Cowboys' player rep. That responsibility belonged to fullback Robert Newhouse. Very quietly he supported the cause of the players union as they sought to negotiate a new collective bargaining agreement with league owners.

But then came a meeting with Schramm, from which White emerged as a fence-rider, unsure of where he stood on the issues at hand. After another meeting, White was all in support of an immediate settlement, turning his back on the players union and pledging his support for the cause of the owners.

"I'm making $250,000 playing football, and I challenge any guy on our team to make more than that outside football," White said. "The owners own the football team. They don't have to pay us a penny. I guess that's a thought from the old school, but I'm a bit old-fashioned. If what I felt mattered, we would be playing football."

Watching White step out of line and attempt to dictate terms to every NFL player rankled dozens of Cowboys in Dallas. Just who did White think he was? Captain America?

"There was a lot of dissension," running back Tony Dorsett told Gary Myers in *The Catch*. "There was a lot of dislike towards Danny White because of what players were thinking he was doing. There is no question if guys had a chance during that strike to string him up and give him a hundred lashes, they would have been more than happy to dish out those lashes.

"We kind of thought he was working both sides of the fence. He was trying to give information about the players. He was spending too much time with Tex. He shouldn't have been doing that."

The strike was eventually resolved and, though a tension had settled over the clubhouse, White was able to lead the Cowboys back into the NFC Championship Game for a third consecutive year, but once again ran into hardship. A big hit from Washington defensive lineman Dexter Manley knocked White from the game near halftime with Dallas trailing 14-3. In stepped Gary Hogeboom, a third-year quarterback out of Central Michigan with a rifle for an arm, to try his hand at a comeback while White sat on the bench with a towel over his head, courtesy of a ringing concussion.

Hogeboom started well, throwing touchdown passes to Pearson and Butch Johnson to draw the Cowboys to within 21-17 after three quarters. The rally was thwarted by a pair of late-game Hogeboom interceptions, allowing the Redskins to win going away 31-17. But an outpouring of postgame support for Hogeboom after the defeat signaled to Landry that he was going to have to shake things up in order to prevent an outright revolt.

With the locker room divided and the quarterback debate growing increasingly toxic, Landry attempted to settle the issue once and for all by bringing in a new young face to guide the franchise. It was a plan that could have changed everything.

In the days leading up to the 1983 draft, the Cowboys had a deal worked out with Baltimore that would send White to the Colts in exchange for the No. 1 overall draft pick, which Landry planned on using to acquire the rights to Stanford gunslinger John Elway. But Colts owner Carroll Rosenbloom nixed the trade at the last minute, causing a quarterback controversy to officially break out in Dallas the following summer.

Danny White-versus-Gary Hogeboom was all the rage during the Cowboys' 1983 training camp in Thousand Oaks. Some soft whispers from the locker room offered full support for young Hogeboom, citing a need for a new direction and a new leader. Others, fearful of causing waves with a new season directly ahead, gave their vote to White. Still more Cowboy players chose to remain silent on the subject.

Caught in the middle of this tussle for supremacy was Landry himself, who was desperately trying to come across to his team and the media as an unbiased participant in the matter. He didn't want to appear to cater to the malcontents on the team publicly undermining White's leadership capabilities by giving the job to Hogeboom, but he also didn't want influential veterans accusing him of playing favorites in the event that he retained White as the Cowboys' starting signal-caller.

The end result of White and Hogeboom racing across the preseason finish line in a dead heat was probably the best situation that Landry could have hoped for. Then he was able to fall back on an old rule which applied to every position on the team, maintaining that an up-and-comer must clearly outplay a veteran in order to win a starting role. Based on that precept, White was declared to be the winner and the Cowboys' No. 1 quarterback for 1983.

Landry had experienced enough quarterback controversies to know that this one had yet to be decided. The players could respect the rule, but that didn't necessarily translate into respect for White's leadership. Danny's doubters still lingered, murmuring quietly in the background.

White responded exactly as Landry hoped he would, by guiding Dallas to a fast start and the top of the conference standings. But when the 12-2 Cowboys stumbled down the December stretch, losing their final three games by a combined score of 97-44, the cries for White's job returned in full force.

The doubters were singing again, harmonizing over a sad song of Cowboy shortcomings. A tidal wave of negativity was threatening to swallow White whole, in spite of the fact that the eight-year Cowboy veteran had compiled one of the more impressive passing resumes the league had ever seen.

By the end of the 1983 season, White stood as the second-highest rated quarterback in NFL history, had tied or broke eight club records, and fell just 20 yards short in 1983 of becoming the first Cowboys QB to throw for 4,000 yards in a season. Only five quarterbacks had ever accomplished that feat: Joe Namath, Dan Fouts, Brian Sipe, Lynn Dickey, and Billy Kinney. Had White not been relieved early in the regular season finale blowout loss to San Francisco, no doubt he would have reached that mark.

Statistics were nice, but they weren't enough to prevent players from hearkening back to when the quarterback in Dallas went by the name of Staubach, and victories were served up on a royal platter of drama, flair, and the finger-drawings commonly associated with a sandlot.

Said Cowboy wide receiver Tony Hill shortly after the 1983 season: "When Roger was here we used to adlib a lot more. With Danny, they had so many things on his mind that I couldn't come back to the huddle and tell him I could beat a guy…maybe have it called two or three plays later.

"For example, in the Philadelphia game [Nov. 12, 1979] when I caught passes for two hundred and something yards [213], two of the plays weren't even in the game plan, but I told Roger I could beat the guy and Roger hit me with both of them. One of them was a 75-yard touchdown and the other about 50 yards for a touchdown."

Invariably, where Danny was, the conversation always came back to Roger. Danny & Roger. Roger & Danny. One was a shadow of past conquest, the other a constant companion of crunch-time defectiveness.

The 1983 season has been regarded by so many to have been White's finest passing campaign as an NFL quarterback.

But it was hard for those clinging to the hope of another Cowboys run to the Super Bowl to forgive White for the 10 turnovers he was responsible for over the final three games of that season. Just days after the Cowboys had taken an early fall from the playoffs at the hands of Los Angeles in the Wild Card round, a letter written to one of the local newspapers suggested that "if Danny White isn't replaced by Gary Hogeboom at quarterback right away, the Cowboys can expect to go through another losing season, just like they did this year."

White's most glaring mistake of the 1983 season came, ironically, during the biggest game. Dallas trailed Washington 14-10 during third quarter action of a high-stakes December tilt at Texas Stadium, with first-place in the division and home-field advantage in the playoffs on the line. The Cowboys were faced with a fourth-and-1 from their own 49-yard line.

A lengthy timeout provided Landry enough time to formulate a plan. Rather than attempt to acquire a first-down, Landry ordered his quarterback to simply make a try at drawing the defense offsides. But White had other ideas. Tired of coming up short in critical games, White was going to try to silence some of his doubters with a risky gamble. White approached the line of scrimmage. He used the hard-count, but no Redskin jumped across the line. Then he checked the formation. Nose tackle Dave Butz and Darryl Grant were aligned just across from Dallas center Tom Rafferty, negating the possibility of a successful quarterback-sneak.

"We had no play at all," Rafferty said. "We were at midfield, we had good field position, it seemed we'd been out there forever. We should have taken the penalty and punted and held them down there."

Instead, White yelled out the signals for an audible that called for a handoff to tailback Ron Springs. Rafferty couldn't believe what he was hearing.

"Don't run it," Rafferty pleaded.

"Shut up and run it," barked White in response.

Like any good center, Rafferty relented to the wishes of his quarterback. With cries of "No, Danny! No!" coming from the mouth of Landry over on the sideline, Rafferty hiked the ball, and White placed the ball in the belly of Springs. When Springs was stuffed for a 2-yard loss, the air went out of the Cowboys' sails. Dallas lost the game and the NFC East crown that day by a 31-10 final, and looked but a lethargic shell of their former selves for the remainder of the season.

"This is what killed Danny," defensive back Dennis Thurman said in *The Catch*. "That's where guys were done with him. To me, that was the pressure of not having accomplished in 1980, '81, and '82. Now it's 1983, after four seasons of being the starting quarterback of the Dallas Cowboys, even though you've been in three championship games, you've lost them all. People are saying you can't win the big one. And now you are in the biggest regular season game, and you feel like you got to make something happen."

Danny's gamble gone wrong also sparked the unraveling of the Dallas locker room. Dissension and resentment hung thick in the air, as players separated into position groups and silently steamed over differences, perceived slights, and game-day failings of fellow teammates.

In late December, a few veterans called a 30-minute meeting supposedly to re-instill a sense of camaraderie. It's safe to say that it didn't work, leaving the team a veritable mess of conflicting interests as the postseason neared.

Before the playoff game against the Rams, certain members of the Dallas locker room were grumbling about the lack of respect the players were receiving from a media contingent who said the Cowboys weren't playing up to par.

Tight end Doug Cosbie, when asked to give a Christmas wish by a local television station, said he would like a present of "every sportswriter in Dallas-Fort Worth getting fired."

After the collapse of what had once been such a promising season in 1983, the negative fan reaction was emphatic in its denouncement of everything and everybody - except the place-kicker - as a problem on the team. "Meaning that kicker Rafael Septien…is the only player who can walk the streets without fear of flying bricks," wrote Frank Luksa in *Dallas Cowboys Weekly* magazine.

Landry and Tex Schramm were now in a bind. Up to this point, Danny White's career had been filled with all of the wrong kind of storybook endings, bitter failures that those in Dallas would tell their grandchildren about for generations. White, instead of being the franchise savior, found himself the butt of every playoff joke in town, a caricature of misguided intentions. He was perceived to be the problem, rather than the solution. No captain – whether his name be Staubach or White – could lead if the soldiers were determined not to follow. What to do with their franchise quarterback?

In the end, after much deliberation on the subject, Landry did what he had done the year before; declare an open competition for the starting quarterback job. It was White vs. Hogeboom II. Now, things were getting serious.

In May of 1984 the *Dallas Morning News* contacted thirty-four Cowboy players for a quarterback poll consisting of two point-blank questions.

Question No. 1: Which QB did they want to win the starting job? Results: Hogeboom, 20; White, 4; no comment, 10.

Question No. 2: Which QB did they think Landry would choose? Result: White, 23; Hogeboom, 5; no comment 6.

Obviously, a good portion of the team didn't think Landry was interested in holding a fair competition, which made for a full summer of intrigue as White and Hogeboom battled it out on the practice fields at Thousand Oaks. Both quarterbacks played well at training camp and through the preseason, but it wasn't until the annual Welcome Home Cowboys luncheon on a Tuesday afternoon in late August that Landry publicly selected his starting quarterback for 1984.

With White and Hogeboom seated next to each other at a nearby table in full dinner attire, Landry approached the podium to declare the winner. Apparently, the head coach was suffering from a bout with nerves. He made small talk about first one thing then another, before finally getting down to the important business at hand.

"Well, I had just as soon be with Bud Grant on some lake fishing right now," said Landry, "then making a decision like this."

Opined Blackie Sherrod for the *Dallas Times Herald* on the following day: "The way he looked and acted, Landry would have rather shared a canoe with Beelzebub himself, much less a retired coach. He did not *like* what he was doing. He was in an awkward position, and Landry, as any other proud captain, does not fancy being caught with his breeches at half-mast."

His hemming and hawing having run its course, Landry finally dropped the name of the lucky winner onto his audience.

"...Phil Pozderac..."

Uh, come again, Coach?

Landry, even in his awkward pose in front of the microphone, managed to crack a smile at his own slip of the tongue. Phil Pozderac was the Cowboys' newly-christened starting left tackle, not the starting quarterback.

That honor, informed Landry, belonged to none other than a fellow by the name of *Hogenbloom.* A quick checking of name-tags proceeded. Hogenbloom? Who invited that guy to the party?

The third time worked a charm for the head coach. Landry finally ironed out the kinks in his diction. Hogeboom, Gary.

There! The secret was out.

The crowd of 1,400 was as stunned as White was displeased. Landry's ensuing explanation for his decision only served to raise attending eyebrows even higher.

"Hogeboom is excitement," said Landry. (Or did he mean Hogenbloom?) "That is one thing about Hogeboom. He's got the strong arm, and what he does is pull himself out of holes. He's just like Roger in that respect."

Just like Roger? You don't say! That was all the insight the fan base needed to pile on the newly-assembled "Boomer Bandwagon" in expectation of another thrilling ride to Super Bowl country.

Come to find out, the new kid quarterback on the block wasn't such hot stuff after all. Hogeboom opened the season with a franchise-record 33 completions for 343 yards in a 20-13 win over Los Angeles on Monday Night Football. He completed at least sixty-percent of his passes just once in what were four sub-par performances following the opener, leading up to a Week 6 matchup with St. Louis when he was replaced by White in the second half. That 31-20 home loss to the Cardinals was the first of three consecutive games in which White came on in relief, forcing Landry to demote Hogeboom to second-string status.

A game of musical quarterbacks then broke out. With White as the starter in Week 9, the Cowboys defeated a struggling Indianapolis team in convincing fashion. On the following Sunday versus the New York Giants, a bruised shoulder sidelined White in the second quarter, allowing the "Boomer Bandwagon" another opportunity to start rolling. But Hogeboom was so ineffective that White, having been successfully passed through the X-ray machine, returned for the fourth quarter. A few plays later, White walked off the field after re-injuring the same shoulder. Back out came Hogeboom, who promptly put the game out of reach by tossing an interception.

But there was more than one cause for the 1984 Cowboys underperforming early in the season. The locker room was a mess. If not pouting over a less-than-desirable role, teammates were using every chance to point fingers in private while using the press to backstab each other publicly. It was a common happening for a player to hold court in front of his locker and wax eloquent on the struggles of a fellow Cowboy.

In the middle of the season, Landry, tired of reading negative things about the Cowboys' inner workings in the morning newspaper, called a team meeting and imposed a gag order on his players. From here on, they were to be fined $1,000 for leaking details of team meetings to the media. Alas, Landry's stern message fell on ears of stone. The next day, a story on the imposed silence was in the morning paper.

The dysfunctional Cowboys from Dallas continued to keep pace in the standings while living on the brink of implosion. Going into Week 12, their 7-4 record, while certainly below franchise standards, was still good enough to have them tied with Washington atop the NFC East.

And then...Buffalo.

Four days away from the Thanksgiving Day holiday, the Cowboys were decked out in their road blues for a bout with the 0-11 Bills inside frigid Rich Stadium in Orchard Park, New York. A grand opportunity to gain some ground in the playoff race was in front of them. Buffalo, the worst team in the league that year by a wide margin, had dropped thirteen consecutive games, including eight in a row on their home field.

The thermometer showed 36-degrees at kickoff, with swirling wind gusts of nearly twenty miles-per-hour, putting the chill-factor in the high teens. Intermittent snow showers fell throughout the afternoon, with balloons blowing throughout the seating sections, occasionally even across the playing field. Accompanied by a low, gray cloud ceiling, it was a gloomy and miserable setting indeed for a football game.

No more miserable, as it turned out, than the Cowboys' performance that day. Rookie Buffalo running back Greg Bell broke through the Dallas defense for an 85-yard touchdown run on the game's first play. Timmy Newsome lost a fumble on the Cowboys' opening possession, the first of his career. The Bills blocked a Danny White punt in the first quarter, leaving Landry visibly upset as he paced the Dallas sideline.

The Bills entered the weekend allowing a league-high average of 29 points-per-game. The Cowboys would not get close to that mark on this day. Gary Hogeboom would not be able to take advantage of a porous Buffalo defense that had already yielded an alarming 25 touchdown passes in only 11 games.

Hogeboom, the starter after a solid outing the previous week in a critical victory over St. Louis while filling in for the injured White, played poorly yet again. But he wasn't alone. Early in the game Hogeboom was guilty of throwing into double-coverage, resulting in an interception. Later in the second quarter, Cosbie was flagged for pushing off in the end-zone, wiping out a Dallas touchdown. Two plays later, Hogeboom was intercepted again.

A listless 14-3 loss having reached its dreary conclusion, Tony Dorsett blew a fuse in the postgame locker room and didn't hesitate to let more than a few teammates hear of his displeasure with the team's effort.

"I'm totally embarrassed," he said. "I'd like to stick my head somewhere and hide. If we're not going to play any better than we did today, we might as well pack it up and take it home."

The loss was not without critical consequence. From a degenerative dynasty, the Cowboys slipped into the rankings of the mortals, even to the outside of the playoff picture. For the first time in ten years, and only the second time since 1965, the Cowboys did not participate in the NFL postseason, coming up short in the standings by a single game.

But all during the spring of 1985, the Dallas head coach clung to an invaluable consolation prize that went directly back to that miserable beating at the hands of the Bills. The disgrace that was Buffalo did more for the Cowboys than Landry would have likely been able to accomplish with one bloody off-season of heads rolling.

Through the humiliation of an unforgivable defeat, long-standing differences among team members were put aside and old wounds began to heal. The ongoing quarterback debate was shelved too. Nobody even dared to question Landry's decision to start White over Hogeboom for the annual Turkey Day game versus New England. It had taken awhile – nearly three full seasons to be exact - but the Cowboys had finally started becoming a team again.

"We weren't a football team after the '82 strike, and we never came together as a team until after the Buffalo game last year," recalled Landry after the 1984 season. "The whole atmosphere changed after Buffalo. Every member of the team started to receive support. The atmosphere totally changed. And I look back on what happened last year as a good experience for Gary, because it has made him a better quarterback…

"…Danny had a very difficult time last year. He was our No. 1 man for four years, and it's pretty tough on a guy when somebody else takes his place. He had a tough mental situation to overcome, and I think he performed well."

"He came back strong in the end. He still wasn't where he wanted to be, but at least he gained the confidence of the team and everybody felt like he could win for them."

Buffalo had been a tough pill for Landry to swallow at the time. He and his team had been embarrassed. But without it, Landry's chances of fending off Tex Schramm's pending takeover of his coaching staff would be as good as nil. The Cowboys no longer had the star power and the depth to overpower opponents. If Dallas was to make any noise in the NFC during the 1985 season, it would have to be on the strength of a complete and thorough collective effort, with no room for stragglers or complainers.

Before Buffalo, Landry would not have believed it to be possible. And even then, looking back upon it, he had to admit the odds were not in his team's favor to rebound into the playoffs. The Cowboys, compared to their former selves of the previous decade, were not much of a team. But at least now they could lay claim to being one. Not the most talented team out there, but a team nonetheless. And Landry knew from experience that players who fight for each other on Sundays very often wind up surprising themselves.

Even amidst troubled waters, and even with his dynasty on the cusp of becoming permanently submerged, Landry was still benefitting from an uncanny sense of timing in his coaching career. Buffalo had not been the closing of a door like so many had suspected at the time, but in fact was the very opening Landry needed in order to make one last attempt at preventing America's Team from falling into the hands of outsiders, and into inevitable ruin.

CHAPTER 8

THE HOPEFUL & NEEDY

"The Cowboys computer would short all its circuits if a 5-9 quarterback were offered."
Dallas Morning News **columnist Blackie Sherrod, on the possibility of the Cowboys drafting Doug Flutie**

The pixie dust of high-stakes excitement had settled softly over the efforts of an entire season, sanctifying the blood and sweat of all who participated in the NFL's 1984 campaign. Now, with the captivating clash between Joe Montana and Dan Marino in Super Bowl XIX in the rearview mirror, the focus of the pro football world looked ahead to April's NFL draft in New York City.

In years past, the city of Dallas had welcomed this event with eager anticipation, confident that their beloved Cowboys would find a gem or three from a crowded field of college talent. Even from very humble beginnings, the Cowboys had climbed out of the muck and mire of an expansion project on the strong right arm of innovation, using the draft to replenish and stockpile a roster that was destined to be world champions multiple times over.

Defying the age-old sentiment which classified brute strength and manly toughness as the primary traits necessary to win football games, it was the Cowboys in the 1960s that proved to a skeptical league that football could be a thinking man's game as well. Aided by computers and an intensive grading process, Gil Brandt sought players from even the smallest of schools for those that fit Tom Landry's complicated brand of football. Brandt scoured the football fields of America, the gyms, and even track and field programs. For more than a decade, the results left competitors flabbergasted, as the Cowboys grew from small-team to America's Team.

Bob Lilly was an All-American defensive end at Texas Christian University who blossomed into a Hall of Fame tackle. An Olympic track legend with the label of "World's Fastest Human," Bob Hayes struck fear into the hearts of every NFL defensive back with bullet-like speed from the wide receiver position. Like Lilly, Hayes too has a bust in Canton.

Roger Staubach is another example of the franchise's scouting brilliance. The Cowboys took a tenth-round flyer on the Heisman Trophy-winning quarterback from Navy, waited four years for him to complete his tour of duty, and were rewarded with one of the most brilliant quarterback careers in league history. Even Mel Renfro, a speedy All-American halfback while at Oregon, found success with the Cowboys, intercepting 52 passes as a Cowboy cornerback on his way to the Hall of Fame.

Jethro Pugh, defensive tackle. Harvey Martin, defensive end. Cornell Green, defensive back. Dave Edwards, outside linebacker. Lee Roy Jordan, middle linebacker. Charlie Waters, strong safety. Cliff Harris, free safety. Calvin Hill, halfback. Robert Newhouse, fullback. Drew Pearson, wide receiver. Billy Joe Dupree, tight end. The list goes on and on of players who came through Brandt's scouting factory and prospered on Sundays in Dallas.

In recent years, though, the Cowboys had been beaten shamefully at their own game, allowing one prize after another to slip past them, while their star-studded roster slowly deteriorated with age. The wheel of first-round misfortune started spinning in 1978 with the selection of Michigan State defensive end Larry Bethea. Cowboy coaches raved about Bethea's athletic ability during practices. Their reviews of his in-game performance spelled something else. Bethea bounced around as a backup end and tackle in his six seasons along the Dallas defensive line, before parting ways with the Cowboys after the 1983 season.

Robert Shaw, a highly-rated center out of Tennessee who coaches expected to one day fill the shoes of standout veteran John Fitzgerald at the position, experienced the brutality of a good draft-pick gone bad. Gifted with All-Pro talent and a rare competitive nature, Shaw's career was cut short after only eight NFL starts, a severe knee injury in a 1981 regular season matchup in San Francisco sidelining him for good.

Two rounds after grabbing Shaw in the 1979 draft, Landry authored what in retrospect proved to be one of his worst war-room blunders. Rather than go the usual route and select the highest-ranked player remaining on the team's draft board, Landry chose to pass on Notre Dame quarterback Joe Montana, thinking that the Cowboys – with Roger Staubach, Danny White, and Glenn Carano on the roster – were more than set at the position. Instead, Landry opted to select Doug Cosbie, a pass-catching specialist at tight end from Santa Clara. Cosbie soon developed into a Pro Bowl player, but it was Montana – a certifiable Hall of Fame talent – who became the chief tormentor of the Cowboys throughout the 1980s.

Missouri guard Howard Richards (1981) was supposed to add some athleticism to the interior of the Cowboy offensive line but couldn't stay off the injured list. Rod Hill (1982) was a highly-touted cornerback from tiny Kentucky State University but was traded away after two disappointing seasons.

The Cowboys' luck proved to be just as poor with their No. 2 draft selections. Fullback Todd Christiansen (1978) was cut before his second season in Dallas and went on to become an All-Pro tight end with the Raiders. Aaron Mitchell (1979) was traded to Tampa Bay. Doug Donley (1981) was told his shoulder injury made him a bad risk, and the Cowboys cut him loose shortly after the 1984 season. Linebacker Jeff Rohrer (1982) had yet to graduate from special teams duty. Linebacker Mike Walter (1983) was waived after one season and went on to start for the world champion 49ers. Victor Scott played so poorly at cornerback as a rookie in 1984 that the Cowboys switched him to safety in the off-season.

Indifferent to whatever rankings or charts that Brandt and staff may have compiled over the course of the winter, fans around Dallas began clamoring for a different approach and a fresh start in 1985. Weary of early playoff exits and an annual quarterback debate, the locals were admittedly anxious for the Cowboys to alter their April tendencies and go for the bold. Bold as in gold. Gold as in Boston College quarterback Doug Flutie.

The Flutie flair had been in full view of a nation during the 1984 college football season, the scrambling, ducking, dodging, do-it-all, signal-calling savior leading the Golden Eagles to a wildly improbable berth in the Cotton Bowl. Even after critics spent a large portion of the holiday season pointing out apparent flaws and shortcomings in his game, Flutie remained a beloved figure as much for his unblinking competitiveness and an unquenchable will to win as the fourth quarter miracles he produced on a weekly basis.

Eagles fans had seen comeback victories from Flutie before, last-gasp drives that grabbed victory from the jaws of familiar defeat. The Boston College rally over Alabama from Week 3 of that season was still being talked about. Flutie, though, saved his best miracle for the very last day of the regular season, his desperation fling at the end of regulation resulting in a touchdown that shocked the rival Miami Hurricanes and had football nerds in Texas hearkening back to a hero from yesteryear.

"This kid is Capt. America to football fans everywhere," wrote Dallas Morning News columnist Randy Galloway. "He threw the most famous pass since Staubach's Hail Mary in the Orange Bowl that November day."

Flutie was rendered a bona-fide magician for his efforts at the college level, a folk-hero who handled all the media attention with admirable ease. And yet a fear remained in the minds of general managers and scouts everywhere that the Flutie magic was nothing more than a fad, a cute gimmick destined to be smothered by the bigger, faster defenses of the NFL.

"At his size, of course, life expectancy in the pros may not exceed that of a mosquito," Galloway readily noted.

There was no denying this obvious truth. Flutie was, as every eye-ball test had suggested, a short little fella. The most generous descriptions painted Flutie as a football giant standing 5-feet-9-inches in his socks. On the field in cleats he looked even shorter.

All of which mattered little to the locals of north Texas, whose confidence in Brandt's system had been severely compromised by one costly misdeed after another. From brainy intellectuals, the Cowboys' front office appeared to be fast-devolving into an unruly circus, enthralled far too much with cute charts and minute measurements than with raw ability. Prior to the 1985 draft, only fourteen selections from the previous eight draft classes were still on the Cowboys' roster.

Who could say for sure whether the Cowboys could actually recognize a roster stud anymore? Despite vehement claims to the contrary, Cowboy scouts had struggled in recent years to accurately quantify the heart and competitiveness of a highly-touted prospect, as evidenced by choosing to bypass on Mike Singletary in 1981 and then drafting Rod Hill one year later. By the end of the 1984 season, Singletary was an established All-Pro middle linebacker for Chicago, while the lackluster Hill had already been shipped from Dallas to Buffalo for a mere pittance.

"In Tom, Tex, and Gil, we used to trust," wrote Galloway. "But that was back when the Cowboys worked the draft as if they owned the bones in a crooked dice game. The numbers always rolled the right way. But now? How long can one team continue to throw craps in the draft?"

But would not a new quarterback in the mix change everything? The future always appears to be brighter with a young franchise quarterback to build around and cheer for. From the perspective of many bleacher thinkers, the Cowboys had been without such a commodity since Staubach's retirement five years before. The Dallas locker room, by and large, was a dark den of similar sentiment.

The players had lost their once-unshakeable confidence in Gary Hogeboom. The paying public had yet to trust Danny White. A fresh start with Doug Flutie seemed to be the logical solution for everyone involved.

Except, that is, in Brandt's office, where numerous shudders of dismay were uttered over Flutie's diminutive nature and lackluster arm strength. So peculiar was Flutie's skill-set, so uncertain was his potential, that it is doubtful whether Brandt dared to punch any of the young quarterback's measurables into the system, for fear of a database meltdown.

Said Blackie Sherrod: ""The Cowboys computer would short all its circuits if a 5-9 quarterback were offered."

Only Donald Trump's sweeping courtship of Flutie, which culminated in a $7 million contract to play alongside Herschel Walker as quarterback of the New Jersey Generals, could relieve Brandt & Staff from the enormous public pressure surrounding the focus of college football's latest craze. Even then, Flutie's jump to the United States Football League couldn't completely wipe his name off the Cowboys' radar. Rumors of the USFL's imminent demise had seriously undermined the league's efforts to sign college prospects to rookie contracts for the 1985 season, allowing the Establishment to cancel the supplemental draft, which had been held the previous few years so that NFL teams could claim the rights to certain players in the event that the USFL did in fact fold.

Moral: If the Cowboys were to claim the rights to Flutie, they would have to do so at some point during April's draft. With Flutie now in New Jersey, no longer could Tom Landry be expected to gamble a first-round selection on a player who certainly wouldn't be able to contribute anything to the upcoming season. But, say a fifth-round selection, well, that was different altogether. That was a hope, to many a layman in the bustling suburbs of Dallas, well worth holding onto.

Far removed from the Flutie Fandom Tour and the rife instant-fix professors waving their magic wands over an ailing Dallas franchise was a group of pragmatic prognosticators attempting to unlock the secret formula for what was certainly a critical draft for the Cowboys. Both Tex Schramm and Tom Landry had strongly indicated that they were bent on avoiding a full-scale rebuild, and were determined to regroup and reshuffle around either Danny White or Gary Hogeboom. So it wasn't a quarterback that the Cowboys would be pursuing with their early selections. Based upon an abnormally disproportionate graduating class, it was hard for even the experts to diagnose just which strategy Cowboy executives would choose to employ.

"It's a funny draft in that you don't have that many sure-fire hits," Joel Buchsbaum of Pro Football Weekly said. "There are no great-great players. But there are a lot of ifs and maybes. You might have hit on a good player in the fifth-round just as well as you might in the second round."

That was good news for a team like Dallas, which had two selections in each of the fifth, sixth, and seventh-rounds. Conversely, if the Cowboys were hoping to use these middle-round selections to procure high-quality players with the capability of stepping immediately into a starter's role, they were likely to be disappointed.

Nerds with hearts of Cowboy blue grabbed every available football magazine within hands reach and began searching for likely selections. Linebacker was a good launching spot. After all, the Cowboys had never been able to replace either Thomas Henderson or D.D. Lewis, and had even selected outside linebackers in the first-or-second-round of the past three drafts. Jeff Rohrer (1982) was still a backup, Mike Walter (1983) had been traded away, and Billy Cannon Jr. (1984) had just been placed on the reserve/retired list due to a congenital defect in his spine. It was hard not to imagine the Cowboys grabbing another linebacker in the upcoming draft. Sooner or later they were bound to hit upon one.

But wait! Hold everything! Come to think of it, linebacker wasn't the Cowboys' greatest position of need. No, not by a long shot!

Suffering from a wave of cataclysmic departures, the wide receiver position, in fact, stood in urgent need of an upgrade going into 1985. So urgent was it that Randy Galloway applied the "Disaster-Area Tag" to this position in a column for the Dallas Morning News. Not so very long before, Landry's team had been jealously accused of having the finest corps of pass-catchers in the entire league. What an unpredictable set of circumstances that served to change all of that, and left Schramm scouring the waiver wire in the desperate hope of filling in the resulting holes.

Since the late 1970's, when the golden-arm of Staubach was still launching rainbows inside Texas Stadium, the triumvirate of Drew Pearson, Tony Hill, and Butch Johnson had struck fear in the hearts of every defensive coordinator, their big-play abilities on weekly display making the Cowboys a threat to score at any juncture of the game, from any position on the field. But this embarrassment of riches did possess one conspicuous drawback. With only one ball to be spread among three targets, and only two starting positions available, someone had to show a bit of deference in order to maintain cohesiveness. What's the old saying? Sharing is caring.

Johnson, after seven years spent with the team mostly as the No. 3 wide receiver, decided he cared for it not at all. For several seasons, Johnson had been persistently lobbying Landry to award him a starting job over Pearson, who Butch deemed to be of an inferior athletic ability. Johnson, you see, never suffered from an inferiority complex. Big plays were the forte of his existence, his "California Quake" touchdown celebration a redoubtable gift from God. He was always the highest-jumping toughest-handed best-dancing Cowboy there was. If only he could have convinced his head coach on the matter.

After the 1982 season, Johnson's patience finally ran out. He held out during the following summer's training camp, and only an assurance from Landry that the Cowboys would trade him once the 1983 season concluded could persuade Johnson to return to the team.

Less than three months after Johnson thought he had played his final game in Dallas, Pearson suffered a career-threatening car accident. After being rushed to the hospital with a broken clavicle and internal bleeding, Pearson was informed that he had a hole in his liver the size of a softball. Recovery would be a long, tedious process.

A few days later, Landry said the Cowboys would have to reevaluate the wide receiver position. But Johnson, itching for new surroundings, quickly reminded Landry of his earlier promise, resulting in him being dealt to Houston in exchange for Oilers receiver Mike Renfro later that April.

It wasn't long before doctors confronted Pearson with the harsh reality that his days as a Cowboy were over. His health status was too precarious to permit him to ever step on a football field again. Were Pearson to get hit in the wrong place during a game, he could start bleeding inside yet again, with fatal results possible.

First Johnson. Then Pearson. Of the Cowboys' "Big Three", only Hill remained. The big-play magic was, predictably, gone. By the middle of the 1984 campaign it was obvious to everyone watching that, with no Pearson running underneath the defense, Hill couldn't go over it, leaving the quarterback with no downfield options, and the running backs with no room to roam. Doug Donley was a speedy option opposite Hill, but his diminutive stature and slight build left him, not only invisible on deep patterns, but also vulnerable to injury. Donley suffered from shoulder and hamstring ailments for the majority of the season.

The news only got worse for Landry when Donley failed the end-of-season physical due to the condition of his injured right shoulder. The doctors didn't mince words in Donley's case. Second and third opinion notwithstanding, the time had come to put the ball down and start looking at other ways to make a living. In the blink of an eye, Donley's career was over too.

So it didn't require a supreme level of intelligence to guess which area the Cowboys were likely trying to improve on their roster for the 1985 season. Said Schramm before the draft: "I asked Tom Landry if he had the opportunity to find one player in the draft, which would it be, and he said he hoped to get 'an impact wide receiver.' That is, a player who can make a difference on the club immediately."

Schramm, to his credit, scoured the veteran market leading up to the draft, but was unable to pull off a deal. Rumors swirled in early spring about a possible trade for Green Bay wide receiver John Jefferson, a Dallas native who attended Roosevelt High School. A noticeable deterrent to striking a bargain was Jefferson's $350,000 salary, an alarmingly high number for a seven-year veteran who caught only 26 passes the year before.

Undaunted by such an obstacle, Packers head coach Forrest Gregg said he would try to make swinging a deal with Dallas as easy as possible, so offered Jefferson to the Cowboys in an even-up trade for Danny White.

"I'm sure Forrest would like to make that trade," Landry said. "Who wouldn't? But he's not going to get very much interest from us."

Over the next few weeks, Gregg remained immovable from his hold-up asking price. Schramm continued to ignore the offer.

Meanwhile, draft day drew nearer in Dallas, bringing with it an assignment so simple in depth and proportion as to have been written by a child. How the Cowboys managed to then flub it remains today as one of pro football's all-time brain-twisters.

CHAPTER 9

DALLIANCE WITH DUTY

"There are goals to chase and tolls to face, ambitions for fate to bestow. But to this simple fish, my only wish is to win or to place or to show."
Blackie Sherrod

"It should have been Eddie Brown – Tom knows it, Tex knows it, Gil knows it. Case closed, and that's a big 10-4."
Dallas Morning News **columnist Randy Galloway, in the aftermath of the Cowboys' failed 1985 draft**

For a man who gave more money to the school and bled more Aggie maroon blood than anyone else, Bum Bright did a strange thing in the spring of 1985. He resigned his post as the chairman of the board of regents at Texas A&M. He had been honored to serve, but had ruffled too many feathers along the way. It was time to step aside before he got in the way of progress.

Bright remained as ardent a supporter of Texas A&M as he

had ever been. He still poured millions into the scholarship fund, and still planned on attending every home football game later that fall at Kyle Field. But for now, duty called him elsewhere.

Back in Dallas, there was plenty of business awaiting his attention. Not just Bright Banc business. Football-related business.

There was the matter of those new Crown Suites at Texas Stadium to see finished. And Blackie Sherrod, his ear to the ground from behind his brand-new office desk at the headquarters of the Dallas Morning News, insisted that Bright was also going to have to re-light the peace pipe for some of his partners.

Wrote Blackie: "Grapevine insists that all is not peaches and cream among Cowboys' new ownership, and some partners may sell interests back to Bum Bright. But then, you know those gossipmongers."

The last thing Tex Schramm needed to have piled on his plate was an all-out war among the ownership group. Schramm was confident that Bright could handle matters himself. If somebody really wanted out of the deal, Bright would probably buy his share, before blackballing him on the local business scene. That's how strongly Bright felt about reneging on a deal.

But Schramm knew the fallout from such an occurrence would likely be costly for himself, not to mention Tom Landry. The more money Bright invested – and he had already promised a pretty penny for those suites – the more expectant he would be of a quick return.

If Schramm were annoyed at these new developments, he never showed it. Looking back, it's probably safe to assume that he didn't have time to.

It was on a sleepy Tuesday morning in April when duty became imminent, the fiftieth edition of the NFL Draft having finally arrived, vanquishing all of the talk and needless speculation in and around the football-crazed city of Dallas. For Tom Landry, Tex Schramm and Gil Brandt, this was the long-awaited moment of truth.

With roster holes aplenty demanding their immediate attention, the time for war-room freelancing had become a thing of the past. More than any other year in recent memory, the Cowboys had to make every draft selection work for them. This was one day they had to stick to the plan. This was one day they had to get right.

Had the Cowboys' roster not been so decimated by recent poor drafts and untimely injuries, the front-office could have used the 1985 draft as an opportunity to stockpile rookie "projects", raw players with potential who would need a few years to develop before contributing significantly on Sundays. The 1985 graduating class may have lacked in star depth, yet promised great rewards if a team could be patient while grooming young rookies for future starting roles. But the Cowboys appeared to be fading, and the pressure to win in Dallas was higher than ever. Bum was the owner. Landry was on the hot seat. With such a backdrop of desperation, being passive on draft-day didn't seem like such a good idea.

The weeks leading up to this annual selection meeting had provided nothing to alter their original strategy. If anything, the long wait had only served to strengthen it. There had been no trades and no surprise signings to grab local headlines, leaving front-office management united in their effort to bring a game-changing wide receiver to the Cowboys.

Ordinarily, the Dallas head coach was a busy man during the early hours of the draft. Landry had the final say on which player the Cowboys were to select in the early rounds, so could be constantly seen engaging in a free-flowing discourse with Schramm and Brandt, going over notes with scouts, anything to help him make a more educated decision when the Cowboys' turn came up.

When Landry walked into the war room on the morning of April 30, 1985, it was with the anticipation of being primarily a spectator to begin with. The decision had already been made. The matter was out of his hands.

Landry's directive had been simple. If at all possible, he wanted Miami Hurricanes wide receiver Eddie Brown to be a Cowboy. If Brown couldn't be had, either one of the other two standout receivers (Wisconsin's Al Toon or Mississippi Valley State's Jerry Rice) would do just as well. Landry had to have another difference-maker at wide receiver in the lineup across from Tony Hill. It was up to the duo of Schramm and Brandt to make it happen.

Schramm, as the general manager, was responsible for initiating and negotiating trade talks with other teams. He decided whether the Cowboys would strike a deal or not.

Brandt, wearing an official tag of vice president of player personnel, offered more than merely an expert knowledge of the strengths and weaknesses of every collegiate prospect on the board. He was also an essential part of the Cowboys' strategy team on draft day. It was Brandt who attempted to accurately project the strategy of other NFL teams, alerting Schramm and Landry throughout the day as to the most likely landing spot for each available player.

Predicting the future wasn't nearly so hard for Brandt during the early rounds as it may initially sound. At its most fundamental level, NFL front-offices are filled with just two kinds of people; the copycats and the adapters. The 1984 season re-emphasized the reality that quarterbacks were having more success than ever by simply delivering the ball quicker. Joe Montana made defenses look foolish on a weekly basis, guiding the 49ers to a 15-1 regular season record on the way to a convincing victory in Super Bowl XIX. And Dan Marino, the young Miami signal-caller with a lightning-quick release, wowed the pro football world by surpassing 5,000-yards passing in a single season for the first time in league history.

Instinctively, the copycats would seek to find another quarterback in the same mold as either Montana or Marino. But since both passers were generational talents, finding better pass-rushers along the defensive front would inevitably become the more common reaction to the offensive outburst the league experienced in 1984. As always, there weren't enough good quarterbacks to go around.

So Brandt, along with many other football geeks around the nation, knew that defensive ends would be in high demand for the 1985 draft. The first-round, though, was too fluid with possibilities for Brandt to make Landry any promises concerning which particular wide receiver Dallas would wind up with. When it came right down to it, Brandt didn't know where Eddie Brown was likely to land. His guess was just as likely to be wrong as the next guy's.

There was nothing wrong with the player. Brown was acknowledged in every war room as a top-ten talent. Brandt, during the intensive grading process, even went so far as to say "Eddie Brown may be the only impact player in the draft."

One pre-draft rumor even had Brown going as high as No. 2 overall to Houston. But then on April 9 – exactly three weeks before the draft - Houston traded away that pick to the Minnesota Vikings, who thought they were now positioned perfectly to acquire the premier quarterback in the draft.

Standing head and shoulders above the rest of the quarterbacking crowd was Brown's buddy from the Hurricanes. At 6-feet-5-inches and 215-pounds, Bernie Kosar didn't have the athleticism of John Elway or the quick release of Marino, but there were scouts in abundance who thought he possessed all of the intangibles of a Montana. Just like Cool Joe from the Bay, Kosar did enough things on the field very well that, when coupled with his knowledge and competitiveness, made for an exemplary leader at the position.

Minnesota's trade with Houston up the board was supposed to have settled Kosar's ultimate NFL destination. Instead, a dispute broke out over Kosar's eligibility. Cleveland, having just acquired the rights to the No. 1 overall pick in July's supplemental draft (an event the league promised to hold were Kosar available) from Buffalo, held that Kosar wouldn't graduate from the University of Miami until later that summer, making him eligible for the supplemental draft at the very earliest. Minnesota contended that Kosar had already filed the paperwork to enter April's draft.

In stepped Pete Rozelle to settle the matter. Caught in a no-win situation, the NFL commissioner did the best thing someone in his position could do; he allowed Kosar the freedom to choose which team he wanted to play for. Would Kosar, a Youngstown, Ohio native, graduate early and become a Viking, or prolong his college experience by a few weeks and go home to play for the Browns? In the end, Kosar cast his vote for Cleveland.

Brandt knew bad news when he heard it, and Kosar's decision was definitely all of that for the Cowboys. By pulling his name out of the list of available players for April's selection meeting, Kosar had produced an inevitable ripple effect, increasing the likelihood of other teams seeking out the very same wide receivers the Cowboys had their eye on. (While Landry, Schramm, and Brandt were collectively shaking their heads out of frustration at the turn of events, fans in Dallas were secretly thrilled. Cleveland had been the only NFL team to publicly express interest in Doug Flutie. Now that they were chasing after Kosar, Flutie just might be available for Dallas to scoop up in the later rounds of the draft.)

Brandt didn't pretend to know what Minnesota's unpredictable general manager, Mike Lynn, was proposing to do with the No. 2 pick, now that Kosar had been removed from reach. Lynn might want a defensive end. Then again, he might prefer the services of a defensive back. Or Lynn just might make the Cowboys sick by selecting Brown. There were too many possibilities for Brandt to feel comfortable anticipating one particular move from the Vikings.

One thing Brandt did know. The draft pool wasn't deep enough in outstanding talent for the Cowboys to sit on their hands with the No. 17 selection. "Impact players," those with the ability to step immediately from college into a starting role in the NFL, were all too precious and rare a commodity, projected to be gone by no later than the No. 15 slot. After that, teams were all but guaranteed to be drafting backup players, a practice that had put the Cowboys in this predicament to begin with.

There was no getting past it. For Dallas to wind up with one of the three blue-chip receivers on their radar, the Cowboys would have to trade up. Depending on how the dominoes fell, each of Brown, Toon, and Rice could very well be off the board by the time Houston's number was called with the No. 11 overall pick. Dallas entered the draft knowing they would likely need to acquire the rights to one of those first ten selections, no matter the cost.

The only thing set in stone leading up to the draft seemed to be in Buffalo, where it was already predetermined that the Bills would select Virginia Tech defensive end Bruce Smith with the No. 1 overall pick. When that decision was formally announced by Rozelle on a podium inside the Omni Park Central Hotel in New York City, the rest of the draft-day puzzle began to slowly assemble itself, piece by piece, pick by pick.

The Cowboys may have been desperate for a wide-out, but they also recognized the futility of trying to trade up into the top handful of spots. In years past, moving up that high would require the sacrifice of an arm and a leg. The sellers took advantage of their position by driving a hard bargain. But for the Cowboys to jump all the way to, say, the No. 2 spot in the 1985 draft would demand a complete decapitation.

Minnesota, the original owner of the No. 3 overall selection, had already given Houston its first-and-second round draft choices for the rights to the No. 2 overall pick. Schramm and Brandt shuddered to think what Dallas would have to give up since they were coming from as far down the list as No. 17.

Lo and behold, everyone in the Cowboy war room was in agreement. Waiting it out early was the right way to go. The Vikings eventually swapped the No. 2 and No. 4 selections with Atlanta, allowing the Falcons to pick Pittsburgh guard Bill Fralic second overall. Moments later, Houston made Texas A&M defensive end Ray Childress the No. 3 overall selection.

Only then did Schramm reach for the telephone. Schramm phoned Lynn in Minneapolis to see if the Vikings were interested in trading down again. But he caught the Minnesota general manager in a bad mood. Lynn was apparently weary of bouncing up-and-down the draft board. He had watched Kosar slip through his fingers, then was forced to trade down with Atlanta after Fralic insisted he would not sign a contract with the penny-ante Vikings. Lynn was done with all of the wheeling-and-dealing. After a thanks-but-no-thanks memo to Schramm on the phone, Lynn tabbed Pittsburgh defensive end Chris Doleman as Minnesota's long-awaited selection at No. 4.

Now the Cowboys were sweating. Indianapolis and Detroit were both unresponsive to Schramm's trade queries. Both teams were content to stay put, leaving management in Dallas with a helpless feeling in the pit of the stomach, their quarry poised to finally elude them.

Schramm need not have worried. The Colts weren't on the trail of Brown. Neither were the Lions. Indiana linebacker Duane Bickett went at No. 5, followed by Florida's outstanding offensive lineman Kevin Glover.

Not until Schramm phoned Buffalo general manager Bill Polian did the trade wheels finally begin turning in Dallas. The Bills, in the midst of a full-fledged rebuild under head coach Kay Stephenson, were actively trying to move down from the No. 7 spot in order to accumulate as many draft picks as possible. The Cowboys expressed interest in striking a deal, as did several other teams. A fast-paced high-stakes auction ensued.

Schramm made an offer, a generous offer. The Cowboys had plenty of pieces to throw out there, whether draft picks or players. Remember, everyone not named Tony Dorsett or Randy White was eligible to be traded. And Schramm could not have cared less about the majority of those mid-draft selections. For the Cowboys, the 1985 draft was supposed to be about quality over quantity.

Now Schramm had Polian's ear. The Bills were listening, to Schramm, and to the other interested parties. The competition was keen. Schramm upped his offer. But nobody offered more than the Packers. A flurry of last-minute bids having subsided, Green Bay walked away with the grand prize under its arm, having coughed up their first-and-second-round draft picks, while receiving Buffalo's fourth-round selection in 1986, for the rights to the No. 7 overall choice in 1985.

The missed opportunity didn't sit well in the local press. Schramm was well known to be a sharp negotiator, even a tightwad on occasion. But nobody had ever accused him of being incompetent.

"Dallas has to beat that offer, period, and topping it shouldn't have been that difficult," wrote Randy Galloway in his Wednesday column. "If the Cowboys could receive an impact contributor such as Brown at a position of need, why would they be worried about giving up a No. 2 and No. 3 pick? They must provide an offer that blows the doors off Buffalo. An Eddie Brown makes this draft for Dallas, regardless of what comes after."

Lady Luck continued to ride the shoulders of the Cowboys deeper into the first-round. Nine selections had been made. Schramm had still not pulled off a deal. But all three wide receivers remained on the board.

The New York Jets were on the clock. Gathered inside the Omni Park, a small contingent of Jets supporters began chanting Brown's name. "Edd-ie Brown! Edd-ie Brown! Edd-ie Brown!" Schramm and Brandt were sweating again. By this time, Landry probably was too.

In fashion so typical of the franchise, the Jets then proceeded to send everyone present, and those watching the cable television coverage on ESPN, into immediate shock. Rozelle stepped to the podium to announce the pick. The Jets had ended the standoff. They had selected a wide receiver. But it wasn't Brown they wanted. Only Al Toon.

Nobody was happier than Schramm, who immediately began dialing the Houston Oilers with the earnest intention of making a deal happen. Schramm offered Houston the Cowboys' first-and-second-round selections in exchange for the No. 11 overall pick. Oilers management turned the deal down, citing a desire to draft Wisconsin cornerback Richard Johnson, who they didn't think would be available at No. 17. Schramm had been stood up again.

Eddie Brown finally landed somewhere when Cincinnati snatched him up with the No. 13 pick, much to the dismay of everyone back in Dallas. But, as Gil Brandt was quick to remind the many sad faces in the Cowboy war room, all was not completely lost. The kid from Mississippi Valley State was still on the board.

Considering Rice's small-school status, it was only natural that a debate broke out between Dallas staffers concerning his merits for a first-round selection. There were those in the room who didn't think the Cowboys should take the risk on such an unproven prospect. Cowboy scout Ron Marciniak thought differently.

"I can remember Ron Marciniak actually getting up on my table in my room to plead his case for Jerry Rice because of the fact that Jerry Rice was not all that fast," Bright told USA Today. "And I think that very few people realized Jerry Rice could run as fast with a uniform on as he could ... in shorts."

The argument was soon resolved. The Cowboys, by popular vote and a nod from Landry, wanted Rice to play in Dallas. But which strategy to employ? Should the Cowboys sit and wait for Rice to fall to them, or have Schramm start tearing the phone lines up again? And what about the new elephant in the room from San Francisco?

Indeed, the million-dollar question on everyone's lips, as the first round of the draft neared the halfway pole, centered around the undefined intentions of the San Francisco 49ers. Bill Walsh was up to something, that much was for certain. Why else would the 49ers head coach give New England all three of San Francisco's top draft choices in exchange for the No. 16 overall pick? But which player was it who attracted the all-seeing eye of The Genius?

Brandt didn't claim to know exactly, but he was adamant that it couldn't have been Rice. "We thought that we were going to be able to draft Jerry Rice because we didn't think you all knew as much about him or felt as strongly about Rice as we did," Brandt told then-49ers personnel man Michael Lombardi during a 2009 NFL Network conference call with reporters.

In assuming the defending Super Bowl champion 49ers hadn't done their homework on Rice, the Cowboys made the fatal mistake of thinking they were smarter than their greatest competition. Walsh had been onto the obscure wide receiver since turning on the television set in a Houston motel room the previous October and watching the highlights of a game in which Rice scored four touchdowns. Oh yes, Walsh knew all about Jerry Rice, so much, in fact, that he made the Mississippi Valley State phenom the sixteenth player chosen in the draft, thrilling 49er executives back in the Bay while forever embalming April 30, 1985 as a day of doom to those from Dallas.

A grand opportunity to fill a glaring roster need had somehow eluded the Cowboys. What a moment of waste! What an hour of failure! The one and only Tex Schramm could not pull off a simple trade. Gil Brandt dared to underestimate the mighty 49ers and their resident genius head coach.

    Left to pick up the pieces was Tom Landry, who emerged from the draft not only without his coveted big-play wide receiver alongside him, but as the new caretaker of a hulking defensive end from Michigan whose words proved to be as alarming as his play was unimpressive.

CHAPTER 10

MAKING AN IMPRESSION

"He is a man now, but there is still plenty of kid and adventure in him."
Detroit Free Press **writer Tommy George on new Cowboys rookie Kevin Brooks**

The deed was done. The pick was in. The time had arrived for Cowboy agents to go into full damage-control mode.

Up in New York City, Pete Rozelle was just stepping away from the lectern, having completed the formal announcement of the Cowboys' selection at No. 17 in front of God, man, and ESPN cameras.

Back in Dallas, sportswriters were rolling their eyes out of frustration and wonderment while simultaneously scrambling for any available notes on the latest Cowboy draftee. Just who was this Kevin Brooks?

Enlightenment in the form of a cryptic player profile did little to dispel the spirit of drudgery which had taken hold of everyone in the room. All those half-finished stories for the next day's printing centering around the rebirth of the Cowboy offense could be torn up and tossed into the wastebasket. All because the Cowboys couldn't pull off a trade. All because of a big man named Brooks.

Why, Tex Schramm had been a newspaper man once upon a time. Surely he remembered the fact that local readers soaked up all those tantalizing stories about the next offensive star? A hot-shot wide receiver on the way into town was front-page news every time. But a defensive tackle from the Big Ten? Not exactly compelling material, even if it was to be consumed on a Wednesday, the dullest part of the sports week.

Eddie Brown would have been a playmaker in Cowboy blue. Jerry Rice would have scored touchdowns. Kevin Brooks, on the other hand, would be lucky if he ever got both of his hands on a ball during a game.

The draft continued to roll on, with Dallas selecting Virginia Tech linebacker Jessie Penn in the second round and Florida offensive tackle Crawford Ker in the third, but the interest from local reporters waned. The story of the Cowboys' entire draft was supposed to be wrapped up in their first selection. In Brooks, they recognized the only potential draftee that could make a significant impact upon the upcoming season for the Cowboys. Doubts as to that ever happening were in abundance.

The media had to verse a far different tale than the one they were expecting to begin the day. But first they would need some answers from Cowboy management.

As soon as Gil Brandt poked his head out of the Cowboys' war room, reporters with skeptical frowns were waiting there to pepper him with salty questions. *So, what happened, Gil, to all those big draft-day plans? Why pick Brooks when defensive line is one of the Cowboys' smallest needs? Why not trade down after Rice was taken off the board? Why, Gil? Why?*

Brandt, as he so often did in those days, delivered a bold message dripping with the sweet nectar of positivity. "He's an outstanding player," Brandt said of Brooks. "We got a defensive lineman who has a chance to be a dominating player... You just don't pass up a defensive lineman of his caliber."

But Dallas was a tough town to con where football was concerned. Brooks had all of six sacks during his final collegiate season with the Michigan Wolverines in 1984. If that was indicative of NFL greatness to come, then obviously Brandt knew more than the rest of the Metroplex did. Yes, Brooks was a two-time All-Big Ten selection in college, but he wasn't a player that jumped out at you on the television screen.

At this point, Brandt might as well have been speaking to a bunch of dumb rocks. His audience wasn't listening. And they certainly weren't buying what he was selling either; hope. The last grain of hope in this draft had been Rice. And by now, everyone was aware that Rice - more likely than not - would be feeding the city of San Francisco a plethora of 49er touchdowns for the next decade. As if they needed another scoring machine for Bill Walsh to tinker with in the Bay.

Once cornered, Tex Schramm's account of the first-round proceedings proved to be quite compelling, though equally mystifying. In spite of what many fans may have been thinking, the Cowboys did actually try to move up in the selection order. No, sitting pat for three hours didn't suit their fancy either.

"We made our most concerted effort to trade up in 10 years," Schramm said, "but things just didn't work out. There were times in the early going when we felt we had things worked out, but they fell apart at the last minute."

To provide additional support for his claims, Schramm let it be known that he had placed no less than 15 long-distance telephone calls to Buffalo during negotiations for the No. 7 overall selection. He had been just as persistent in trying to persuade Houston to part ways with the No. 11 pick. Schramm was frustrated with the end result as much as fans were.

The head coach sounded like a man bored in waging the common war against negative perception. Tom Landry, a longtime company man, found the company line to be somewhat stuffy on this day, especially when dealing with the obvious disappointment of missing out on every single one of a handful of prospects who could have changed the fortunes of the Dallas offense.

Landry was complementary of Rice, describing him as the kind of "possession" receiver who would thrive in San

Francisco's West Coast offense. "But we wanted Ed Brown speed," he said, in a tone that clearly indicated a sincere regret that the Cowboys did not get it.

Concerning Brooks, Landry was pragmatic if nothing else. "He's not a guy who is going to impact this season," said Landry. "But he's a good athlete, who has good speed and is very active. His presence, with the age we have in the defensive line, will really help us in the long run." Of that future possibility, Landry sounded more hopeful than actually convinced.

The Dallas defensive line, though getting a bit long in the tooth going into the 1985 season, was still considered a strength of the unit. Three of the four starters (defensive end Ed Jones & tackles Randy White and John Dutton) had each crossed over the other side of thirty, but had yet to slow down. White was still regarded by many to be the best defensive tackle in the league. Other than Dutton, who had slimmed down to maintain optimum effectiveness in a limited role, all the starters were full-time contributors for Landry's Flex defense. Even though the Cowboys planned on moving Brooks from tackle to end, Brooks' role as a rookie was bound to be a limited one.

With management having done their part to provide Brooks a positive platform to work from, it was now up to the rookie to dissuade the skeptics of their negative convictions by making a good first impression. Ironically, just like all those earlier trade overtures from Schramm over the phone, Brooks nearly pulled it off.

His Cowboy debut started so well. Brooks walked into the crowded room at the team's offices for his first press conference on late Tuesday afternoon. He was dapperly dressed in a gray suit, black tie, all the works. This young man obviously understood that football, at the highest level, was serious business. He appeared to be in shape too. That showed commitment and a good work ethic. He smiled, a clear sign of a healthy disposition and a clear conscience. Better and better. If only Brooks didn't have to open his mouth.

Brooks' enthusiasm in being a Cowboy was very transparent, despite admitting he was surprised to land with

Dallas at No. 17, thinking all along that he would be taken by the New York Jets.

"It was a total shock. I had heard I was going to New York (No. 10 overall) and I was all set to go. I was kind of disappointed about that. Then I thought there was an outside chance I would go to San Francisco."

But the 49ers had their eye on Rice, leaving the Cowboys to take Brooks.

Given all that was at stake for the Cowboys in this draft, the pick didn't add up. Come to find out, neither did the player. Brooks was undoubtedly a big guy. But just how big was he?

Apparently, there was room for debate on the issue. In one scouting book, Brooks was listed as 6-feet-5 ½ inches tall. According to Michigan officials, he was 6-feet-6-inches tall and weighed 245-pounds. Over the phone just minutes after he was selected, Brooks told reporters he was 6-feet-7-inches in height and tilted the scales at 272-pounds. And at the press conference, after flying to Dallas from his native Detroit later that afternoon, Brooks claimed he stood 6-feet-7 ½ inches tall.

Evidently, Brooks not only drank milk for breakfast every morning, but he also claimed distinctive ownership of being the fastest-growing Cowboy in America. At that rate, it wouldn't be very long before he dwarfed Dallas' All-Pro defensive end Ed "Too Tall" Jones, whose 6-foot-9-inch frame had towered over every other player in the league for eleven seasons.

The plot surrounding Brooks only thickened from there. Brooks, who was preparing to graduate with a degree in Communications, had a way with words. Or, rather, they had a way with him.

"I didn't think that Dallas needed any defensive ends," Brooks said during his brief phone interview with reporters. "I thought Ed Jones and Harvey Martin were playing well." That statement raised more than a few eyebrows in the audience

Former Cowboy pass-rushing great Harvey Martin had actually retired from football after the 1983 season and was rumored to be busy at that moment working on his autobiography, not to mention preparing to venture into the business world as a real estate agent.

Later, during his news conference in Dallas, Brooks referred to second-year Dallas defensive end Jim Jeffcoat as Jud Heathcote. Heathcote just happened to be the head basketball coach at Michigan State.

"I'm not very good with names," Brooks admitted with a shrug.

For the record, and in the spirit of fairness, Brooks wasn't the first athlete to ever trip over a frozen tongue when confronted by a crowd. Randy White was once that shy rookie in front of a microphone when Dallas picked him No. 2 overall in 1975. But no reporter was going to inform the "Manster" that he looked uncomfortable and just a bit awkward out in public, for fear of winding up in a permanent headlock. White, for all his southern country boy charm, possessed a can't miss persona that demanded instant respect. That's what a chiseled figure and a pair of abnormally-large biceps can do for a man.

But Kevin Brooks was not to be confused with Randy White, a fact evidenced by the rookie's next move. Brooks took exception to reporters making note of his discomfiture in Dallas-area newspapers during the next few days. He didn't care much either for the slanted views bouncing around town that suggested he lacked awareness and certain of the social graces, compelling Brooks to take an unusual course of action in an attempt to preserve his good name.

At the team's rookie orientation camp in May, Brooks told Gary Myers of the Dallas Morning News that he would find out what the Cowboys expected of him in training camp "after talking with Coach Starkey." In this instance, "Coach Starkey" just happened to be defensive line coach Ernie Stautner. At the sight of Myers' blank stare, a bell went off in the head of Brooks. Uh oh. He had done it again. But he was quick to defend himself by admitting to having conducted a locker room poll of 80 rookies which revealed that more than half did not realize that Harvey Martin had retired. A spasmodic pause followed Brooks' revelation. The sound of crickets filled the air. If Myers had not cut the interview short, there's no telling where it would have ended up.

Brooks thought that publicizing the results of his poll would get the local media off his case. And, technically, it did.

Before very long, the beat writers and columnists were placing bets as to whether the royally inept Rangers of baseball would reach one-hundred in the loss-column. They weren't out to destroy Brooks. They had no reason to.

But private musings persisted about the future prospects of this young Cowboy. He seemed a nice enough young man, and had proven to be more than gracious to the media in the short time he had been in Dallas. But was he a player? Or was he a headcase? It was hard to forecast his future amidst such present confusion.

Though the amusing story of Harvey and Starkey faded away into the summer heat, a wondering admiration remained for Kevin Brooks. Reporters and fans alike wondered about him, because everyone agreed that he was a wondering sort of guy.

Though the popular vote designated the selection of Kevin Brooks as a decidedly underwhelming first-round selection, the Cowboys did pique some interest among the fan base with their first choice in the fifth-round. Just a few minutes after picking Georgia Tech running back Robert LaVette to add some depth behind Tony Dorsett in the Dallas backfield, Tex Schramm took a gamble that a high-profile USFL star, and former Heisman Trophy winner, would one day soon become an NFL standout with the Cowboys. No, his name was not Doug Flutie. (Flutie eventually landed with the Los Angeles Rams in the eleventh-round.)

Herschel Walker was still under contract to carry the ball for the New Jersey Generals, and his employer, Donald Trump, had pockets deep enough to keep him there for the foreseeable future. Walker, apparently, seemed content playing the starring role in America's second-tier football league, running roughshod over opponents on a weekly basis, accumulating over 3,100 rushing yards and scoring 33 touchdowns in his first two seasons.

But Schramm was banking that the USFL experiment would eventually fold, and that Walker would then become the heir-apparent to Dorsett's starting role. It was a long-term gamble, with no guarantees of success. But what did Schramm have to lose at that point? Walker was, by far, the highest-rated player remaining on the board, and though he wouldn't contribute to the team in 1985, there was always the possibility that he would emerge as a Cowboy game-breaker some time after that. Which is more than could rightly be expected from any of the other players Schramm chose on draft-day.

CHAPTER 11

THE LONGSHOT

"They wouldn't let me talk about the game, so I wanted to give them something to talk about."
Former Cowboys wide receiver Drew Pearson, explaining his reason for trading in a broadcasting career for a chance at a comeback.

Tex Schramm had a reputation for being somewhat of a genius, but he definitely could be a glutton for punishment. As the president and general manager of the nation's marquee football franchise, Schramm heard loud and clear the whispering going on behind every keyhole and at every newsroom desk in north Texas during June of 1985. Those Cowboys, said one and all, no matter their glorious past, could no longer lay claim to being the kings of the NFL highway. Tex, Tom, and Gil – the entire organization, for that matter – looked more akin to buzzard meat than any tiffany-hoisting cavalry of yesteryear.

Whether at the office or at home, Schramm was ever aware of this growing spirit of local negativity. Such was the benefit of not only reading the sports page every day but also having a listed telephone number. Each morning Schramm read all about it, and that same evening came home and heard the latest craftily-worded messages from frustrated fans awaiting him on his machine. If the opportunity suited his purpose, Schramm might even make a return call and argue his case with a fan. It was a setup that Schramm, mysteriously enough, reveled in.

Schramm could appreciate the common points of current contention. John Jefferson was still wearing green and yellow for Green Bay. Eddie Brown was getting acclimated to his new digs in Cincinnati. What in the wide world of wide receivers were Schramm and Co. doing back in Dallas? Not enough, apparently.

After mini-camps had concluded, and with training camp looming large on the horizon, rumors began circulating that the Cowboys – as desperate teams will do – were spending their final days of summer vacation shopping for someone, anyone with enough potential or pedigree to line up opposite of Tony Hill. On one particular Sunday morning, one Dallas newspaper featured a story suggesting that the Cowboys were close to making a deal for Washington wide receiver Charlie Brown. The other paper said the same about a trade with the New York Jets that would bring Wesley Walker to Dallas. But no deal ever happened. Reality was beginning to set in. Maybe it never would happen.

Schramm knew the score. He had flunked any and all trade opportunities. He had failed to find a wide receiver in the free agent market, as well as the rookie pool of talent. But the door of opportunity didn't turn on the same set of hinges for Schramm as it did for the outside world. While the press printed articles bemoaning his inaction and disgruntled fans were leaving telephone messages questioning his mental health, Schramm was searching out other avenues for a solution at wide receiver.

Time was running out. The season was almost here. And Tex Schramm still had one more swing at the plate, one more hope to rectify an off-season gone, oh, so wrong. It was a long shot, for sure, but one that Schramm believed was well worth keeping his fingers crossed for.

Pay heed now to a story whose infancy is laced with the bitter taste of irony. On the evening of October 20, 1984, Bill Walsh was unhappily sequestered within the restricted confines of a Houston hotel room. Ordinary people outside were enjoying their Saturday night. Dining. Partying. Or simply shooting the breeze on the front porch. Walsh, the brilliant mastermind of the resurrected NFL franchise from San Francisco, envied them. If only he were so lucky.

Walsh's preparations for a Sunday afternoon meeting with the Oilers was complete. The game-plan was flawless, the final meetings with the rest of his coaching staff long since over and done with. Now Walsh was faced with a different kind of challenge. He was bored. Walsh couldn't abide boredom. It made him fidgety.

The natural reaction for the average man would have been to jump at the opportunity to grab a few extra winks in anticipation of a long workday ahead. But not Walsh. Even though it was only a winless Oilers team the 49ers were set to face on the morrow, the night before a game always found him nervous and on edge. To try to sleep at such an early hour would be an exercise in futility.

So Walsh grabbed a remote and turned on the television set in his room. He began flipping channels. It wasn't long before he came across a local newscast that was running through the sports highlights from earlier in the day. Walsh sat mesmerized through the rundown of the Texas Southern-Mississippi Valley State football game, as a Delta Devil wide receiver made one big play after another to lead his team to victory.

Walsh called Michael Lombardi, who was involved in personnel at the time, into his room. "Who's this kid on the TV set I'm watching," asked Walsh. "This is incredible. Can you get me every tape on this guy?"

"Coach, that's Jerry Rice. I'll see what I can do," Lombardi assured Walsh.

Lombardi eventually delivered on his promise, locating some film of Rice in action a few weeks later. After studying the footage, Walsh left a little note on the film describing Rice as "John Jefferson...with speed."

The Cowboys, six months later, were rendered incapable of obtaining the rights to Rice in the draft. They couldn't even acquire the authentic Jefferson, he of the undersized production rate and oversized salary. Not that anyone in Dallas was bemoaning that fact, considering the ridiculous terms the Green Bay front-office were stubbornly demanding.

But the irony doesn't end there. The afternoon following Walsh's discovery of Rice on a hotel television set in Houston, the Cowboys were tarred and feathered at the hands of the Washington Redskins at RFK Stadium. The 34-14 final was thorough, leaving Tex Schramm boiling mad and scrambling for solutions for what ailed the Cowboys.

The 1984 season was just seven weeks old, and Schramm was already tired of watching a conservative Dallas offense be stymied on a weekly basis. The offensive line was banged up and, when not crowding the line of scrimmage to stop Tony Dorsett, defenses were blitzing Gary Hogeboom with increasing regularity.

Schramm recognized, even back then, that the Cowboys needed a big-play weapon opposite of Tony Hill to loosen up defenses and re-energize the Dallas offense. On the very next day, while Lombardi was beginning his quest to get his hands on some footage of Rice by making calls to the Mississippi Valley State athletic department, Schramm put through a telephone call to Drew Pearson and asked if the former Dallas wide receiver was interested in making a comeback. Schramm promised him that if the doctors gave him a clean bill of health, a roster spot would be awaiting him. Pearson declined the offer, citing a desire to make a new career for himself in broadcasting.

Only six months before Schramm's call, Pearson had been anticipating his twelfth season in Cowboy blue, the opportunity to put the finishing touches on what, to so many around Dallas, was a Hall of Fame-caliber career spurring him onward. Pearson was beloved by fans in Dallas, due to his outgoing personality and his penchant for making the clutch catch.

From the time he stepped onto the field as an undrafted rookie out of the University of Tulsa, Pearson had a habit of emerging in the fourth quarter when the game was on the line. In 1973 he hauled in an 83-yard touchdown bomb from Roger Staubach to beat the Los Angeles Rams in the Divisional playoffs. On Thanksgiving Day in 1974, it was his 50-yard touchdown reception from the right hand of backup quarterback Clint Longley that capped a thrilling comeback over Washington.

One year later in the Divisional round of the postseason, Pearson caught another 50-yard game-winner, the original "Hail Mary" pass from Staubach to down the Vikings at the old Metropolitan Stadium. And in the 1980 playoffs Pearson made two scoring grabs in the final four minutes from Danny White, as Dallas beat Atlanta 28-27.

But Pearson's career hit a roadblock during the early morning hours of March 22, when he and some eight players were returning from Colgate, OK where they had played an exhibition basketball game.

In the back of the bus, while his younger brother Carey slept, Drew was sharing a few laughs and a couple of beers with teammates while playing poker with fellow wide receiver Doug Donley. Drew remembers being in a good mood on the ride back. He should have been. He was cleaning up good.

About an hour later, while driving his brother home on I-635 in a Dodge Dart that he had on loan from a local dealer, Drew crashed the smaller-sized sports car into the rear of a tractor-trailer rig. To this day, Pearson has no recollection of the crash. No memory of screeching tires, nor of the awful collision. It's all just a blank.

"I remember getting on the freeway. That's all," Pearson told the *Los Angeles Times* in July, 1985. "I didn't hear or feel anything. I was stunned when I woke up. My brother's head was on my shoulder. I tried to wake him up, but I couldn't." Carey, 27, was pronounced dead at the scene.

According to the police report, Pearson had been driving at an "unsafe speed." He took a Breathalyzer test. His blood-alcohol level was .063, well below the level of .10 classifying legal intoxication. Pearson has always been adamant that he wasn't drunk.

"I don't understand how I could just fall out like that. I'd had just two beers on the bus. I was winning too much money in the card game.

"I was tired, but not sleepy. Maybe I got on the freeway and did nod. It's the only explanation. But [Carey] wasn't asleep.

"I can't piece anything else together. I've racked my head trying to remember, but I can't."

Pearson suffered a broken clavicle and a lacerated liver in the crash, so was transported immediately to a local hospital. Once there, doctors drained his liver, and in order to insert tubes, they were forced to crack two ribs, an intensely painful experience.

On top of the emotional pain of having his brother die in his lap, Pearson was also told that he would be saying goodbye to his playing career. His liver ultimately healed, but the scar tissue made him, in the words of Gary Myers, "a walking time bomb if he got hit in that area." Tackle football was out of the question.

Pearson didn't last long on the unemployment line. CBS scooped Pearson up as a color analyst for their coverage of the NFL and assigned him eight games during the 1984 season. For a rookie, Pearson did all right in the television booth. Said *Dallas Morning News* sports media columnist Cathy Harasta: "He's articulate, personable, and he has a lot of credibility."

But about a week before the draft, just when Pearson thought he had discovered a second career for himself, he got a call from Terry O'Neill, the executive producer of the network's NFL coverage, telling him that his contract would not be renewed. Pearson was floored. For the second time in a year, he was a free agent.

"I didn't think it was a question of whether they wanted to renew or not, and I never had any indication that I was close to being let go,' said Pearson. "Then what Terry O'Neil told me was that he didn't think I had the potential to show enough enthusiasm, to be excitable enough. He said that was the main reason for letting me go. I thought it was a pretty weak reason. I never could be a yuk-yuk type of guy."

It was a source of consternation for Pearson that he was released so late in the spring, hurting his chances to land a gig with another network for the upcoming season. Pearson's agent, David Falk, approached ABC, ESPN, NBC, and WTBS for potential employment. But the former NFL star had no intentions of waiting around and hoping that his reputation would do the trick. He was going to strike out and make something happen on his own. So Pearson got into contact with Schramm, and informed the Cowboys' general manager that he was working out again, with his eye on making a comeback for the 1985 season.

"They wouldn't let me talk about the game, so I wanted to give them something to talk about," explained Pearson. Pearson started lifting weights, trying to regain the strength lost during his lengthy recovery period. Pumping iron was simple. It could also be qualified as monotonous. If not for his daily runs, Pearson might have gone crazy.

When his stamina had reached a certain level, Pearson went out onto the practice field and caught some passes from Danny White and Gary Hogeboom. Sweat rolled off his body in the warm spring Texas sunshine, as he snared one zinger after another. Now it was starting to feel like old times.

Proper conditioning was paramount. But, once Pearson stepped between the lines, running precise pass patterns became his major concern. Pearson didn't have to worry about his 40-yard dash time. He had never been the fastest receiver on the field anyway, relying instead on superior quickness and a cunning, crafty mind.

Pearson's vision of the field belied his status as a former college quarterback. He understood angles and was sensitive to openings that a passer naturally perceives from his position in the backfield. He understood timing, and the importance of proper body position on in-breaking routes. He never hung his quarterback out to dry.

Schramm, from behind his desk, kept abreast of Pearson's progress on the practice field. For more than two months, all incoming reports were positive. Pearson appeared to be regaining some of his old form. Schramm couldn't have been happier, for the player, and for himself.

Playing football may very well have been the only dream remaining to Pearson. His surrounding family had never gone out of its way to make him feel loved after his car crash, making the burden of guilt that much heavier for Pearson to carry. His broadcasting career was in jeopardy. He was divorced. If Pearson couldn't make a comeback, Schramm didn't know what the future would hold for him.

As for himself, Schramm just needed a break. He needed something good to happen. He needed to give Tom Landry another wide receiver to work with. He needed Drew Pearson. But later that July, Pearson's longshot bid ran into the same immovable obstacle that had ended his career in the first place.

The liver. Even more than a year after suffering the injury, the diagnosis from doctors remained the same. One collision on the football field could split his liver, resulting in massive internal bleeding.

Oh well. Pearson had done his part. He had tried. And Tex Schramm, for his part, had just struck out. His last hope for finding a trustworthy wide receiver before the outset of training camp had just been dashed. Unlike Pearson, Schramm had no consolation to cling to. Simply trying wasn't good enough for a man in his position, something the public had been all too willing to remind him of lately.

By the time the Cowboys' plane landed in Thousand Oaks, Schramm was ready for a break from that noisy answering machine.

CHAPTER 12

THE FIRST MILE

"The Pied Piper of Hamlin may not have rounded up as many rats as the Cowboys did wide receivers this summer."
Mike Rabun, *Dallas Cowboys Weekly*

The record does not lie. It was in quite the relaxing fashion that the 1985 Dallas Cowboys officially started the long, grueling, annual climb up the NFL mountain. Under overcast California skies, a cool breeze fanning their faces, all 114 players present were – of all things – sprawled in neat rows across the expanse of a soft green lawn. Nearby, a handful of kids hung on a fence lazily, while across the way, a few of their friends amused themselves by tossing a football around the parking lot.

At first glance, an innocent bystander would have assumed the only thing missing from the scene was a large red-and-white checkered table cloth. But this was no picnic at a family reunion, and that wasn't a pitcher of lemonade that Tom Landry was carrying through the crowd. By sitting down, the Cowboys were actually moving forward with their first task of the day – a routine period of stretching. Landry, as he always did, walked up and down the rows while exhorting his players to maintain diligence.

"Let's get that stretching done right so you can show something special today," the head coach called out through his bullhorn. "Stretch that leg. Can you feel that thigh muscle stretch?"

The first day of training camp was always a bit odd. Of the 97 rookies and 17 veterans Landry was addressing at that moment, few had a realistic chance of making the regular season roster. Most of them he did not even know by name. He would be afforded little time to remedy that. When the rest of the veteran players reported in 10 days, Landry would be forced to cut several dozen of the faces in the crowd.

Nevertheless, these first handful of training camp practices were not without importance for the Cowboys. More than any other camp in the previous two decades, Landry and his staff were not only on the lookout for young players to add to the roster, but resolved to also insert them in the game-day lineup.

The rookies would be tested, with the coaches looking for signs – any sign – to indicate a keeper. It was a form of bargain-basement shopping that circumstances demanded the Cowboys employ in 1985.

There was no hiding the fact that the Cowboys were keeping a sharp lookout for help on the offensive side. There were 63 rookies in camp trying to make the offensive unit, and just 28 on defense. But coming off a sub-par 1984 season, the Cowboys would gladly accept help in any area on the team.

"This is the year – and the coaches feel the same way – that we have to take some gambles that we haven't taken in the past, and go with more younger players," said Tex Schramm. "...The most important thing: I think the coaches are looking for those kinds of player and want to play them – where in the past, the experience factor prevailed. Our coaches, just like everyone else, don't want to go down the same trail again."

The trail may have been different for the coaching staff in 1985, but the road on the first day of camp was very much the same for the players. Once stretching had been completed, everyone was split up into position groups, where they then awaited the sharp report of a whistle to begin a conditioning run that both rookie and vet would momentarily realize a mutual disdain for.

Landry liked to get the attention of his players early in camp. He also preferred to have an accurate gauge of each individual's stamina level. He knew of no better way to kill these two birds with one unforgivable stone than to re-enact the "Landry Mile" every July.

Since the early 1960s, The Landry Mile had been heralded as the most demanding trial that Cowboy players would face during the six-week training camp period. This winding, bumpy, off-road excursion on the campus of California Lutheran College would have been bearable if not for the fact that Landry had turned it into a mandatory sprint. Players from each position group had minimum time requirements. To fail meant to invoke a frown from Landry's normally expressionless face. Depending on who you were, it might even get you fired.

The smart player showed up to training camp already in shape. But many, back in those days, did not. There was nothing easy about the Landry Mile. It tested the endurance, the will, and the competitive fire of each participant. More than one player, over the years, had given up his breakfast during the battle. Still others had yielded instantly to the newfound desire of a new career.

Legends of this annual foot race to please Time and Tom grew over the years, as did the course itself. By 1985, the Landry Mile was so long that it was actually one-and-a-half miles in distance. Nobody on the Dallas coaching staff bothered to volunteer this piece of information to the participants. What they didn't know, they wouldn't know could hurt them.

When the players were properly situated, the whistle sounded sharply. No encouragement was needed. They took off like so many eager thoroughbreds, leaving a cloud of dust behind to sanctify their passing.

The picnic was over, the cool breeze forgotten. The 1985 edition of the Dallas Cowboys was now climbing the football mountain in earnest. Along the way, their ultimate destination was an intriguing topic indeed, graced through the sweat of endeavor, seasoned by the spirit of hope, disputed by skeptical man, known only to an omnipotent God.

From the perspective of the entire Dallas coaching staff, the initial training camp practice sessions that July were spirited, trying affairs, aesthetically-challenged moments in the history of the franchise when youthfulness and eagerness emerged as preeminent elements, often at the expense of proper execution. There were times when the practice fields looked to be more of a mess than the organized teaching grounds they were alleged to be.

When coaches encouraged zigging, a player could often be found zagging. A deep post could often turn into a fly pattern. An outside running play to the left could end frequently in a quarterback takedown, after he turned the wrong way upon receiving the snap from center.

Mistakes. They were in abundance. But such is often the case when more than 100 rookies are desperately trying to make an impression.

While the majority of the group floundered day-to-day under the California sky, there were a handful of standouts who caught the eye of Cowboy coaches. That young man from Georgia, one and all agreed, was as tantalizing a prospect as they had hoped he would be. Mel Lattany was his name, and speed was his game.

An international track-and-field celebrity, Lattany was a bright-eyed 26-year old with a reputation as a world-class sprinter. He was also facing a stacked deck in trying to secure a roster spot. Lattany was one of 21 wide receivers that the Cowboys had invited to camp. But if anybody was capable of standing out from such a large crowd, assistant coaches all agreed that it was Lattany.

In 1980, while attending the University of Georgia, he earned a spot on the United States Olympic team in Moscow, where he was scheduled to compete in the 100 as well as the

4x100 meter relay. But when President Jimmy Carter opted to boycott the Moscow Games, Latany was denied his chance of winning Olympic gold.

Since then, Lattany had been ranked near the top of the annual world rankings in both the 100 and 200 meters. He ran the fastest legitimate 100-meter dash ever recorded at sea level (9.96). At the 1981 World Cup Championships in Rome, he took top honors in the 200 meters. In 1983, just outside of London in Gateshead, England, Lattany established a new world-record in the 300-meter dash (31.15). And in 1984, he qualified for the 100-meter Olympic finals in Los Angeles. A back ailment contributed to his last-place finish in the race.

Seven years had passed since Lattany last stepped onto a football field as a member of his high school team in Brunswick, GA. Cowboys scout John Wooten insisted that Lattany showed no rust from the layoff during his tryout earlier that spring. Wooten recalled the day vividly. He was in Athens on an innocent scouting trip, when a Bulldogs assistant told him that Lattany was interested in an NFL career.

"After learning that," Wooten said, "I asked the coach if I could borrow one of his scout team quarterbacks to throw some to Lattany. During the drill I had the guy throwing the ball in front of him, behind him, high and low, and Mel was catching everything. And, of course, he went through a 40 like nobody I'd ever seen before."

Wooten was hardly exaggerating. Lattany ran a 4.29 in the 40-yard dash that day, faster than "Bullet" Bob Hayes ever ran for the Cowboys during the 1960s when he was billed as "The World's Fastest Human."

"I knew right away he was somebody you take a chance on," said Wooten.

Lattany's first few days in camp were an adjustment period. He had to get used to wearing a helmet again, and to running with pads on. Finding the ball on deep patterns sometimes befuddled him. But Lattany's biggest challenge may have been simply slowing down.

"The thing I'm learning is that in football, as a receiver, you have to control your speed when you're running patterns," Lattany explained early in camp. "Early on, I was told to, say, run four steps and cut. I'd do that and would be beyond where the ball was supposed to be thrown because I was running those four steps too fast."

Lattany was certainly raw at wide receiver, but he had potential and a speed that – when managed properly – would strike fear in the hearts of defensive backs around the league.

Another rookie drawing attention to himself was Jesse Penn. There had been some concerns over whether the Cowboys' No. 2 draft choice would struggle in transitioning from a hybrid defensive end/weakside linebacker in a 5-2 scheme while at Virginia Tech to an outside linebacker's role on Tom Landry's 4-3 Flex defense in Dallas. Penn was doing his part to put all those doubts to rest.

A 6-3, 217-pound pass-coverage specialist, Penn had a natural athleticism that reminded linebackers coach Jerry Tubbs of former Cowboy All-Pro Thomas Henderson, and a wingspan that, according to Penn's college defensive coordinator Bob Brush, was comparable to Dallas Mavericks forward Sam Perkins. As a senior, Penn finished second on the Virginia Tech squad with five interceptions and was credited with eight pass breakups.

According to Jarrett Bell of Dallas Cowboys Weekly, Penn was "perhaps the most outstanding player on the defensive unit" over the course of those early practices. In scrimmages the first week, despite dealing with a series of migraine headaches, Penn intercepted four passes.

The only hiccup during "rookie camp" derived from the brief absence of Kevin Brooks, who, along with twenty-four other No. 1 picks around the NFL, was holding out for a more favorable contract. Without Brooks' participation, the Cowboys didn't have enough rookie defensive linemen to properly organize certain drills, which left the head coach predictably irritated.

"You have to be disappointed," Landry said after the first day of practice. "Brooks is a player. We wouldn't have taken him if he wasn't. The longer he stays away, the further behind he gets.

"The agents seem to feel they have to prove something. But it will work out. When the dam breaks and a few of them sign, then there will be a lot of people in camp."

Lo, and behold, Brooks signed his deal on the following day, a four-year $1.525 million agreement that included $500,000 in deferred payments. The deal pleased both parties.

The Cowboys had avoided the burden of a front-loaded contract, while Brooks had negotiated financial security for later in life. Gil Brandt, who was responsible for negotiating all rookie contracts for the Cowboys, shook the hand of Brooks' agent, Mike Trope. It had been a pleasure.

Ten days later, Tex Schramm was feeling something not so pleasurable rising within him, a sincere wish growing that he could have been shaking that same hand. Trope's former client, Tony Dorsett, had done the unthinkable; gone AWOL and refused to report to training camp, leaving Schramm in the lurch and Tom Landry with a noticeable hole in the Cowboys' backfield.

CHAPTER 13

THE HOLDOUT

"As hardnose as Tony is about football, he's also not the kind of person who will play the kind of hardball in negotiations that Slusher wants."
Gil Brandt

"I guess you could say we've got a lot of things to worry about."
Tom Landry during training camp

    Tex Schramm – a likely candidate for Life's Victim of the Year if there ever was one – always maintained a smug appreciation for being such a misunderstood member of the human race. He'll have you know he came by that status honestly.
    Schramm always considered it to be one of the imperative ingredients for long-term success that he – in his role as the Cowboys' general manager – be portrayed as a man with an iron chin. Nobody – whether player or coach – was going to run him over or push him around. Schramm enjoyed slamming his fist down on the negotiating table to get his point across. He loved being portrayed as a tough guy.

But despite what the common perception about him was among players and fans, Schramm was not inhuman. He had a heart, a fact that Tony Dorsett knew better than most. Dorsett had joined the Cowboys as the No. 2 overall selection in the 1977 draft as the reigning Heisman Trophy winner. He was an undersized runner whose primary goal – outside of bringing another Super Bowl title to the city – was to endure five seasons in the league. Even as a rookie Dorsett was possessed by a cocky attitude, but he still thought he would be extremely fortunate to last that long against the mammoth defenses of the NFL. He wanted to get in, then get out, life and limb preferably intact.

Eight years later, "Tony D" had a ring and was fast closing in on the 10,000-yard rushing mark. His goals had changed. Dorsett no longer wanted to merely endure. He wanted security, a commodity that he figured Schramm owed him – in cash.

From the moment he had been awarded a substantial workload as a rookie, Dorsett had been a certified star. Rare speed made him a threat to turn the corner on any play, and he was as tough as a brick on inside running plays. But all of Dorsett's on-the-field attributes couldn't disguise the fact that he needed guidance off the field. Like a lot of NFL players making six-figure salaries, he was vulnerable.

John Wooten worked five years as an agent before joining the Cowboys as a scout. His list of clients included more than 100 players, including former Cowboy tight end Billy Joe Dupree and wide receiver Drew Pearson. Wooten was familiar with many of the temptations and pitfalls that befell the common athlete. Some players want to get rich overnight. Others simply want the thrill of a big fling. Either way, hard-earned money has a habit of disappearing quickly.

"There are a lot of good sound investments out there and there are a lot of bad ones, too," said Wooten. "What's sad is that a lot of players will talk to anyone who comes up to them. Some players would put their money in snowshoes in the Sahara desert."

One of Wooten's most vivid memories happened in 1975, the same year that Miami Dolphins stars Larry Csonka, Paul Warfield, and Jim Kiick all jumped to the World Football

League. With a healthy percentage of the Dolphin payroll having been reduced, Wooten was able to renegotiate a new contract for Miami running back Mercury Morris. Included in that deal was a large signing bonus, which he handed Morris one day just before noon. That same day, Wooten recalled, still pained at the thought, Mercury went shopping and bought a Cadillac, a Porsche, and a yellow Corvette.

The Cowboys had a team of advisors to not only try to discourage impulsive shopping sprees, but also to provide information that would help players evaluate the merits of business deals they were approached with. While many Cowboy players took advantage of these services, Dorsett did not. It cost him dearly.

Fortunately, Schramm had been there to get him out of more than one jam. In 1980, at Dorsett's request, Schramm reworked his contract to help him settle his debts. And when a divorce settlement of $250,000 and a series of additional poor investments plunged him deeper into red ink, Dorsett's employer promptly reached into his pocket and handed him $500,000. Schramm had a heart. He just wondered when – if ever – Dorsett would find himself a brain.

Tony had contacted Tex with the details of his latest problem six months earlier, in January of 1985. The Internal Revenue Service claimed that Dorsett owed them over $400,000 and, in addition to placing liens on his two Dallas homes, had been appropriating his paychecks since October. Schramm listened, but didn't think too much of it, figuring that, after all the team had done for him, Dorsett would work something out and show up on time for training camp. But he never did.

Dorsett called shortly before the July 25 veteran reporting deadline and asked Schramm for an extra 48 hours to come up with an agreeable payment plan with the IRS. Schramm agreed, only to have Dorsett hire a special advisor and declare a holdout. The only way Schramm could get Dorsett into camp, he insisted, was to give him a new contract.

Schramm had no choice but to believe Dorsett in that regard. Not because his running back had a history of being a stiff-necked mule when in a tight spot, but due to the presence of a new player in the room coaching Dorsett's every move.

Howard Slusher was infamous throughout the NFL and NBA for coaching his clients through long holdouts – months certainly, at times even a full season. Slusher had been the man behind Randy White's five-week training camp holdout in 1984, and now Dorsett wanted him on his side because, in Tony's words, "no one knows the Cowboys better" than Slusher.

With Slusher in his corner, Dorsett thought he could bully Cowboy management into submission. Schramm balked at such a notion, sparking a contentious standoff between a pair of Hall of Fame egos that became the story of training camp.

Dorsett claimed he was only waiting for his due, that the Cowboys had promised to give him a giant contract like the one All-Pro defensive tackle Randy White was given the year before.

Schramm cried shame. Dorsett, in response, applied a common strategy of Slusher's by refusing to come to California and negotiate with Schramm face-to-face, staying hidden from sight back in Dallas with his team of lawyers, expecting at any moment the Cowboys to come crawling to his door.

Dorsett's strategy in the matter, it is safe to say, was curiously naïve. Did he really expect Tex Schramm to bend an inch? It is barely possible that, in some bygone year, a disgruntled player short of funds once referred to Schramm as creepy, but never crawly. Dorsett was wasting his time.

Dorsett's hopes may have been misplaced, but his stance was certainly in vogue. Holdouts were happening all across the league, as if in direct reply to the NFL owners' recent resolution to try to keep salaries down.

In addition to Dorsett for the Cowboys, running back Eric Dickerson of Los Angeles, Miami quarterback Dan Marino, and Chicago linebacker Mike Singletary were all demanding reworked contracts. So too was linebacker Dennis Winston of New Orleans and offensive tackle Marvin Powell of the New York Jets.

In Philadelphia, it seemed the entire Eagles roster was holding out for more money. In the middle of training camp, Eagles general manager Harry Gamble said the team planned to place holdouts running back Wilbert Montgomery, wide receiver Mike Quick, linebacker Jerry Robinson, offensive tackle Dean

Miraldi, and defensive end Dennis Harrison on suspension without pay for one year.

Schramm, through the press, insisted that a holdout was not necessary for Dorsett, that the Cowboys had some big financial favors planned for him. Schramm liked Dorsett as a person, and he appreciated his flashy style on the field, believing it only enhanced the Cowboys' image as a sleek, high-tech franchise. But Schramm couldn't negotiate with someone who refused to come out of hiding.

Dorsett continually used Randy White's contract as a blueprint for the new deal he wanted. Just how had he managed to become familiar with the fine print in White's contract? According to fellow Cowboys running back Ron Springs, Dorsett made a few calls to the Players Union and learned the terms of the latest contracts signed by both White and Gary Hogeboom, and then got disgruntled because he didn't have the same. Oh yes, Tony was being sly in renegotiating his renegotiations.

"One wonders how White, for example, will react to a teammate taking it upon himself to use Randy's private business to benefit his own. Or is that how it's done these days?" queried Blackie Sherrod in the *Dallas Morning News*.

Schramm had been caught off guard by Dorsett's sudden change in manner. He had never dreamed of a holdout scenario affecting training camp. But when Dorsett laid out his cards, Schramm rolled the dice without hesitation, betting that a looming season and the accompanying paychecks would lure Dorsett to Thousand Oaks before very long. If Tony wanted to hold out, that was fine. It was only costing him $1,000 a day, a hard-and-fast rule which applied to all players who reported late to training camp.

A year ago, Slusher had told White to stay in hiding until further notice. White responded the best way he knew how, by grabbing his gear and tackle and heading to East Texas for what turned out to be a five-week fishing trip.

Playing the waiting game did not suit Dorsett's personality. He wasn't a country boy who enjoyed solitude. Dorsett wanted to be noticed by more eyes than those on some slimy fish. He liked the bright lights and all of the attention that went along with being a Dallas Cowboy. T.D. preferred to be scoring touchdowns.

It was all Dorsett could do to stay hidden away for a week. After that, he started talking. First it was to *Sports Illustrated*, then to Dallas sportswriters from the *Times Herald* and the *Morning News*.

Everything was a hunky-dory mutual disagreement into the first week of August, with both contestants dancing around the ring indifferently, until Dorsett's team, from the far corner, threw a hammer into the ring. The Cowboys were traveling to Dallas for the first preseason game when Dorsett's other agent, Witt Stewart, called Schramm to task for allegedly lying about the promise he had made to Dorsett about a considerable raise, adding that the Cowboys had also cheated his client out of his original $662,000 signing bonus from 1977. Dorsett admitted it as a public fact, whereupon he demanded to be traded. If Schramm refused to oblige, Dorsett promised to retire.

Meanwhile, due to the holdout, the Cowboys coaching staff was having to adjust the offensive formula on the fly. Initially, when Dorsett didn't show up for training camp, Tom Landry had penciled in James Jones at the No. 1 tailback spot. But when management divined that Dorsett and his agents were hunkering down for a lengthy standoff, Landry called an audible and moved Springs up to the No. 1 spot.

No matter how much he may have wanted to, Landry couldn't bring himself to have faith that Jones' knees could endure a full workload. Since November of 1979, Jones had undergone surgery three times on his left knee. The first time, as a senior at Mississippi State, was for cartilage damage and stretched ligaments, then twice more with the Cowboys due to bone spurs. He missed all of the strike-shortened season of 1982. He was used only on special teams in 1983 and carried the ball just eight times in 1984.

Landry chose to preserve Jones' health as best he could for the regular season grind, where he hoped to use the sixth-year runner in a complementary role, preferably to Dorsett. But Dorsett was nowhere to be found.

During the preseason opener versus Green Bay at toasty Texas Stadium, about thirty Cowboy players, "rather like teenage club members" in Blackie Sherrod's opinion, wore "33" on their wristbands to commemorate Dorsett's absence. Schramm was bored with the gesture.

Soon after arriving back to camp in Thousand Oaks, Schramm alluded to certain "financial problems" of Dorsett's while speaking on KRLD radio. Reporters continued to pump Schramm on the issue, approaching him with information alleged to be from sources familiar with Dorsett's plight. While trying to be close-mouthed on the issue, Schramm was obliging enough to tell them whether their figures were in the ballpark, or not.

When word got back to Dorsett, the running back blew his top, claiming that Schramm had intentionally leaked all of his financial problems to the press. Not one to sit idly by and let public opinion pile against him, Schramm took complete control of the situation by rolling out detailed documents showing when and how the Cowboys doled out Dorsett's original signing bonus of $662,000, as well as the critical features of his current contract. It was all there, black writing on white paper. The Cowboys were innocent of any wrongdoing in the matter.

Just before publicizing those facts in front of the press, Schramm's frustration with the situation boiled over in front of Dallas Morning News columnist Bob St. John. "This whole thing…this is just what happens when I [!@#$%!] around and try to help somebody. I know better. They turn on you every time."

Dorsett's response? "It's a matter of who is lying," he was quoted as saying from back in north Texas. Then, in an attempt to throw more fuel on the fast-growing flame of ill-will, Dorsett said that he would love to play in Miami because he considered Don Shula to be the best coach in the business. Or did he just want to go to South Beach so he could play alongside Dan Marino? Was this another low-blow aimed at Danny White?

Dorsett's bargaining position was hardly desirable. He was 31, beyond an NFL tailback's normal productive age. He had three years remaining on his existing contract. He had to face-off against a front-office that had long shown a reluctance to renegotiate contracts.

Oh, and Schramm wasn't about to let Dorsett forget that 1984 had been his worst as a professional. Through the first eight weeks of the season, Dorsett failed to rush for 100 yards in a game. His longest run of the season was just 31 yards.

And it wasn't as if Dorsett had a myriad of money-making options outside of football. What position in the corporate world could he immediately acquire that would compensate him at a comparable level to his running back gig with the Cowboys?

Dorsett had nowhere to turn, not if he was going to make an honest effort to get the IRS off his back. He needed the Cowboys. But did the Cowboys need him?

It wouldn't be the ideal situation for a head coach needing to impress the general manager with a big season, but the fact that the Cowboys had drafted Herschel Walker might convince Landry to go with an inexperienced cast at tailback for one year and plan on welcoming Walker to the lineup in 1986. (The USFL is going to fold, right Tex?) What about Dorsett, you ask? Well, he could go jump in the creek!

Dorsett had suggested a trade, but the likelihood of that ever happening was unlikely for all of the above reasons. Trying to drag Schramm through the mud wasn't helping him any either.

Public sentiment was set against Dorsett because he had managed to squander so much money in the space of a few years. His accusations against Cowboy management only made him look worse to the world.

The fact that Bum Bright was not sympathetic to his cause hurt Dorsett even more. Yes, even the owner had to chime in on this drama.

"I don't understand it," Bright told Gary Myers of the *Dallas Morning News*. "He says he has a problem with his contract and needs to get it straightened out. I thought he had a contract. That, to me, is very clear. He can read, I presume. I don't understand a guy welshing on it. My only advice to Tony is to act like he has a contract and do what he is supposed to do."

But the longer Dorsett stayed holed up in Dallas, the more irritable Schramm became out west. He had been clearly shaken in late July at the news of his 42-year old son-in-law being hospitalized for a heart attack, and annoyed at the rumor that the

Cowboys' ownership group was falling apart back in Dallas and that Bright was seeking confidential bids to replace his other partners. By the second week of August, Schramm's nerves had been worn to a frazzle.

Earlier in camp, Dallas assistant coach Gene Stallings had extolled the performance of defensive lineman David Ponder, telling Schramm to keep his eye on Ponder during a scrimmage with the Rams. Schramm paid close attention, yet failed to see anything to get excited about. He mentioned this to Stallings after the scrimmage. A few moments later, they were both embroiled in a heated shouting match.

"That's [!@#$%!]," said Schramm, his voice booming across the field. "I watched him and saw nothing. He's just like some of those other greats who turn out to be nothings."

"That's because you don't look for the things coaches look for," retorted Stallings. "You just don't know what to look for."

"[!@#$%!] You guys always think you have some great secrets. But you see what you see!"

The face-to-face argument lasted for a few more minutes, before Schramm and Stallings each went their separate ways. Everyone – even the kids in the audience – knew that Schramm was in a bad mood. Fortunately for Schramm and the entire coaching staff (especially Stallings), the cloud of doom and gloom would soon be lifted.

The Cowboys' running back situation was hardly comforting as the sun peaked above the horizon on August 14. Dorsett was holding out. Ron Springs had a Sep. 9 court date, his availability for the regular season very much in question. And James Jones was nursing another knee injury. Had the regular season started tomorrow, it may very well have been rookie Robert LaVette taking the lion's share of the carries against the Washington Redskins.

Back in Dallas, Dorsett's camp was coming unglued. Slusher had just found out about a clandestine meeting between running back and general manager over the weekend. He wasn't happy. Slusher wanted Dorsett to refrain from talking to the press and, above all, stay away from Schramm. Another two weeks of hiding out, Slusher promised, and the Cowboys would be forced to roll out the red carpet.

Stewart and Dorsett disagreed. They wanted to begin negotiations right away, fearful that a longer wait would affect the regular season and hurt any chances they had of inking a big deal.

In what was reported to be an amicable split, Slusher resigned as Dorsett's negotiating agent that same morning. Stewart immediately contacted Schramm. The three met later that day for five hours in a closed-door meeting, Stewart rolling out his client's needs, and Schramm explaining to Dorsett, in a booming voice that was heard by nearly everyone in the building, the many misunderstandings the two parties had been operating under.

"I guess we should have talked in a soundproof room," Schramm said afterwards. "…When you're upset, you say things you don't mean. I feel very good about the situation now." Upon emerging, a new $6 million contract was declared to have been agreed upon. Dorsett had his security. Schramm had his running back. Even the IRS was pacified.

As quickly as it had begun, the twenty-day holdout was over. Now, maybe Schramm could watch some football at Cowboys camp, instead of worrying himself to death over financial issues that could have been resolved in a much easier fashion and, not to mention, oh, so long ago.

CHAPTER 14

HELLO AGAIN, GOODBYE FOREVER

"Drew's a good communicator. He's able to translate through language his talent – how he played the game – to us as players."
Cowboys wide receiver Mike Renfro speaking of new assistant coach Drew Pearson

Drew Pearson was back. From catching passes on the practice field in Dallas in hopes of a comeback a few weeks before, Pearson had arrived in Thousand Oaks in the employ of a San Antonio television station. His playing career may have been over, but at least Pearson's value was not being completely overlooked in broadcasting. He was at camp to interview former teammates and deliver credible daily reports to his audience back in south Texas.

Pearson didn't have to strain himself to find a story. Spirits were noticeably high after Dallas' 27-3 preseason-opening victory over Green Bay, an outcome that had dozens of Cowboy rookies soaring with confidence. Yes, even during preseason, winning could be a contagious ingredient.

After so many uninspiring practices in a row, Robert LaVette had shown the coaching staff a few flashes of brilliance in live action, breaking loose for 50 yards on 8 carries, including a 7-yard fourth-quarter scoring run. Jesse Penn was all smiles after his 77-yard interception return for a touchdown. And Kevin Brooks was now talking smack on the practice field, as a result of his two-sack performance against the Packers. Brooks didn't care that one of those sacks had been officially wiped from the record book because of a Dallas penalty. The quarterback had felt his presence. That's all that mattered.

"It was the best rookie show we've had in some time," said Landry after the game.

And, in the event that Pearson got tired of the rookie ravings, he could always attempt to dig up the juicy details of Tony Hill's story, a one-of-a-kind mystery that had provoked more than one laugh amongst reporters over the previous three weeks. Hill had reported to camp in late July weighing 220-pounds, a full 18-pounds over his prescribed playing weight. Hill, wearing a poker face, claimed he had enjoyed "a big dinner" the night before checking into camp, making his weight misleading. *Uh, Tony, could you tell us exactly what was on the menu that night? Come on, Tony! Just for historical purposes, you know.*

Pearson played the role of reporter well for a few days, but it was only a matter of time till his competitive juices took over. A credentialed spectator on the sideline, Pearson – his perfectionist spirit leaking through his armor – couldn't help but notice a series of fundamental errors hindering several of the Cowboys' young wide receivers one afternoon. Pearson was initially hesitant to inject himself into the flow of practice. After all, he was supposed to be an indifferent observer. He was supposed to be holding a microphone, not a football.

But it went against the grain to just sit by and do nothing. He was still a Cowboy at heart. Moments later, Pearson was seen easing out onto the practice field offering instructions.

Before long, those same players were eagerly plying him with questions.

Leon Gonzalez, the Cowboys' eighth-round draft choice out of Bethune-Cookman, needed help getting off the line of scrimmage. Mel Lattany asked for Pearson's philosophy on tracking the ball in flight. And Karl Powe, a seventh-round selection from Alabama State, soaked up Pearson's teaching on body control.

These talks were often technical, dealing with small details that the average fan failed to comprehend during a full-speed practice. Route concepts. Footwork. Shoulder levels. Hand placement. Even eye placement. But Pearson was quick to point out that all of the long hours working on proper technique wouldn't amount to a hill of beans if the receiver didn't understand his primary job on the field.

"He says, 'Catch the ball. That's the biggest thing,'" said Powe. "If you run the wrong route, don't worry about it. Just catch the ball. That's the most important thing to a receiver. Whatever you have to do. Drew says that if it comes high, you turn into a bird. If it comes low, you turn into a mole. Just catch it."

A few days later, Pearson was awarded a temporary position as an assistant to wide receivers coach Dick Nolan. No matter how hard they tried, doctors just couldn't keep him away from the game and the team he loved. Drew Pearson was still a Cowboy, both in heart and in service.

The Tony Dorsett saga now firmly in the rearview mirror, Tex Schramm was back to the grind of trying to locate another wide receiver. For several weeks, he had been keeping one eye glued to several of the young Cowboy wide-outs in camp. And while they did make some plays on occasion, it was also apparent that they were green, too green at this date to burden with starting duties in September.

Though considerably weary with the process, Schramm was resolved to try his rotten luck once again at procuring a veteran from an opponent's roster. He and Gil Brandt had called around to different teams and were soon involved in trade negotiations with Miami for Dolphins wide receiver Anthony Carter, a USFL transfer. Schramm was so close to a deal he could almost taste it. But then it all fell apart. Miami head coach Don Shula insisted that the only way the Cowboys were going to get their hands on Carter was to include Jesse Penn in a trade.

Brandt reported back that the team was not interested. Carter's rights were eventually traded to the Vikings. Schramm threw up his hands in despair. Well, he had tried. God knows he did.

The wide receiver search had been fruitless for so long that one reporter decided to test just how desperate for one the Cowboys were, asking Tom Landry during the preseason if he would consider signing Butch Johnson in the event that the former Cowboys wideout was released by the Denver Broncos.

"Butch Who?" grinned Landry. "I'm too old for that."

Drew Pearson had been paying close attention to Mel Lattany. The rookie wide receiver had looked uncomfortable for the entire afternoon practice, stumbling and bumbling his way around the field like someone suffering from either dizziness or exhaustion.

Lattany's accomplishments for the day were noteworthy, though certainly forgettable. He had dropped passes, slipped several times while making cuts, and appeared off-balance more often than not. In short, just enough to make Pearson wonder what was up with the former Olympic sprinter.

Pearson approached Lattany after practice and asked him what was wrong. The rookie had no answers, shaking his head resignedly. Lattany had gotten hurt early in camp when he crashed into a fence while trying to avoid running into some children who were sitting close to the practice field. He had shaken it off after a couple of days, thinking that a forgettable chapter of training camp was over for him. But he was wrong there.

Ever since the veterans showed up in camp, Lattany had sensed a roster spot slipping away from him. He was fast on his feet, alarmingly so, but that wasn't always good enough. Lattany needed cunning to win battles consistently against NFL cornerbacks. He needed seasoning. But those attributes took time to acquire, of which he didn't have much remaining. The Cowboys were preparing to break camp in a few days, with the preseason slate set to expire a week later. If he was going to win back the confidence of Cowboy coaches in time to avoid being released, he needed a change of luck.

Or, according to Pearson, a change of shoes. Pearson had been examining Lattany's equipment and discovered that he was wearing shoes one-half size too large. He checked with equipment manager Buch Buchanan and brought back a new pair to be worn the next day.

On the following morning, Lattany trotted out onto the field with his new cleats, eager to impress. Little did Lattany know that it wasn't to be the coaching staff that he imparted an impression upon. A few minutes into practice, Lattany lost his way in the end-zone and ran headlong into the goal-post, injuring his wrist in the process.

"It just shows how much I help," Pearson sarcastically observed afterwards.

A bandaged wrist preventing him from participating in practice afterwards, Lattany kissed his dreams of being a Cowboy goodbye at the end of training camp when the team announced his release.

The news for Pearson in late August was of a much different variety, as he accepted Tom Landry's offer for a full-time position as the Cowboys' wide receivers consultant.

Drew Pearson's timing in leaving broadcasting momentarily behind was impeccable. Intriguing storylines at Camp Cowboy were fast disappearing.

The vortex surrounding the status of Tony Dorsett had disappeared the moment his holdout ended. Dorsett had reported to camp like a good soldier and was entrenched as the No. 1 tailback, just as if he had never been gone in the first place. Less than a week later, Tom Landry officially announced that Danny White would be the Cowboys' opening-night starter on Sep. 7 versus Washington, ending what had been a very mundane quarterback competition between White and Gary Hogeboom.

Fortunately for the beat writers who followed the team around every day, there remained one final surprise before regular season's greetings were administered. Prior to the final preseason game in Houston, the Cowboys raised a few eyebrows by shipping starting outside linebacker Anthony Dickerson to Buffalo in exchange for a seventh-round draft choice. Evidently, the Cowboys really were serious about a youth movement, though insiders suggested the move had been in the makings for some time.

Dickerson had not played at all during the Cowboys' Monday night preseason contest against Chicago. Afterwards, Landry had said not to read too much into it, that coaches simply wanted to see more of Jesse Penn, Jeff Rohrer, Brian Salonen, and Scott Strasburger. But it was difficult for those familiar with the team not to divine the fact that the Cowboys were anxious to move on from Dickerson.

For several seasons now, Dickerson had harbored the feeling that the Cowboys were actively trying to get rid of him. One year after another, the team had selected an outside linebacker with a high draft pick, then went out of their way to pump the rookie up during camp. This pressure from behind had served to motivate Dickerson for a time, but not even that could save his job in the end.

Dickerson enjoyed a career year with the Cowboys in 1983, his first as the starting weak-side linebacker, leading the team in solo tackles (81) and finishing second in total tackles (114) and sacks (10 ½). He knocked down six passes, recovered three fumbles, and forced two additional fumbles.

More than merely stuff the stat sheet, Dickerson impacted that season with a couple of memorable plays. His takedown of New Orleans quarterback Ken Stabler in the end-zone for a safety with 1:58 to play provided the difference in a 21-20 Dallas victory. Later in the season, Dickerson's pressuring of New York Giants quarterback Scott Brunner allowed Dextor Clinkscale to intercept a pass and return it for the decisive touchdown.

But the following year, Dickerson proved to be a resounding disappointment, falling to tenth in total tackles while recording just two sacks. He attributed his poor 1984 performance on three things: (1) a deep shoulder bruise that never properly healed. (2) reduced playing time. (3) an inability to shake off his demotion and play well when he was on the field.

"I was discouraged because my playing time was cut – they didn't give me a reason for that," said Dickerson. "I found myself sitting on the bench a lot, and that tore me up inside. I found myself thinking more of why it was happening, instead of playing football. It really hurt my play."

Having played out his option, Dickerson became embroiled in a contract dispute with the Cowboys during the spring of 1985. A veteran of five NFL seasons, he was tired of being one of the lowest-paid members on the team, and felt that Tex Schramm should finally reward him for his starter's status.

When Schramm shuffled his feet, Dickerson flirted with the Memphis Showboats of the USFL, before eventually signing a new three-year pact with the Cowboys.

With Dickerson now in Buffalo, Landry was free to announce another noteworthy decision, christening Rohrer, an outspoken linebacker from Yale, as a member of the starting unit. Rohrer, a second-round draft selection in 1982, had been seldom used on defense during his first two years in the league, drawing criticism from fans for being long on wit and toughness but lacking in athleticism. Once upon a time, Landry had designs on watching Rohrer take the torch from Bob Breunig at middle linebacker, awarding Rohrer a preseason start in the middle in 1984. But it didn't work. Rohrer was ousted by

Eugene Lockhart during training camp, before being moved back to the outside.

Penn, the big-play rookie who faded late in training camp with "dead legs," was slotted as Rohrer's backup. More than one Dallas assistant felt that Penn, once he got his head completely wrapped around the Flex system, would be starting in Rohrer's place by mid-season. But for now, he was simply a youngster learning the ropes, watching Rohrer and the rest of the Cowboy squad storm out of the regular season gates and serve notice to every other NFL camp that Dallas was not yet dead.

CHAPTER 15

THE GREAT BIRTHDAY BASH

"For the first time in my career, I saw Joe Theismann totally rattled."
Cowboys safety Dextor Clinkscale

"It was the cruelest moment I've ever been through. We were getting our [butt] handed to us, and I sat on the bench and all of Texas Stadium was singing 'Happy Birthday' to me."
Redskins QB Joe Theismann after his five-interception performance on opening night

Game day had arrived in Dallas, which meant that Dennis Thurman was busy putting on his game-face. Though no longer a starter, and obviously lacking the credentials of a Randy White, Thurman certainly posed as one of the most important members of Tom Landry's Flex defense. He was, at the ripe old age of 29, the unquestioned leader of an underwhelming group of Cowboy defensive backs.

Thurman knew the doubters were everywhere. He had been hearing them ever since the Cowboys made the All-American defensive back from USC an eleventh-round selection in the 1978 draft. The experts said he was too small and too slow to last at the NFL level. Seven years later, Thurman was doing more than enduring as a professional. He was thriving. Twice he had led the Cowboys in interceptions, and was already ranked second on the franchise's all-time list for playoff thefts, behind only Charlie Waters.

Going into 1985, Thurman had admittedly lost a half-step, a fact which had cost him his starting cornerback job during the previous season. But Thurman continued to make plays on the field in a backup role. Whether as a nickel cornerback or a safety in the Cowboys' 4-0 defense, Dennis continued to be a defensive menace who relied heavily on superior fundamentals and uncommon instincts.

His knowledge of the opponent and the Flex defense impressed Landry so much that the head coach allowed Thurman to serve as a player/coach during training camp. The move enabled Thurman to take a more hands-on approach with members of the Cowboys' secondary, all of whom shared a common bond. Of the eight defensive backs on the Dallas roster to begin the regular season, only one had been drafted higher than the seventh-round, and five were not even drafted at all. But Thurman's diligence and uber-confidence had rubbed off on his pupils, allowing them to play loose and fast while defending some of the NFL's best receivers.

Thurman knew that the combination of Joe Theismann and Art Monk had provided the Cowboys a number of problems in previous meetings with Washington. The Redskins loved to pound the ball with John Riggins, then sneak in a long throw to Monk over an unsuspecting defense. This formula had worked to perfection in 1984 when Washington swept the season series from Dallas. But Thurman believed the Cowboys would be ready this time.

A few hours before the Cowboys were scheduled to kick off their 1985 season, Thurman telephoned his younger brother to offer an encouraging word. USC cornerback Junior Thurman was feeling good about himself after intercepting two passes against Illinois on Saturday. But Dennis, like every older brother has done down through time, was there to remind Junior that he could have done more.

"I'll think you done something when you run one of those interceptions in for a touchdown," chided Dennis, little realizing that a touchdown of his own was on the horizon later that night, when he and the rest of the Cowboys' unheralded defensive backfield thrust themselves into a limelight they could not -and would not - avoid.

The radiant glow of the *Monday Night Football* caravan provided a bright spotlight and an unquenchable buzz within the sweltering confines of Texas Stadium. For the 62,292 fans in attendance and the millions more watching on ABC, this evening of September 9 was undoubtedly the end of a tediously long wait that had rendered patience thin, nerves frazzled, and expectations nearly non-existent. After months of practices, hype, and countless verses of melodramatic harmonizing, the stage was finally set. The flag had been saluted, the coin dutifully tossed, and, under the comfort of darkening summer skies and nearly triple-digit temperatures, the Dallas Cowboys' 1985 season was now prepared to commence.

Fueling this scene of anticipatory fervor was the antagonizing presence of the Washington Redskins on the visitors sideline. No opponent in the history of professional football in Dallas could provoke more derision and ungentlemanly behavior from the locals than the Redskins. By the early 1970s, what started out as a front-office feud between Tex Schramm and then-owner George Preston Marshall had developed into an all-out war on the field between Tom Landry's Cowboys and George Allen's Redskins. And though Allen was no longer around to stoke the fires of ill will with his wit and sarcasm, the dislike remained very much the same into the ensuing decade, as Dallas and Washington tangled annually with the NFC East title at stake.

As of late, Joe Gibbs' crew had owned the upper hand in the rivalry, dealing Dallas three consecutive losses. Clearest in the minds of Dallas fans was the most recent encounter from the previous December, when Washington rallied from a 21-6 deficit to claim a 30-28 victory, thus preventing the Cowboys from clinching a playoff berth. Adding insult to injury was the suspicious behavior of quarterback Joe Theismann, who drew the ire of certain Cowboy defenders for allegedly dancing a jig in the backfield while the Redskins were running out the clock. Theismann claimed he was only trying to burn a few extra seconds before kneeling down. To Randy White, Ron Fellows, and others wearing silver and blue, it appeared that Theismann was in fact dancing on the Cowboys' grave.

Nearly nine months later, with their Week 1 showdown in north Texas just days away, the animosity remained a very stark reality, as the two teams traded barbs through the press as if their very lives depended on it. White pointed a finger. Theismann stuck out his tongue. The two head coaches, meanwhile, did their best to downplay the incident and the buzz surrounding it.

So it was that when Rafael Septien put his foot into the ball to signal the beginning of the game and the regular season, there was an unacknowledged understanding among everyone present that this was to be one night when the sparks of competition would be seen in all the brilliant colors that only a fierce rivalry and a primetime stage could induce. The only astonishment that followed came when one of these sparks set light to a birthday candle, provoking a song from the throngs that would come to define Joe's worst night as a professional, when the Cowboys drove the Redskins to their knees and Theismann to the bench.

While the press spent the better part of the week preceding the season opener dealing with the drama surrounding Joe

Theismann's alleged misconduct, Tom Landry was busy fretting over a bigger man and a much bigger problem. Whether he was in the film room or on the practice field, Landry stressed to his defense the importance of slowing down Washington's one-man wrecking-ball, John Riggins.

If ability were a quality gleaned from first impressions, Riggins might have qualified as one of the least talented players that the league had to offer. The Redskins' media guide inclined to the theory that Riggins stood 6-foot-2-inches in his socks, and consisted primarily of 230 pounds of well-tempered steel. But to behold Riggins in person provided a very different impression than what his measurements indicated. Whether it was his sallow complexion or stooping posture, Riggins looked very much like a pudgy redneck whose disposition and waistline seemed more suited to standing behind a bar or in a Nascar garage than in any NFL backfield. Only when trying to bring him down with a tackle during a game did defenders realize the true capabilities of Riggins' suspicious physique.

"The Diesel," as Riggins was known around the nation's capital, implicitly reflected the personality and the mystique of Joe Gibbs' Redskin teams of the 1980s. Tough. Resilient. And thoroughly devastating against the Cowboys. Especially in recent meetings.

Versus a Dallas defensive system predicated on stopping opposing rushers, Riggins had overpowered Landry's trademark Flex scheme in both 1984 encounters, totaling 276 yards while averaging nearly 5 yards-per-carry. That Washington scored at least 30 points in each meeting was no surprise to the Dallas head coach, for it only provided additional support for Landry's philosophy pertaining to Riggins' overall impact on a game. As Riggins rolled, so rolled the Redskins.

To prevent "The Diesel" from rolling right over the Cowboys yet again would require more than just attention to detail and unwavering faith in the Flex system. Landry needed his players to also prove themselves affluent in the art of swarming the ball-carrier with steadfast numbers in the backfield. Hit him early, hit him often. Get him, before he gets you. Because once Big John got his legs churning downfield, the fun was over for anything or anybody unlucky enough to be in his path.

It was a long-established fact of football that there was nothing friendly in the sight of Riggins' massive thighs barreling straight ahead at you. There was nothing serene about the struggle to bring him down that would then surely ensue. Football, it must be acknowledged, ceased to be a game when attempting to tackle Riggins in the open field. It was more akin to a brawl, a brutal battle of wills that stretched and bent mind, limb and protective equipment to the breaking point.

As it so happened, there were simultaneous concerns growing among the Washington media that it might be Riggins himself who was nearing the breaking point heading into his fourteenth season. At age 36, Riggins was the oldest starting running back in the league, yet it was more than mere questions of his physical durability that encircled him during the summer of 1985. After watching him exceed the 10,000-yard career rushing mark and earn a Super Bowl MVP trophy to cap the 1982 season, the newspapers were now openly speculating whether Riggins had become too much of a headache to the organization.

It has been rumored ever since Riggins arrived at his troubles through an honest mistake, that instead of relieving the pain of another 1,000-yard rushing season in 1984 by immersing himself in a tub of ice as team doctors recommended, Riggins inadvertently drowned himself in a bottle of firewater. Thus transported to a level of physical tranquility, Riggins stumbled his way into the Salute to Congress dinner at the Washington Sheraton hotel on an evening in late January where he immediately made another inauspicious error by downing one glass of Scotch, then another.

After an expeditious navigation through the crowd, Riggins found himself nearing his own table, and the unmistakable figure of Virginia Senator Chuck Robb. "Gooo-be-na-toor!" Riggins said in greeting. "I understand that we're going to be seated at the same table tonight!"

Dinner began with all the fussiness commonly associated with a black-tie event, which only allowed Riggins to further distinguish himself from the many dignitaries around him.

Staying true to his small-town roots in the Midwest, Riggins claimed he didn't care for the fancy food of politicians. So while everyone else ate, he continued to drink. And drink. And drink...

By this time, Riggins was fast becoming disoriented. He knocked one bottle of red wine over. And when the waiter brought two more bottles to the table, Riggins proved adept in knocking those over too.

Soon after, it was announced that Supreme Court Justice Sandra Day O'Connor would be leaving early due to an engagement on the following morning. Upon hearing this, Riggins managed to get to his feet and approach her seat, where he put his arm around the neck of O'Connor's husband, and looked directly at the female justice while authoring his infamous plea for her to remain longer. "Aww, come on, loosen up, Sandy baby, you're too tight."

"Sandy" departed in the pursuit of a good night's sleep. Riggins accomplished as much by staying, snoring on the carpeted floor through the entirety of George H.W. Bush's speech. As a guest of People magazine, Riggins was afforded helpful, attentive service by the hotel staff at the conclusion of the dinner, who guided Riggins to his awaiting taxi. Recalls Associated Press photographer Ron Edmonds: "They took him out the VIP door. They were dragging him, feet first."

Nearly six months later, Riggins was arrested in Reston, Va. on a charge of public intoxication. His friend, Stuart, was charged with driving while intoxicated. Though Riggins maintained his innocence in the case, there was the feeling around Washington that the Redskins might give up on the aging running back and shove all their chips toward George Rogers, whom they had acquired via a trade with New Orleans during the draft.

But after due deliberation and a 16-day holdout from training camp, Riggins signed a one-year incentive-laden contract valued at $825,000, with player and franchise declaring their undying commitment to each other in a grand public display.

This show of solidarity between Riggins and the front-office provided a sense of stability at the running back position for the Redskins. It also gave the onlooking crowd from Dallas something to chuckle about.

From the verbose fountain of Blackie Sherrod's pen flowed this simple poem:

Title: John The Tapis

Redskins are fiercely protective,
Of their bull-dozing one-man mob,
They say he may sleep on the carpet,
But never does he sleep on the job.

While certainly humorous, Sherrod's bit of poetry possessed a moral that Landry hoped his team would keep in mind for Monday night's matchup. The big stage, the bright lights, and the presence of the Dallas Cowboys were all familiar ingredients for a John Riggins masterpiece performance. To categorize him as an aging, fading has-been would be an open-handed invitation to a primetime bludgeoning, not to mention a season-opening defeat.

Those pre-game prognostications from Landry and the Dallas coaching staff were rendered properly prophetic in the early moments of action on Monday night. The only ineffectual service seemed to be the many hours of preparation that Landry insisted upon from his players.

Safety Bill Bates started at weakside linebacker in place of Jeff Rohrer, a move that was supposed to bolster the Cowboys' ability to cover Washington's misdirection passing attack. Instead, it played right into the hand of the Redskins, who started the game with an unbalanced offensive line, tackles Mark May and Joe Jacoby both lining up on the left side where they could take advantage of the smaller Bates.

Washington received the opening kickoff and duly stuffed the ball in the belly of their veteran steamroller. Once…Twice… Four times in succession did Riggins receive a handoff to start the game, barreling over the left side for an accumulative total of 24 yards, forcing Landry to call an unanticipated timeout.

Out came Bates and in went Rohrer, adding some much-needed beef to the Dallas front. Whatever else was said in the huddle – whether words of encouragement or those of a technical variety – appeared to effect a change in the Dallas defense. Passive punching bags to start, a wall of angered Cowboys emerged from the stoppage, thwarting a Redskin march of once promising proportions with a manly helmet-to-helmet collision between Eugene Lockhart and Riggins, followed by a third-down Randy White takedown of Joe Theismann at the Dallas 48-yard line.

While the Cowboys had spent their week in preparing to defend the uncommon force of Riggins, the Redskins were busy formulating their own set of priorities. No. 1 on their to-do list was to diagnose the health status of Danny White. White had suffered rib cartilage damage in the second exhibition game at San Diego's Jack Murphy Stadium, forcing him to watch from the sidelines over the next two weeks as the Cowboys completed the franchise's first unbeaten preseason since their Super Bowl championship campaign of 1971. Much to Gary Hogeboom's disappointment, team trainer Don Cochren said that a flak jacket designed to shield the rib area would enable the 33-year old White to suit up versus Washington.

White felt confident that he would be able to play all four quarters because he knew something that the Redskins did not. The Cowboys had spent the entire off-season overhauling their passing attack, completely eliminating seven-step drops by the quarterback from the offensive playbook. This was a move to copy the quick-pass formula that the high-flying offenses in San Francisco and Miami were employing. By calling for pass plays that required a quick delivery, Landry felt that he could not only limit negative plays, but also better protect his quarterback.

White liked the subtle change, feeling that it would frustrate an overeager team like the rush-happy Redskins. He also approved of Landry's first play-call of the game, a quick pass to Tony Hill on the left sideline requiring only a three-step drop. Surely this was the perfect way to allow White to shake off the rust of a long layoff and gain an early rhythm.

But the Redskins weren't going to be delayed in achieving their goal. They had talked all week about putting a licking on White and, by golly, that's what they were going to do. So out came the defense, out came the gloves, and down went White in the backfield at the conclusion of Dallas' first offensive play, courtesy of an after-the-bell hit by Washington's Charles Mann.

White got to his feet, his tender ribs still intact and seemingly none the worse for wear. Which was more than could be said for the Washington defense. The infraction for roughing-the-passer warranted a fifteen-yard walk-off, and sparked a Dallas scoring drive capped by a 53-yard Rafael Septien field goal.

The game then settled into a series of big hits and near-blows, with players from both sides laboring in the summer heat, their sweat-streaked faces and soaked shirt-fronts belying the oppressive conditions inside Texas Stadium. The brand-new suites that Bum Bright bankrolled during the off-season were, as Tex Schramm had promised they would be, the very latest in luxury. They also qualified as a first-class nuisance for the common patron seated in the open-air conditions of the arena.

Blocking what for the past fourteen years had been the most natural avenue for the outside breeze to filter down into the stadium's bowl, Bum's Bright idea of a money-making scheme had turned a once-veritable football palace into an oversized oven. Tex Schramm had attempted to off-set this problem by installing 145 fans inside the stadium, a strategy that sounded like a good idea beforehand. But on the night of Sep. 9, nothing could persuade a breath of air to move inside Texas Stadium during the course of the game.

Even the scoreboard seemed to have wilted in the uncommon temperatures, as Dallas clung to a 3-0 lead into the second quarter. But then the Cowboys began marching out of the shadow of their own goalposts, wearing down the Washington defense on a lengthy drive that started at the 2-yard line. Danny White, after completing just 1-of-5 pass attempts during the opening frame, had found a groove, connecting with

Hill, Mike Renfro, and Tony Dorsett on a series of short, quick throws.

After running off seventeen plays in succession, the Cowboys were faced with a third-and-6 from the Washington 17-yard line. White had designs of throwing to Renfro once again, but when that didn't materialize, the quarterback was forced to scramble from the pocket. Running to his right, a winded Mann huffing and puffing in pursuit, White scanned the field for an open target. Renfro was still blanketed in the end-zone. Hill was on the other side of the field. And rookie Leon Gonzalez was running away from him.

Just when it appeared that he would have to toss the ball into the seats and allow the field-goal team to come onto the field again, White threw across his body toward fullback Timmy Newsome, who was being closely guarded at the 10-yard line. The pass was a dangerous one, with the potential for the ball to be deflected in the air and intercepted by a nearby Redskin. But White was in a gambling mood, his resolve and determination at an all-time high after re-claiming his rightful position as the Cowboys' starting quarterback. Risk notwithstanding, White rifled the ball downfield, confident that a combination of skill and luck would preserve the Cowboy march. As the Redskins defense can attest, White's confidence was not misplaced.

Newsome not only made the reception, he spun away from the defender and turned upfield. Linebacker Monte Coleman latched onto the ball-carrier at the 6-yard line, but Newsome kept his legs churning forward. As Newsome began falling to the ground near the 1, rookie defensive back Barry Wilburn entered the picture and delivered a crunching blow to the runner, sending the ball rolling into the end-zone, where it was scooped up by All-Pro cornerback Darrell Green.

Green's runback, and the collective gasps of 60,000 Cowboy fans in attendance, were cut short by the piercing whistles of the officials signaling that Newsome's knee had touched the artificial turf before the fumble occurred, constituting the end of the play. Joe Gibbs, along with many of his players, pointed to the new Diamond Vision replay screens inside the stadium as evidence that Newsome's knee was, in fact, not down before he coughed up the ball. But their efforts were wasted. Officials were still not allowed to use replay to correct an error in judgment. The ruling had been administered. The discussion was over.

The NFL had experimented with instant replay during the preseason of 1985, but it was not in effect for the regular season. While the league office was evaluating the usage of instant replay from the preseason, the Redskins were getting fleeced by the Cowboys.

On the very next play, Newsome bulled his way over the goal-line to give Dallas a 10-0 advantage, while a troop of weary Redskins stormed angrily toward the visitors bench, still bemoaning the injustice done to them.

"That drive took a lot out of them," White said after the game. "When we got to their 40, you could see they were tired."

With the Washington defense trying to catch their breath over on the sidelines, Theismann engineered an impressive 77-yard march to close the gap. After connecting with Calvin Muhammad on a 32-yard bomb and then with tight end Clint Didier for a 16-yard gain, Theismann simply handed off to Riggins, and watched The Diesel rumble into the end-zone from one-yard out, shaving the Dallas lead to just 10-7.

What Landry later referred to as "the big play of the game for us" came during the final minute of the first half. Following a Washington punt, the Cowboys had regained possession at their own 39-yard line with 38 seconds remaining. Fans were hoping that the offense could advance far enough to get within Septien's kicking range, but Landry had designs on more than just scoring another field-goal.

A simple six-yard pass to Renfro advanced the ball to the 45, but left the clock running. When Tom Rafferty next snapped the ball back to White, only 15 seconds were showing on the clock. White didn't bother to glance over in the direction of Hill, who had been double-covered all game long. The play was designed for Renfro, who was lined up, man-on-man, across from Wilburn. Like a lot of rookies, Wilburn was a bright bundle of eagerness in his first game, as Newsome discovered near the goal-line earlier. But he still had a lot to learn about situational football.

Renfro made a quick move toward the boundary, but when Wilburn stepped up to deny the short completion, Renfro turned upfield and into the clear. White's downfield throw was perfect, allowing Renfro to run under it and into the end-zone for a 55-yard touchdown.

"They were running a lot of outs," recalled Wilburn. 'I don't know if it was a setup or not. They may have been setting me up, but it was inexcusable on my part. I just got beat."

"It's an old high school play called a 'sideline-and-go'" said Renfro. "We'd been wanting to call the play earlier. But it couldn't have been run at a better time than it was. Washington uses a gambling defense and the NFL knows it, and we just wanted to try to take advantage. I got the cornerback to bite (on the fake to the sideline) and usually, there's a safety who comes over to help out. But he never came over."

The Cowboys talked during the halftime break about avoiding a collapse like they endured the previous December, when Washington erased a 21-6 deficit at Texas Stadium and rallied for a 30-28 victory. A ten-point lead was not insurmountable, despite the fact that the Redskins were a team that thrived on playing from ahead. The Cowboys had dominated the first-half but, to put this one in the win-column, they would have to avoid a third-quarter letdown.

With Riggins limping around from a strained hamstring suffered late in the second quarter, the focus of the Dallas defense shifted from stopping The Diesel to making life miserable for the Birthday Boy. Joe Theismann was celebrating his thirty-sixth birthday on this Monday night in Irving, Texas, while making his league-leading sixty-first consecutive start at quarterback. During the week, Theismann had day-dreamed about throwing himself an unforgettable party by beating the Cowboys on national television. But without his backfield sidekick there to shield him, Theismann proved ripe for a once-in-a-lifetime birthday meltdown.

On Washington's third offensive play of the second-half, Theismann's sideline pass intended for Muhammad was behind the receiver, allowing Everson Walls to rally and make the interception. The turnover led to Septien's second field-goal of the game, giving Dallas a 20-7 cushion.

Gibbs tried to calm his quarterback down by trying to lean on George Rogers, but that plan backfired when Eugene Lockhart forced a fumble, leading to a Dallas recovery. Another Septien trey a few moments later had the patrons throwing their own party, doing the wave while the teams prepared for the ensuing kickoff.

Trailing by 16 on the scoreboard, Gibbs put the game in the hands of his quarterback in an attempt to rally. But Theismann had lost his touch and his focus. The field was a blur of blue-and-white jerseys frolicking on a green carpet, his right hand a shaking instrument of uncertain accuracy. On the next Redskin possession, Theismann thought he saw Don Warren breaking open downfield. His pass, instead of landing in the arms of his tight end, wound up in the mitts of Dallas cornerback Ron Fellows. Fellows had spent some time on the sideline early in the game after a Redskin player fell on his leg while covering a first-quarter punt. Fellows appeared to have mended well from his accident, looking considerably spry on a 26-yard cross-country runback that reached the Washington 14-yard line.

A batted ball late in the third quarter allowed Bates to record the fourth theft of Theismann for the game, prompting Joe Namath on the ABC-TV broadcast to remark, "I don't think Joe likes this birthday present that he's getting from the Cowboys." The gifts continued to roll in, adding humiliation to insult for the beleaguered Washington quarterback. Second-year safety Victor Scott, who had dropped an earlier interception and inadvertently batted another away from Clinkscale, finally came up with one of his own in the fourth quarter, snaring another errant throw from Theismann and returning it 26 yards for a touchdown, diving inside the pylon to give the Cowboys a 37-7 lead. As Theismann came back onto the field for Washington's next series, the Texas Stadium faithful began serenading him with the "Happy Birthday" song.

Birthday Joe managed to lead a garbage-time touchdown drive, before giving way to backup Jay Schroeder. Not even a few extra moments to collect himself was enough for Theismann to fully explain to inquisitive reporters how he could have played so poorly.

"It really got out of hand in the third quarter," he said. "...There is a reason for everything that happens on a football field. That's what game films are for. To answer the questions that begin with 'Who' and 'Why' and 'What the . . .'"

While Theismann watched from the bench wearing a dazed expression, Schroeder's first pass attempt was intercepted by Dennis Thurman, who rumbled into the end-zone from 23 yards away to punctuate the Cowboys' resounding 44-14 victory. With music blaring over the public-address system, the remaining fans added to the embarrassment of the visitor by singing "Happy Birthday" one more time while the Redskins and Theismann exited the playing field.

"It was the cruelest moment I've ever been through," Theismann later said of that night. "We were getting our [butt] handed to us, and I sat on the bench and all of Texas Stadium was singing 'Happy Birthday' to me. If it had been natural grass, I would have been able to crawl under a blade of grass."

In the jubilant Dallas locker room, the praise was naturally funneled toward the group of Cowboy defensive backs, all six of whom had recorded an interception. Danny White, marveling at the six-man support system that paved the way to a runaway victory, offered up the quote of the evening when he said of the Dallas secondary: "They were like thieves – Thurman's Thieves."

And a legend was born.

CHAPTER 16

THE GREAT UNEXPECTED

"In just six calendar days the Cowboys went from super men to super skunks..."
Randy Galloway, *Dallas Morning News* **columnist**

    Satisfaction is rarely accused of loitering within the confines of a pro football camp. During a long six-month season, there is always more work to be done, another game to be won. Duty is an ever-present burden and companion, pointing the way forward to January and the Super Bowl.

    Tex Schramm had long since learned to master the art of the short-lived celebration. On Tuesday, seated beside Tom Landry at the Cowboys' weekly press luncheon, Schramm gladly availed himself of the opportunity to crow at the expense of the Redskins. By the time he arrived at his office on Wednesday morning, the emotional high of thrashing Washington had been placed behind him, Schramm's energies and attention already focused ahead toward a Sunday date with the Lions.

    Of course, it wasn't always required that Schramm be such a model of self-discipline. Living in a wide-open football town like Dallas offered its own set of natural limits. There was always something happening around the Cowboys to bring the dreamer back to reality. Yes, even after a thirty-point victory over their arch-rivals.

Even if he hadn't already done so, the news that filtered down to Schramm's ears on Wednesday afternoon would have made him forget all about the Redskins. Schramm couldn't believe what he was hearing. With one win under his team's belt and a full schedule still ahead, Landry had allowed several Cowboy players to skip Wednesday's practice in order to offer support for former teammate Ron Springs at a court hearing. It was enough to make Schramm do a double take. *Landry did what?* It was enough to make Schramm mad.

During his six seasons in the Cowboys' backfield, Springs had never been close to landing on Schramm's favorites list. Springs was a part of the new type of bold, opinionated players coming into the league, an outspoken breed that Schramm strongly disapproved of. From Schramm's perspective as general manager, nothing in life or in football was ever good enough for them. They always wanted a bigger stage, a bigger salary, and always more playing time. Schramm approved of their boldness on Sunday afternoons when they were dancing a jig in the end-zone, but didn't care for it off the field. Springs fancied himself a comedian and voice of reason within the Cowboys' locker room all at the same time. When popular veteran cornerback Benny Barnes was cut at the conclusion of the 1983 preseason, Springs thought it an ingenious idea to hold a "revival" meeting in protest to Barnes' release. Standing up on a bench in front of his locker – smack in the middle of "Ghetto Row," the name given by the black players to the section where many of them lockered side-by-side – Springs addressed his rapt audience in the manner of Martin Luther King Jr.

"How long are we going to take this?!" Springs shouted.

"Not long, Brother Ron!" his teammates answered.

"How long?!" he shouted.

"Not long!"

Had Landry not walked through the locker room just at that instant and given Springs the evil eye, there's no telling what list of specifics the crowd of preaching chanters may have discussed at the meeting.

There had long been whispers emanating from the Cowboy locker room that black players viewed Landry as something of a snobby, stiff-necked racist. Schramm never paid much attention to this, perceiving the frustration of men whose best Sunday efforts had been critiqued by a perfectionist, their pride stung by a head coach who refused to be friends with his players. Only when these whispers turned into rumblings during the early 1980s did Schramm become concerned that Landry was losing clout in the locker room.

Drew Pearson's tragic car accident in the spring of 1984 gave Landry the opportunity to show his players a human side of him that many didn't know existed. Day after day, often for hours at a time, Landry took time away from preparing for the upcoming draft by visiting his All-Pro wide receiver at the hospital. No bigoted, indifferent man would do that.

But where others altered their opinion of the Cowboys' head coach and changed their tune in the locker room moving forward, Springs remained his former bold self, much to Schramm's annoyance. Schramm could appreciate Springs' contributions as a player, but he always found his personality to be somewhat disconcerting.

It wasn't too long before that when Springs enjoyed semi-star status around Dallas. In 1983 he caught a team-leading 73 passes as the Cowboys' starting fullback, and accounted for 1,130 yards rushing and receiving while scoring seven touchdowns.

But the wheels of his Cowboy career began falling off on opening night of the 1984 season, beginning a forgettable six-month sequence of events for Springs. While running on a short-yardage play against the Rams on *Monday Night Football*, Springs had his head pushed backwards into a precarious position, causing him to suffer a pinched nerve in his neck. His production dropped off from there, as he suffered from numbness in his right arm over the next five weeks.

When Springs began to feel more like his former self, he then became frustrated at not having more plays called for him. He complained about this openly to the media on multiple occasions during the middle portion of the season, adding but one more volatile ingredient to a locker room already split down the middle due to the Danny White-Gary Hogeboom debate.

As part of the fallout from the November loss to Buffalo, Springs was replaced in the starting lineup by Timmy Newsome for the next game on Thanksgiving Day versus New England. A few weeks later, with Springs still steaming over his demotion, Schramm was quoted as saying the team needed to rid itself of a "negative element." Though Schramm didn't name names during the interview, it was believed that Springs was considered a part of that element.

Rather than attempt to turn over a new leaf and ingratiate himself with management, Springs all but buried himself when he disappeared from the football scene after the final game of the season only to resurface on the party scene. In February, after an incident at a Dallas nightclub, he was indicted on a felony charge of aggravated assault on a female police officer. If convicted, he would face a maximum punishment of 10 years in prison. Springs maintained he accidentally struck the officer, backing the Cowboys' front-office into a corner in the process. Schramm wanted to release Springs on the spot, but refrained from doing so out of fear that it would create unwanted tension in the locker room. In spite of what Schramm may have thought about him, Springs was popular among a good number of Cowboy players. To completely sever ties with Springs while the running back was trying to clear his name could completely dismantle the budding chemistry on the team.

So Springs maintained his hold on a roster spot, allowing him to continue his billowing of discontented smoke in the direction of Schramm and Co. When a reporter asked Springs what his chances were of making the Dallas roster in 1985, Springs spoke from a heart that had long since forgotten to trust Cowboy management, even going so far as to suggest that he preferred a change of scenery.

"I wouldn't bet on it – with your money," Springs said.

"...I don't want to be at a place where people don't want me. I can't perform for somebody that doesn't want me to perform. I can't play for an administration that doesn't want me to play. I don't want to play where I'm not wanted... If they want to trade me, they can do that. It wouldn't bother me at all."

Though he dared not admit it publicly, Schramm was glad to have the veteran in the ranks during Tony Dorsett's unexpected training camp absence. If Dorsett did indeed play hardball to the end and allow his holdout to spill over into the regular season, then Springs would suddenly become a very valuable asset to the Cowboys. With Dorsett sitting back on his couch in Dallas twiddling his thumbs, Springs was listed as the No. 1 tailback on the depth chart. But nothing was set in stone, as of yet.

As the middle of August approached, Landry was already looking ahead to the opening night of the regular season versus Washington, the very same day, mind you, that Springs' court hearing was set for. If Landry was to be able to count on Springs for that game, then lawyers for the defendant would have to convince the courts to reschedule, a concern that was cast by the wayside with the arrival of Dorsett at camp. With Tony D back at practice, Springs' days in a Cowboy uniform were officially numbered.

Schramm and Gil Brandt nearly had a trade worked out with Buffalo in late August that had Springs going to the Bills, but when negotiations broke down Schramm washed his hands of the matter. The Cowboys released Springs after the final preseason game, allowing Schramm to heave a sigh of relief. No, he wasn't a headache to the extent that Duane Thomas had been nearly fifteen years before, but Ron Springs was one running back that Tex Schramm was glad to be rid of.

Until, that is, the moment came when Tex realized he wasn't quite rid of him yet, leaving the general manager fuming at the head coach. It was one thing for them to be testifying on Tuesday, the acknowledged off day for players, but not on company time. *Landry did what?! So what if it is Tom's birthday today? He should know better!*

The players had rallied around Landry's summer plea to focus on winning games in a collective manner in 1985, no matter the cost. "Get The Job Done" was the mantra that defined a very spirited training camp for the Cowboys, and was supposed to carry over into the regular season.

Maybe he was callous or simply dense, but Schramm failed to see how a day spent in court with a friend would help the Cowboys beat Detroit on Sunday afternoon inside the Silverdome. Getting the job done, according to Schramm's way of thinking, meant getting back to practice. This was to be a short week as it was. A Monday night affair in Dallas followed up by an early Sunday afternoon kickoff in Detroit didn't leave much time for preparation.

Landry's defense, explained by the now 61-year old head coach in detail later that afternoon, centered around the needs of the individual. Schramm didn't want to hear it, caring only about the progression of the team. Landry was viewing the problem from the humane side of things. Schramm was too busy being a rigid businessman to listen. It was inevitable that a standoff ensued.

Schramm was beside himself with irritation. At the beginning of the week, he had considered any such problem to be an impossibility. The trial had started on Monday. Surely the case wasn't going to affect the Cowboys. Then it had carried over to Tuesday. But testimony dragged on into the third day of the work week, which wouldn't have bothered Schramm in the least had he known what his head coach's next move was to have been.

Schramm couldn't understand Landry's decision. Springs was a free agent. He wasn't Landry's responsibility anymore. But, Landry reminded him, the remaining players on the team were, many of whom considered Springs a good friend. Landry was of the opinion that allowing a handful of Springs' former teammates to serve as character witnesses would actually benefit the Cowboys in the long run, if only by preventing a firestorm of discontent to break out.

Striking a police officer was nothing to sneeze at. Especially when that officer was a woman. In a case like this, being a Cowboy wouldn't help him. If anything, it would hurt him. Being a Cowboy meant you were held to a higher standard of social conduct, fair or not.

Springs was in a tight spot that had the potential to turn suddenly dark. From the bright lights of a pro football career in Dallas, he was now facing the possibility of some hard prison time. He needed a friend or six to put in a word or two on his behalf.

There were times when Schramm could have cursed Landry and his Christianity. *Turn the other cheek, you say? When has Springs ever put in a good word on our behalf?*

Schramm's was a one-track mind in 1985. He wanted to see the Cowboys back in the playoffs where they belonged. He didn't have time for personal problems, especially those concerning a player who was no longer part of the team. There were better things to be doing than wasting company time by pacifying approximately 18 players whose buddy had lost a grip on the rudiments of proper public deportment.

Schramm wasn't going to change anything with his bellowing. What was done was done. Due in part to Landry's soft heart, Springs was found guilty only of resisting arrest and was given a probated sentence.

But Schramm was able to sleep well that night while resting in the knowledge that he had made his position on the matter perfectly clear to Landry, a position that was bolstered four days later in the domed den of the Lions, when the Cowboys were found guilty of sleepwalking through their first road test of the young season.

A week of distractions and disjointed practices culminated on Sunday afternoon in the Silverdome, an indoor football palace that invoked horrid memories for the visitors. It was here in 1981 that Detroit place-kicker Eddie Murray stole the hearts of every onlooking Cowboy by booting the game-winning field goal on the final play – despite the glaring fact that the Lions were guilty of having too many players on the field. Then-special teams coach Mike Ditka went irate over on the Dallas sideline, drawing attention to the infraction. But the officials hearkened not at all, awarding a 26-23 victory to Detroit that came back to bite the Cowboys in the race for home-field advantage in the NFC playoffs.

Four years later the Cowboys returned to the scene of the crime, allegedly focused on avenging past injustices. By game's end, Tom Landry's bunch was receiving their due credit in the locker room. The Cowboys were not outmanned by the Lions this time. Only outclassed.

There was never any doubt as to the outcome of this Week 2 matchup. The Cowboys were not only flat, they were incompetent. As Tom Landry opined in his very somber postgame briefing, "We were as bad today as we were good Monday night."

For Danny White and the rest of the Dallas offense, the day was long before it was ever old. On the second play of the game, an innocuous screen pass from White sailed over the head of Tony Dorsett and into the waiting hands of defensive lineman William Gay at the Cowboys' 20-yard line. In the end, the Detroit payoff was a short Murray kick through the uprights.

White's aim was better on the next possession, as he found Dorsett with a short third-down pass between the hashes. Dorsett was ready for the pass in front, but not for the probing hand of Detroit safety Alvin Hall from behind. A reception was followed by a nearly simultaneous fumble, leading to another Lion recovery.

This time the Cowboys' charity would cost them more than just a field goal. Flanker Jeff Chadwick easily maneuvered past the coverage of Everson Walls on the right side and hauled in a dart-like pass from quarterback Eric Hipple just inside the pylon to put Detroit ahead 10-0.

The third drive turned out no better for the Cowboys than the former two. White got hot, connecting on a series of passes to Doug Cosbie and Tony Hill, advancing the ball inside the Detroit 10-yard line. But on third-down, Hall was there again to provoke another turnover, blitzing from the blindside and smacking White in the back as the Dallas quarterback was attempting his delivery. The pass was intended for Cosbie, but fluttered like a wounded duck on its final flight and fell into the arms of safety William Graham at the backline. Less than ten minutes had elapsed, and the Cowboys had already turned the ball over three times.

When not simply giving the ball away to the home team, the Cowboys were shooting themselves in the foot with mental mistakes. A lengthy second quarter march witnessed Dallas operating inside the 5-yard line, their sights set on cutting into the 10-0 deficit. But then a flag dropped onto the artificial surface, and the referee declared the Cowboys guilty of a strange substitution infraction.

The short series of confusing events began on the previous play, when Landry left the offense on the field on fourth-down. Needing only inches to convert, Landry sent in the jumbo package, which called for Chris Schultz to replace Phil Pozderac at left tackle, and for Pozderac to report to the referee as an eligible receiver at tight end.

Pozderac informed the official of his intentions prior to Dorsett's fourth-down gain of two yards. But when jumbo package was called on again for the Cowboys' first-down play, Pozderac forgot that he was required to report again, drawing a flag that wiped out Timmy Newsome's plunge that reached inside the 1-yard line.

"That was just a lack of alertness," explained Landry.

Pozderac's mistake proved costly. On the sixteenth play of the drive, Newsome was stuffed on a fourth-down carry at the 1-yard line, snuffing out the Cowboys' best scoring opportunity of the first half.

The beat droned on and on into the afternoon. Rafael Septien missed two field goals, from 42 and 44 yards respectively. White fumbled deep in Dallas territory after tripping over the foot of guard Glen Titensor as he was attempting to handoff to Dorsett.

Shortly after, White attempted to escape another bone crunching hit in the pocket by making an under-handed toss to Cosbie. The ill-advised toss was instead received by linebacker James Harrell, setting up Detroit's final score of the game.

When Landry pulled White from the action after three quarters due to a sore thumb on his throwing hand, the Cowboys trailed 26-0. And though Gary Hogeboom orchestrated a furious fourth-quarter rally that came up just short, there was no escaping the reality of what a miserable afternoon it had been for the Cowboys in MoTown, thoroughly erasing any sense of invincibility that may have subconsciously crept into the locker room after beating Washington.

By a 26-21 final, the 1985 Dallas Cowboys were proven to be very mortal, prompting Tom Landry to circle the wagons, and the rest of the team to refocus and regroup.

Clint Murchison Jr. – the founding father of the Dallas Cowboys – pictured (far right) alongside Tex Schramm, minority owner Bedford Wynne, and Tom Landry during the early days in Dallas.

Longtime general manager Tex Schramm had a lot on his mind after Clint Murchison Jr. decided to sell the Cowboys in 1983.

Tom Landry – minus his customary suit jacket – offers a few instructions for Danny White during the season-opening clash with Washington.

Player personnel executive Gil Brandt made an ill-fated move on Draft Day 1985 when he predicted that Jerry Rice would fall to the Cowboys at No. 17 overall.

The villain of a toxic summer holdout only a few weeks before, Tony Dorsett is seen here acknowledging the applause of the Texas Stadium faithful after surpassing 10,000 career rushing yards in Week 6 versus Pittsburgh.

Once the heir-apparent to the legendary Roger Staubach, a series of big-game failures had Danny White looking over his shoulder in Dallas..

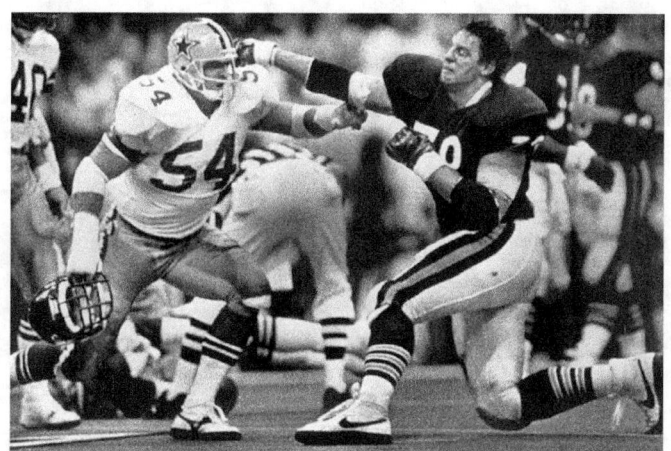

Randy White "The Manster" slugs it out with Chicago's Keith Van Horne during a 1985 preseason game at Texas Stadium. White was ejected.

Wide receiver Tony Hill was a big-play machine for the Cowboys in 1985, setting a new franchise record for receptions (74) in a single season.

Though not gifted with blazing speed, cornerback Everson Walls had a knack for being in the right place at the right time. Walls – in only his fifth NFL season – paced the league for a record-setting third time with nine interceptions during the 1985 season.

Gary Hogeboom was a bright-eyed bundle of untapped quarterbacking potential when he was inserted into the lineup in 1984. But a penchant for turnovers opened the door for Danny White's reemergence as the starter in Dallas.

Jim Jeffcoat's five-sack outing against Washington in Week 10 was one of many superlative defensive performances that carried the Cowboys up the standings in 1985.

Though playing injured wire-to-wire, Ed Jones piled up a career-high 13 sacks in 1985. Here, "Too Tall" towers over Los Angeles quarterback Dieter Brock during the 1985 Divisional playoff game.

Tom Landry (background) had to keep a close eye on Rafael Septien in September, after his normally-reliable place-kicker missed four field goals against Houston.

Mike Renfro shrugged off a pair of bad knees to post a breakout season for the Cowboys in 1985, recording 60 receptions and 8 touchdowns.

At 6-feet-6-inches tall, Doug Cosbie was a can't-miss target at tight end for Dallas quarterbacks during 1985, catching 64 passes on the season, including this reception against Washington at RFK Stadium on Nov. 10.

As the No. 3 quarterback in Dallas, young Steve Pelluer was an all-but-forgotten member of the Cowboys in 1985 – until he was called upon to lead the Cowboys on a fourth-quarter drive that had make-or-break written all over it.

CHAPTER 17

HOME COOKING

"Boy, these people in Texas know their football."
NBC TV's Dick Enberg, after the Texas Stadium crowd silenced Cleveland's hurry-up offense in the first quarter with a deafening din

Texas Earnest Schramm, one hand on his heart and the other on his wallet, had vowed more than once that he was only interested in the welfare of the NFL. No one doubted ol' Tex in his capacity as Chairman of the league's Competition Committee, not he of the innovative marketing mind and cash-stained fingers. An unquestioned character with the vision to introduce overtime into regular season play and move the goalposts out of the end-zone, Schramm was the type of good soldier who would work for $1 an hour and purchase all the potted meat his cupboard would hold. Fortunately for Schramm and the Internal Revenue Service, duty as a front-office dignitary was never so demanding.

Yet, for someone who so willingly denied selfish gain as a motivator, it was certainly uncanny how many times Schramm's Cowboys managed to benefit from various rule changes. Even, as in the case of the 1985 season, proposed rule changes. During the off-season, Schramm was adamant that teams be allowed to combat stadium noise by using radios in their helmets. Schramm was concerned about the competitive advantage for home teams whose crowd disrupts a game by harassing the visiting offense.

According to Schramm, penalizing the fans wasn't the answer. Nor was penalizing the home team, which had no control over the rowdies that walked through the turnstiles every Sunday afternoon.

"He thinks the solution is Radio Station NFL, to be found nowhere on your dial," wrote Frank Luksa in Dallas Cowboys Weekly magazine.

This was Schramm's stance and his soapbox right to the bitter end when the owners voted him down. But after what went down in Week 3 at Texas Stadium, it was fair to speculate as to which side of the argument Schramm was actually on.

Provoked by Schramm's support, the NFL experimented with radios in helmets a bit during preseason play in 1985, but could never get favorable feedback from both parties. Pittsburgh and Minnesota were scheduled to wear them in an August meeting, but Vikings head coach Bud Grant refused to cooperate, preventing his team from wearing the radios. The Steelers did wear them and reported only one bug (which was solved soon after) – if everyone in the stands whistled, that particular noise affected the transmission.

On the last preseason weekend, the Cowboys and Oilers tried their luck. Dallas reported no problems, but the Houston coaching staff complained of interference. Schramm walked away from the preseason disgustedly aware that, after never having completed a game with radios in which both teams expressed their satisfaction, there was no chance of getting the required 21 owner votes to pass the bill.

Though he had no doubt that the majority of NFL coaches were in favor of the proposition and that players would eventually wear radio receivers on the field in the coming years, Schramm readily acknowledged an up-hill battle in breaking down the barriers of traditional thought among owners. In Schramm's world, this radio proffer was nothing but business in its simplest form, an elementary question with an all too obvious answer. Why all the fuss and petty debate? And, furthermore, why use tradition as a crutch to support what was actually another form of intellectual dishonesty?

Here's how Schramm's proposition was supposed to work. The quarterback would have a miniature microphone attached to the interior of his helmet through which he could communicate with the rest of the offense on the field. The quarterback would be able to deliver messages to teammates, but not receive them. It was a one-way communication system designed for the purpose of hearing signals in spite of crowd noise.

All Tex wanted was the installation of the means to help the game function smoother for everyone in the stadium, from players to coaches to fans, even on down to the television and radio broadcast teams on site. Radio communication to the quarterback (at the very least, if not all of the offensive players) would simplify matters for the coaching staff, streamline the process of communication for the entire offensive unit on the field, and allow the fans to make as much noise as they pleased without the worry that game officials would stop the action. No longer would running backs or tight ends have to relay the play-call from a coach on the sideline to the quarterback on the field.

The insertion of particular offensive substitution packages would be effortless. The list of benefits went on and on… But no matter how many times Tex beat on this drum, he couldn't get through to his audience. There were times, Tex felt, when teaching a pig to tap-dance in a mud hole was considerably easier than getting through to a group of stuffy rich galoots at the round table.

Not only were the majority of owners against the proposed rule change, they also complicated matters by taking three different angles of approach to the discussion table, which frustrated a bottom-line operator such as Schramm. "One [party] makes no bones about it. They have domed stadiums and they like the advantage," explained Schramm. "Two, those that have that reason but try to cover it up with other reasons. Such as, 'Now you'll have the coaches sending signals in. How are you going to stop that?' Doing anything to cloud the issue. "Some, like Lamar Hunt, says he feels you're taking the human element out of the game. He's against that and against instant replay."

The furrow in Schramm's brow was deepened at the unspoken acknowledgment that his association with America's Team had done him no favors in the matter. Because he was the president and general manager of a Cowboys organization that, long ago, stole every heart and show in town, Schramm had a difficult time selling some of his propositions to rival owners.

Everyone in the room envied Schramm. Everyone in the room wanted to beat his team on the field in the worst way. For some owners, that was cause enough to vote against whatever Schramm brought before the board, especially a bill that would undermine the efforts of opponents to upset the Cowboys in the upcoming season.

It was no secret that franchises were always on the lookout for competitive advantages, and that crowd noise qualified as one of the biggest when hosting the Cowboys. It was also a known fact that Dallas was scheduled to go on the road early in the season to play the Lions and Oilers, two teams that played their home games in domed stadiums where crowd noise was commonly amplified due to the closed environment and the inevitable reverberations. To expect William Ford and Bud Adams to side with Schramm on the radio receiver issue was too much to expect, what with human nature being what it is. Still, Schramm graced his audience with an all-knowing scowl when leaving the negotiating table, a silent transmission that nobody in the room could misinterpret. Politics and selfishness had won the day, but they hadn't heard the last from Schramm on this issue. Not by a long shot.

A few weeks later, Tex was all smiles at the strange turn of events during the early stages of Dallas' inter-conference tussle with Cleveland. A Texas Stadium crowd renowned for a high-browed laid-back demeanor had just authored a clear-cut example for why Schramm believed radio receivers had a place on a football field, their deafening first-quarter cheers forcing game officials to call a brief timeout and Browns coaches to search for an alternative plan of attack. It was the unexpected beginning of a good day for Schramm, one that afforded him the opportunity of more than a few derisive grins from his skyward perch while watching his team publish a blueprint for future success.

They paid cash, they paid late, which, in retrospect, was certainly better than not paying at all. No, the 61,456 fans who walked through the Texas Stadium turnstiles had not anticipated a critical early-season tilt with Cleveland in time to avoid a local TV blackout, but they came anyway, from all corners of the community. A few from home, a group from church, some at the last hour, many more at the last minute. They came to watch their Cowboys do battle against an uncommon foe, little realizing that they would be called upon to exert their voices to such an uncommon level.

Seven days removed from a turnover-fest inside the air-conditioned dimensions of the Silverdome, Tom Landry reverted to a primitive formula against the Cleveland Browns designed to specifically limit Cowboy mistakes. Gone was the wide-open offense, the big-play passing game, and all of the fancy doo-dads that the locals had come to expect. In its place was an old-school ball-control attack that put a premium on protecting the ball, squeezing the clock dry like a sponge, and playing tough defense to boot. The altered style of play induced more than its fair share of yawns on that warm September afternoon, but nobody could dare question its overall effectiveness.

A pitch to Tony Dorsett going left netted five yards on the first play from scrimmage. A quick handoff, and a short third-down pass to Timmy Newsome, and the Cowboys had moved the chains. Fifty-eight slow-moving yards later, Rafael Septien booted a 39-yard field goal through the uprights to give this new-look Cowboys squad a 3-0 lead, an event which earned them a smattering of applause from the loyal locals.

The team from Cleveland, as it turned out, had their own bag of offensive surprises to unveil. Decked in brown jerseys, white pants, orange helmets, and even high-top sneakers, the Browns' scoring unit marched onto the field carrying a secret weapon; the no-huddle. Working on a short week after an emotional Monday night victory over rival Pittsburgh, 41-year old rookie head coach Marty Schottenheimer devised a plan to upset Ernie Stautner's penchant for substituting on defense.

Rather than play at a traditional pace with huddle and full use of the thirty-second clock, a Browns offense with nine new starters would attempt to stay close on the scoreboard by simply wearing out their opponent with a superior pace. Chasing their second victory of the season, the underdog Browns were of an inclination that a huddle and regular substitution packages would only inhibit their efforts and help that of their opponent.

So, after Willis Adams' first-down reception of 8 yards, quarterback Gary Danielson immediately began barking out signals for the next play. Without pausing to huddle, the Browns quickly lined up, and after scanning the defense Danielson executed a handoff to Earnest Byner, the 215-pound backfield bruiser who burrowed his way through a surprised Cowboy defense for five more yards. The same action was repeated, Danielson yelling and gesticulating before receiving the first-down snap and scrambling away from the pass-rush for a short gain. Another hurried approach, another gift in the belly of Byner, and the Browns had chewed up another five yards. This was looking easy. Too easy.

Not until Cleveland attempted to get set for a third-and-1 play from the 46-yard line did the crowd come out of its stupor and lend a hand to the winded Dallas defense. As Danielson attempted to audibly relay the signals to teammates, Texas Stadium's finest came out of their seats and negated the voice of the 34-year old quarterback to little more than a silent whisper with a resounding roar that grew louder and louder until head referee Fred Silva had to stop the game altogether.

"Boy, these people in Texas know their football," marveled Dick Enberg on the NBC telecast. "Didn't take them long to figure out, 'Hey, we can be a part of this too, if by making noise it takes away some of the audible effectiveness of Danielson.'"

Just how loud was it down on the field?

"I was one of the closest receivers to the quarterback, and I couldn't hear the signals," recalled Cleveland tight end Ozzie Newsome.

With the crowd now in a contrary humor, the Browns were forced to ditch their no-huddle attack for the rest of the game, allowing Stautner to substitute freely as the situation demanded. Thus robbed of their one advantage, Cleveland's first drive coughed, sputtered, and was finally placed to rest in all the banal trimmings of a punt.

A good start for the Cowboys had just been made even better. They were leading on the scoreboard, they had possession of the ball again, and they had a general manager whose good humor was suddenly and unexplainably filled to overflowing.

There is a helplessness in the art of forced inactivity that lends itself to wild presumptuousness. Never has this axiom been felt more pointedly than in America, a land conquered by a people who carved their social posterity with a knife of vigorous effort. Presidents, plebes, and the insignificant catechumen have all sensed the loneliness common with non-participation. And so too did the quarterback of a famous football franchise.

Standing forlorn on the sideline after being pulled from second-half action in Detroit, Danny White harbored numerous misgivings about his future in Dallas while watching his nemesis Gary Hogeboom engineer a near-miracle comeback victory. His thumb throbbing from an earlier hand-to-helmet collision with a Lion defender and his ego smarting from a forgettable first-half showing, White felt sick at the thought that he had just allowed the last chance to cement himself as the starting quarterback of America's Team get away from him so quickly. Through eyes of fear and uncertainty, White envisioned himself being hung in permanent effigy in the streets of Dallas, and serving as an aging piece of trade-bait for Tex Schramm the following spring. Surely this was it, the end of his career as a Cowboy.

Less than two games into a season that was supposed to be entirely his for the making, White was back in a familiar role as an unhappy spectator while the Boomer amused himself by hurling bullets all over the yard. One...two...three touchdown passes later and the Cowboys were back within shouting distance of Detroit. But for a failed onside-kick in the closing seconds, Hogeboom would have been christened as the second coming of Roger Staubach, no doubt, the master of all late-game wizardry.

Even though the Dallas rally fell just short in the end, Hogeboom still emerged from the smoke as the likely figure to be tagged as the Cowboys' Week 3 starter versus a rebuilding Cleveland squad. He had the arm, the confidence of his teammates, and was completely healthy.

If only White were so lucky. In addition to the thumb that CBS cameras continued to provide rapturous attention, White was also dealing with a sprained wrist, a hip pointer, bruised ribs, and the lingering aftereffects of a strained calf muscle that cost him some playing time during preseason. White, in short, was a "real walking infirmary," as *Dallas Morning News* writer Gary Myers so aptly observed.

So it came as somewhat of a surprise to outsiders when Tom Landry gave White his full support after the loss in Detroit, blaming White's regrettable afternoon against the Lions on a concerted "team effort." *Say what? Is Tom off his rocker? Has Landry lost his hat AND his marbles?*

The purpose for Landry's unhesitating stance on such a delicate issue was merely an extension of the team-oriented philosophy which had defined a very therapeutic off-season. There would be no scapegoat for the Dallas locker room to feast on with quiet murmurings this time around, no lone high-profile target of criticism to help overshadow the flawed efforts of the Cowboys' first two games of the 1985 season. Not on Landry's watch.

The game-film did not lie, a fact which Landry ardently hammered home to his players over the next few days. The pass-protection left something to be desired, especially on third-downs. Tony Dorsett, after missing a large portion of training camp, had yet to hit high-gear. And the defense, though certainly opportunistic, had displayed a tendency to miss an occasional assignment. Attention to these areas would benefit the team far more than dwelling on the shortcomings of the quarterback position. The Cowboys had come too far from a year before to fall back into the same trap of pointing fingers at every opportunity.

Given a reprieve from the vultures of circumstance, Danny White determined within himself to do whatever it took to play on Sunday versus the Browns, whether that meant he had to take a pre-game injection for his ribs or even wear a bulky cast to stabilize his newly-injured right wrist. This chance was one that White couldn't allow to slip by, a day in the Texas sun which he had to make the most of. Because, at age 33, there were no promises of tomorrow.

Sporting a heavily-taped wrist and thumb, Danny White disappointed more than a few in the Texas Stadium audience by trotting onto the field and into the huddle for the Cowboys' first possession versus Cleveland. Though his grip on the football was limited and the flak jacket still in place under his familiar No. 11 jersey, White had received the nod from his head coach to start the game, albeit with a calm last-minute reminder to avoid the costly mistakes which had plagued him the week before.

The afternoon began smoothly for White and the Cowboys, with Septien capping their initial march with a 39-yard trey. But on the second time out disaster rolled in like a runaway bowling ball straight into the belly of White, as 270-pound defensive lineman Reggie Camp fell on top of the Dallas quarterback, crushing him to the unforgiving artificial surface.

While Camp got to his feet and while Doug Cosbie received due applause from the home crowd for his 18-yard reception, White lay on his back at the 26-yard line, a perfect picture of misery and discomfort. Team doctors gathered around him, but still White remained down, gesturing mildly to his mid-section, grimace imprinted upon his face.

This pause in the action revealed a variety of responses from onlookers. Merlin Olsen's first inclination led him to hazard a guess to NBC viewers that White's thumb had been sandwiched during the collision, thus re-aggravating his injury from the week prior. After sending his audience to a commercial break, Dick Enberg speculated soberly in the broadcast booth if White had in fact suffered a knee injury on the play. And having digested the replay from the stadium's video board, fans murmured in their seats at the possibility of White having broken one of his tender ribs, which would have required the entry of golden boy Gary Hogeboom onto the scene, a joyous thought for many locals indeed.

By suddenly getting to his feet and walking to the Dallas sideline under his own power, White was able to put to rest the mixed bag of speculations and hopes encircling his status, though the impact from Camp had been plentiful, and though he had stayed down on the turf far longer than was deemed healthy, White had never needed a doctor at all, only time enough to catch his breath. The cobwebs having been cleared, his wind fully restored, White watched from the bench as Hogeboom delighted the fans with another 18-yard strike to Cosbie on the right side, before slapping the Boomer's hand on his way back onto the field. Having dodged yet another painful bullet, White buckled his chinstrap one more time and moved the Dallas offense the final 29 yards to complete the most efficient Cowboy march of the young season, his 10-yard scoring pass to Cosbie giving the home team a 10-0 advantage early in the second frame.

How the Cowboys managed to completely stave off the Browns' attempts to cut into that lead is another entry into the proficient nature of Thurman's Thieves. This particular adventure started with a misstep from Dennis Thurman himself. Lining up across from Glen Young, a lanky wide receiver who had yet to catch a pass on the season, Thurman was caught flat-footed and out of position on a first-down passing play, as Young beat him deep to the corner for a 30-yard gainer that put the ball on the Dallas 3-yard line.

But Thurman's gaffe was soon nullified by his fellow compadre in crime, Everson Walls. Recognizing Cleveland's second-down play as the exact carbon-copy of one which had beaten Dallas a year before against the Bills, Walls anticipated the throw from Gary Danielson, which came in low and flailing after the quarterback was hit from behind by blitzing safety

Michael Downs, and stepped in front of Earnest Byner at the goal-line to record his third interception in as many games.

"It's a pick play, where they use their wide receivers to kind of wall off the defensive backs, and then the running back floats in behind them looking for the ball," said Walls. "I could see what was happening, so I went to Byner. Buffalo beat us with it last year. I wasn't going to let that happen again."

But Thurman wasn't about to finish the game without exacting some kind of revenge upon the Browns, and that's exactly what he did later in the third quarter to nullify an error of royally-poor timing from White. Correctly anticipating that Cleveland would be in a man-to-man defense, Landry's call on a third-and-11 play from the Browns 13 was a halfback throwback pass by James Jones, who would take the handoff and run right on an apparent sweep before turning and throwing back to White down the left sideline. The plan was foolproof, except for the fact that White bobbled the Shotgun snap.

Danielson wasted no time after the turnover, needing only two completions to advance the ball to the Cowboy 22-yard line, from where the Browns tried to sucker Thurman once more. This time Willis Adams tried to beat Thurman on a corner route, and when Walls looked across the field with the ball in flight he saw Thurman trailing the intended receiver yet again. But Dennis, a defensive wizard through long hours of film study, had guessed Adams' intentions before the snap and arrived at an instant resolution.

"I just decided that I wasn't going to get beat on the same route twice. They might beat me on a different route, but they weren't going to beat me on that one," said Thurman.

Danielson's pass following a play-fake was slightly late and just a tad underthrown, allowing Thurman to cut in front of Adams and make a surprising interception.

"It was revenge," said a smiling Thurman afterwards. "…I really wasn't even sure where the receiver was… I saw the ball, and after I caught it I felt like Drew Pearson, trying to get both my feet in bounds."

When informed of Walls' first inclination upon looking in Thurman's direction during the play, the player they called "Coach" smiled once again. "We don't pay Everson to think,"

Thurman said. "I'm the head of the thievery group. When I pay Everson to think, I will give him a raise."

Thurman wasn't the only Cowboy who made the most of a second chance that day. After leading the offense into the Cleveland red-zone for the second consecutive series, White was afforded another opportunity to execute the halfback throwback. The play had been in the playbook section marked "storage" since the Cowboys used it for a touchdown to White during a 1983 meeting with the Los Angeles Raiders, yet here was Landry calling it for the second time in the same game.

"I was surprised the second time Tom called it,' admitted White in the postgame dressing room. "To call the play once in a game is rare. To call it two times is really rare. I was in a little bit of shock... The second time, talk about pressure. I could just hear Tom say if I'd fumbled that one, 'That White doesn't have a cool bone in his body. He gets flustered.' So I was concentrating on catching the snap and saying, 'Let's worry about the pass later.'"

White had no trouble with the snap this time, executing a smooth handoff to an eager Jones. Next, by feigning disinterest at becoming a receiver, White had to convince linebacker Carl Banks that Jones was indeed running a sweep. For a split-second, it seemed as if Banks was too smart to take the bait. But take it he finally did, allowing White to turn upfield into the clear.

"Banks was just sitting out there, so I had to stay," White said. "Finally, he went for it. I guess he was bored."

The high, arching spiral from the right hand of Jones was slow in arriving, allowing White just enough time to haul it in at the 2-yard line before he was belted by a hard-charging Banks from behind. The crowd came out of their seats to give a standing ovation in honor of White, who took his time in rising while checking to make sure he was still in one piece.

"Now I know how receivers feel about quarterbacks who hang the ball," White said. "I sympathize with them. I got hammered."

The spectacular touchdown with 10 seconds remaining in the third quarter upped the Dallas lead to 17-0, and allowed the Cowboys to coast home for a 20-7 victory. Having put the debacle in Detroit now firmly behind them, Landry's crew set their sights ahead to a two-game road trip that began with a visit to the Astrodome and the home turf of their in-state rivals.

The season was now in full swing.

CHAPTER 18

THE BATTLE OF TEXAS

"It was about as subtle as the charge on the Alamo"
Dallas Morning News **writer David Casstevens, on the blitz-reliant strategy of the Dallas defense**

"I'm alive. I'm healthy. Hopefully, I'll still have a job."
Cowboys place-kicker Rafael Septien after missing four field goals against Houston

Water-cooler conversation was certainly a jolly affair on Monday morning in Dallas, as loyalists gloated over the details of Sunday's ho-hum back-to-normal 20-7 conquest of the Cleveland Browns. Danny White, bludgeoned nearly to the point of dismemberment in so many recent outings, had played the entire game without being sacked. And the defense, caught napping on numerous occasions the previous week in Detroit, was nothing short of brilliant while blanking Cleveland throughout the first three quarters of play.

Efficiency and dominance. These, acknowledged the entire city in unison, were the hallmarks associated with a Tom

Landry-coached football team, and was something the Cowboys of 1984 had sorely lacked. Having apparently rediscovered their old habits, and with a promising slate of games directly ahead on the schedule, there was a collective anticipation that the Cowboys would enact their annual early-season march to the top of the conference standings.

But tomorrow's rosy garden nearly withered away in the Wednesday afternoon sun, when the team published a very pallid medical printout for public consumption, turning this seemingly fertile plot of Cowboy revival into a tedious patch of doom, gloom, and thistles. There in plain, ordinary, understandable English was the news that, at first glance, all but guaranteed another lost season. At at the center of a toxic standoff with Tex Schramm only a few weeks before, Tony Dorsett had emerged from the smoke and haze of an otherwise innocuous Sunday beat-down of Cleveland as a fallen man, courtesy of a broken bone in his back which – unnoticed by so many – had cut his weekend efforts short during the third quarter.

For those not steeped in the terminology common to the Physicians' Desk Reference, this simple injury report from team headquarters proved almost too much for fans to initially come to grips with. The very nature and wording of the injury made it hard for them to envision Dorsett stepping onto a football field again in 1985 – if ever. To the layman, a broken bone in the back invoked visions of therapy, wheelchairs and a lifetime of handicaps.

Fortunately for Dorsett and the entire Cowboy coaching staff, the diagnosis from team doctors was not nearly as morbid. When Dorsett suffered a fracture of the transverse process – a non-weight bearing bone in his back – versus the Browns, Landry and his staff had to mull and process a myriad of possibilities relating to Dorsett's status, all while knowing nothing of a concrete nature.

The fracture was so small that the pain had initially been put down to a severe case of back spasms by team doctors. It wasn't until three days later that an X-ray machine identified the cause of discomfort on the left side of his lower back, thus creating a sense of uncertainty at Valley Ranch.

While it was still within reason to suggest that he could suit up on Sunday (Dorsett was actually listed as probable for the next game in Houston), it was also within the realm of possibility for Dorsett to miss one or two games along the way. The speed of recovery would all depend on a pair of factors; Dorsett's pain tolerance and the overall severity of the fracture. Nothing, in this particular case, was an exact science.

Nobody at Valley Ranch was doubting the fact that Dorsett was determined to extend his streak of 68 consecutive games played. With protective padding around his mid-section, Dorsett was a participant at Wednesday's practice, though he admitted the unordinary amount of discomfort he was dealing with.

"I've had cracked ribs and bruises everywhere and everything else," said Dorsett. "This one hurts more than anything else."

To a man, Dorsett insisted he would start on Sunday. But there wasn't a player, coach or doctor who knew just how Dorsett's body would respond during live-game action. Would his back tighten up after being tackled on the Astrodome's unforgiving artificial surface? Would the pain limit his lateral movement and restrict his speed to the point of no return? How many plays would Dorsett be able to participate in? And how many weeks would it be before the pain was no longer a factor?

Any road without Dorsett – however long that happened to be – was bound to be a grueling one for the Cowboys. Though 31, and despite an uninspiring start to the season, Dorsett remained the offense's premier talent, and was the one player who struck fear in the hearts of opponents. Without him in the backfield, there was no doubt around Dallas that Landry's offensive ingenuity would be greatly challenged.

Dorsett's presence, even for a head coach with the intelligence and creativity of Landry, was absolutely imperative for the Cowboys to remain competitive within the NFC East. Over the years, Landry had been guilty of spreading carries among other runners in an attempt to protect Dorsett's undersized frame. But the days of Preston Pearson, Robert Newhouse and Ron Springs as complementary runners were over, leaving Dorsett as the only proven and trusted back in the fold going into the 1985 regular season.

With a suspect wide receiving corps and an inconsistent offensive line, Landry needed Dorsett not only as a big-play weapon, but as the franchise workhorse. The blueprint for recent success in Dallas had been anything but complicated. When Dorsett was fed the ball, the Cowboys feasted on opponents. Since Dorsett's second pro season in 1978, the Cowboys had compiled a 41-5 record when he carried the ball at least 20 times, and were just 27-26 when falling short of that mark.

Proving indifferent to whatever vindictive plans Tex Schramm may have recommended for the franchise running back, Landry had shown patience after Dorsett's training camp holdout, slowly easing him back into the lineup. More than merely a humanitarian touch of kindness, there was certainly method to Landry's gentle touch. By increasing Dorsett's workload in steady increments, Landry was able to circumvent those pesky muscle injuries that so often crop up when a skill player performs at something less than peak conditioning.

Dorsett was noticeably winded on a stiflingly hot opening night and was one of numerous out-of-sorts members of the Cowboys six days later in Detroit. But against Cleveland, Landry had taken the kid gloves off, feeding Dorsett 15 carries in just over two quarters of play before he was hit in the back with the helmet of a Browns defender after catching a third-quarter screen pass.

Had Dorsett actually kept his promise and held out through the start of the regular season, Landry was, at that time, prepared to make Ron Springs the featured runner. But with Springs now in Tampa Bay, Landry was boxed into an unforgiving triangle of youth and unreliability. If Dorsett couldn't go against Houston, then Landry would have to lean on either Timmy Newsome, James Jones or Robert LaVette at running back, a situation that did not appeal to the Cowboys' head coach in the least.

Landry the optimist was holding out hope that Dorsett would be in uniform to play the Oilers in a few days. Yet, being the realist that he was, Landry also was forced to be prepared with an alternative plan of attack, just in case. Because it always paid to be prepared for the worst.

But not even Landry could have anticipated the wild scene awaiting his team at the Astrodome, one which set the Cowboys back on their heels and in danger of another September defeat. Sunday's showdown in Houston was fast approaching, bringing with it a script as unpredictable as the Cowboys' starting backfield.

Gilded with the glistening armor belonging only to a world wonder, the Astrodome rumbled from the disposition of a scorned city. Metaphors unspeakable, imaginations ineffable, and the forgettable, unutterable tones of jealous hearts were the common tributes of the hour.

It was the afternoon of Sunday, September 29 and loud drumbeats of rain, falling from ominous black thunderheads above, danced mournfully on the roof outside, while the climate-controlled confines within echoed the inhospitable ballad of Houston's finest. Brimming with jeers, jabs, and the uncouth cursing of the proverbial sailor, a prolonged demonstration of pithy proportions greeted the visiting Dallas Cowboys as they conducted their pre-game stretching on the Astrodome's green carpet. It was a moment long awaited by Oilers fans and indifferently expected by their targets.

It had always been a thorn in the side of the city of Houston to watch the Dallas Cowboys become, and endure as, the league's crown jewel franchise. To outsiders, Dallas had always been a city of hoarders where greedy bankers stocked their vaults and got rich by charging inflated interest rates. But when the Cowboys rose to national prominence during the 1970s, Dallas became the going thing among American cities. Young families, business investors, even television producers flocked to north Texas to settle down, make roots, and make money. What the onlooking world could see in such a cluster of spongers and desk stooges was beyond the blue-collared, sweat-streaked crowd living just down IH-45.

According to Houstonians, the famed royal-blue star of the Cowboys was an inferior symbol of power when placed alongside the Columbia-blue oil derrick of the Oilers. Sure, the star was flashy and pleasing to the eye, but oil was a symbol of stability and prosperity. The Cowboys, so went the local narrative, may have been America's Team, but they certainly were not Houston's team.

All during the long week of anticipation for this "Battle for Texas," the host city had made it quite clear that they had no love lost for their in-state rivals from the north and that they would do all in their power to make the Cowboys from Dallas feel unwelcome. A rowdy and unapologetically rude fan base was promised to entertain the Cowboys on game day. But the list of assurances didn't stop there.

Crazy Ray, the Cowboys' unofficial mascot who paraded himself on the sidelines of every game as a friendly pistol-toting cowboy, was informed that he would not be welcome at the Astrodome. If security spotted him anywhere in the building – whether near the Cowboys' bench or in the stands - they were under orders to escort him from the premises. As added insurance against an invasion by Crazy Ray, the home team offered 5,000 standing-room only tickets along the sidelines which were quickly snatched up by eager Oilers fans. Needless to say, Crazy Ray played it safe and stayed far, far away from the watchful eyes inside the Astrodome on that day.

Down on the field, with the opening kickoff fast approaching, Dennis Thurman had mental blinders on. Indifferent to the pageantry and the circus-like atmosphere around him, Thurman was building up to a moment of daring that would change the identity of the Dallas defense moving forward in 1985. Thurman, more than any other Cowboy player, had enough clout amongst the coaching staff to have some of his concepts implemented in the weekly game-plan. But even he wondered if this next suggestion would be considered a bit too aggressive.

This bold idea of his had been growing since earlier in the week when Thurman had first started watching game-film of the Oilers offense. It was there, in a darkened room at the Cowboys' Valley Ranch training complex, when Thurman realized that Washington and Pittsburgh had exposed a fatal flaw in Houston's attack over the previous two weeks. The Oilers, quite simply, couldn't protect their quarterback. More importantly, Thurman's film-study convinced him that Warren Moon had cold feet in the pocket, with the second-year NFL pro of Canadian Football League fame displaying an uncommon tendency to forego his secondary receiving options and instead simply tuck the ball under his arm and run with it. Moon's frantic scrambling had resulted in 47 rushing yards against the Redskins in Week 2, keeping Houston close into the fourth quarter. But one week later at Three Rivers Stadium, the Pittsburgh defense closed up all of his running lanes, leaving Moon nowhere to turn to and the Houston offense stuck in neutral. In a 20-0 defeat to the Steelers, Moon accounted for just 92 yards through the air on 10-of-18 passing.

Thurman's notion was a simple one. It wouldn't take a cavalry of Cowboy defenders in the secondary to cover the one – or possibly two – potential targets that Moon would look toward before either (a) directing a pass downfield or (b) running for his life. So why not send the cavalry after Moon in the backfield?

Approaching his position coach, Gene Stallings, just minutes before kickoff, Thurman explained his idea of a double-blitz, which called for two Cowboy defensive backs to blitz off the same side. Stallings approved of the plan, and immediately sought out defensive coordinator Ernie Stautner to inform him of the adjustment. Thurman, over near the Dallas bench, lectured the rest of his Thieves on the intricacies and responsibilities of the double-blitz.

The whistle sounded and Rafael Septien swung his leg through, putting the ball into orbit and into play. At long last, the "Battle of Texas" was underway.

The most aggressive defensive strategy that the Cowboys had ever employed was about to be unleashed in the Astrodome, whether Warren Moon and the city of Houston were ready or not.

Provoked perhaps by the militant vibes of the preceding days, the Oilers came out in the first quarter with bombs on the brain. Spotting Ron Fellows in coverage on speedy wide receiver Drew Hill, Moon unleashed a high, arching spiral down the left side that would have resulted in a first-play touchdown for Houston had it been thrown far enough. Hill had gotten behind both Fellows and Michael Downs in the Dallas secondary, but when Moon's pass was short of his runaway target, Fellows was there for an easy interception at the Cowboy 34-yard line.

Wearing thick padding around his middle to protect his injured back, Tony Dorsett, just moments later, followed the rest of the Dallas offense onto the field for their first possession of the game. Tom Landry wasted no time in giving the ball to his star runner, allowing Dorsett to touch the ball on the Cowboys' initial play from scrimmage. Starting from his usual position directly behind Danny White in the Dallas backfield, Dorsett received the handoff while running to his right. It was then, just when you would have expected him to make a quick dart upfield, that Dorsett calmly flipped the ball to Tony Hill, who was curling back in the opposite direction.

This form of a wide receiver reverse was typical of Landry's aggressive nature as a play-caller. Ever mindful of the many subtleties needed to engineer a big play for his team, Landry thought it a good idea to use a surprise handoff to Hill at the very outset of the game while the defense was zeroed in on the Cowboys' No. 1 health concern of the week – Dorsett.

The strategy was well conceived on Landry's part, especially against an Oilers unit which had yielded nearly 250 rushing yards to the Steelers a week before. The players in Houston had heard it all week from defensive coordinator Jerry Glanville about their need to stop the Cowboys' ground attack, and would be eager to prove their showing in Pittsburgh was but an unfortunate fluke. With the defense leaning one way anxiously attempting to test Dorsett's bruised back with a manly tackle, Landry hoped to sneak the speedy Hill around the other end with daylight in front of him.

But the lane that Landry envisioned for Hill on the left side never developed. Hill ran straight into the arm tackle of linebacker Johnny Meads six yards behind the line of scrimmage. On second-down, Dorsett received a pitch and managed but a short gain before being dragged to the turf, where he was hit again on the back by fast-charging rookie defensive lineman Ray Childress. As Landry, along with every other fan back in Dallas, gasped at the sight, Dorsett bounced quickly to his feet and trotted over to the sideline, giving way to James Jones for the Cowboys' third-down play.

The drive fizzled. Landry's offensive ingenuity had been momentarily foiled. But at least the worries about Dorsett's health were over.

The well being of Cowboys place-kicker Rafael Septien, however, was another matter. Septien, considered one of the truly reliable veterans on the Dallas roster, had been a source of wonderment for fans and coaches early in the season, having missed three field goals over the past two games. Effects from a minor training camp back injury had lingered longer than anticipated, hindering not his distance but costing Septien his trademark consistency.

It bothered Septien that he had cost the Cowboys six points against Detroit in a game they ultimately lost by five. It bothered him more when the Texas Stadium crowd found cause to boo him a week later versus Cleveland for another errant kick. To ensure he avoided another forgettable outing in Houston, Septien spent the following days getting in extra work on the practice field, making sure his timing and mechanics were properly tuned.

By the time game-day rolled around in south Texas, Septien's right leg had grown tired from overexertion. In pregame warm-ups his carriage and kicking motion appeared to be pure. But Septien felt a barely discernible weight preventing him from inflicting maximum punishment on the football. His leg felt heavy and slightly rubbery. Nevertheless, Septien said not a word to assistant coach Alan Lowry, hoping that he would be able to overcome one of a place-kicker's worst nightmares.

On the Cowboys' second possession, Hill caught a 58-yard bomb from White near the sideline. When the drive stalled, Landry – unaware of Septien's limitations – called on his kicker to execute what appeared to be a very straightforward 47-yard field goal. But nothing in Septien's world was to be simple against the Oilers. The dreaded "dead leg" was about to emerge in a big, bad way for the Cowboys.

Septien pushed his first attempt of the game wide right. His 33-yard try to conclude the next Dallas march was bounced off the left upright, prompting Landry to approach his kicker and offer a few words of advice.

The struggle to score was very real inside the Astrodome, much to the delight of 55,000 pom-pom waving fans anticipating an upset in the making. When Septien wasn't missing field goals, the Dallas offense was falling all over itself in an attempt to score touchdowns. The Cowboys had used a halfback pass to stretch out their lead over Cleveland a week before versus Cleveland. They tried to use another version of a halfback pass to break a scoreless tie in the first quarter against Houston, but it didn't work nearly as well.

Dorsett had been slashing through the Oiler defense with ease, picking up huge chunks of yardage without even the smallest indication that he was playing hurt, carrying the Cowboys down the field and into scoring range once again. With the goal-line in sight and the defense growing increasingly anxious to stop No. 33, Landry could think of no better opportunity and moment to turn Dorsett from superstar running back to surprise quarterback.

Dorsett received a first-down pitch from Danny White while running right. Instead of White sneaking out on the backside to play receiver as he had against the Browns, Dorsett's target was Mike Renfro on the same side of the field. But when Renfro was jammed at the line of scrimmage, the play's timing was thrown off. Dorsett had to hold the ball, allowing the Houston defense to close in near the boundary, forcing Dorsett – after momentarily pondering the possibilities of running himself to gain some yardage - to give a precarious last-instant flip of the ball out of bounds.

"That looked like a Chinese sandwich. That was awful. It was really a mess," said Verne Lundquist on the CBS-TV broadcast.

A yellow hankie signaling an illegal shift against the offense did even more to discredit the Cowboys' efforts on the play. It was assumed that Timmy Newsome was the particular offender, but nobody watching the game on television could be absolutely sure since the official's voice didn't come through.

"On a play like that, it seems suitable that the referee's mic didn't work," noted Lundquist.

It wasn't until the end of the first quarter that the Cowboys finally ended a most entertaining of stalemates, Newsome catching a short flare pass and crossing the goal-line from 7 yards out. It was Dorsett who made the payoff even possible, breaking loose down the sideline earlier in the drive for a 30-yard gainer. He would finish the first-half with 90 yards rushing on just 13 carries.

While White had the Dallas offense moving up and down the field at will during the first half of play, Moon was taking a rare beating at the hands of the Cowboy pass-rush. Thurman's cornerback blitz package was giving his former Pee Wee football rival from back in southern California more than he – and the rest of his Oiler teammates - could handle. Every time Houston coach Hugh Campbell looked up, there was his quarterback lying at the bottom of a pile of Cowboys. At one point late in the first half, the Cowboys had more sacks (7) than the Oilers did first downs (5).

When Moon wasn't going down in the arms of a Cowboy, he was either tossing the ball away or – worse yet – throwing it up for grabs. This latter trademark proved especially beneficial to the aggressive ball-hawking tendencies of Thurman's Thieves.

Early in the second quarter, Dennis Thurman intercepted an underthrown pass intended for running back Butch Woolfolk, who had slipped past the Cowboys' coverage. And with the halftime whistle fast approaching, Moon's ill-advised toss into the end-zone – with Jim Jeffcoat grabbing his jersey from behind - snuffed out Houston's lone scoring threat of the first-half, as Bill Bates came down with the third Dallas interception of the game.

"It's tough when you can't take a couple of steps from center and get your feet planted to throw the football," said a frustrated Moon after the game. "…It's tough to throw the football when you can't do that, or when you can't look around and find a guy. They were sending more people than we could block in certain situations…"

In what was a very rough-and-tumble thirty minutes of action for the Houston signal-caller, Moon completed just 6-of-13 passes for 97 yards, with three interceptions.

But no matter the heroics of their defense, the Cowboys simply could not extend their 7-0 advantage on the scoreboard. A pair of heedless personal fouls on Houston moved Dallas into Oilers territory during the second quarter, but when Tony Hill couldn't control a third-down pass in the end-zone, it was left up to Septien to convert from 36 yards out. The snap was slightly high, and Septien pushed the kick wide right. He walked over to the sideline a perfect picture of perplexity, where he met with his equally perplexed head coach once again.

"Septien tried to correct a hook and pushed the next one. When he starts missing, he gets to worrying and missing a lot of 'em," explained Landry. "…When I talked to Septien I was trying to boost his confidence. He wasn't swinging normally and didn't have his good groove."

No matter Landry's good intentions or soft words, Septien continued to battle the demons of every past kicker into the second-half. The Oilers were now loading the box to put the clamps on Dorsett, which meant that White would be afforded a few extra passing lanes downfield to advance the ball. One of these lanes opened up on the Cowboys' initial march of the third quarter, when White found Doug Cosbie running free for a catch-and-run of 32 yards. But another third-down breakdown stalled the drive, forcing the Cowboys' troubled kicker to come trotting out onto the field for a fourth time.

Outside, an awesome thunderstorm drummed heavily on the roof of the Astrodome. Inside, where everyone was snug and dry, an even greater storm raged in the mind of Septien, whose wide-eyed look belied the wonder and apprehension of another impending disaster soon to occur off his suddenly bent kicking toe. Never in the history of the NFL had a former All-Pro kicker been so intimidated by a 40-yard field goal attempt in the third quarter of a regular season game in September. He dreaded the thought of missing again. He dreaded the look Landry would give him when he got back to the sideline. No matter how hard he tried, Septien couldn't bring himself to even conceive the possibility that he would actually suddenly rediscover his old magic. No, there was no way in Houston he was going to make this.

And he didn't. "Reliable" Rafael's fourth attempt of the game was blocked, sparking a wild frenzy of applause from the home crowd, their "Luv Ya Blue" hearts thrilled to no end at witnessing the unraveling career of one of the Cowboys' steadiest performers.

But a penalty on Houston for being off-sides on the play afforded Septien a re-try, this time from 35 yards away. Someway, somehow, Septien's next kick was high, long, and very straight, sailing through the uprights to give Dallas a 10-0 lead.

Yet, Septien's good fortune in making the most of a second chance was not a signal of a return to normalcy, not for him or for anyone else officially riding the wave of the on-the-field developments. This game filled with crazy, unexpected turns would continue to the very end.

Moon finally made the Cowboys pay for their blitzing ways, rifling a quick dart to Drew Hill on a short slant and watched his speedy wide receiver cover the rest of the distance on a 57-yard touchdown play. Moments later, Landry watched from the sideline in disbelief as Houston's Frank Bush broke through the Dallas line to block Mike Saxon's punt, setting up the Oilers with prime field position. With 2:42 remaining in the third quarter, Tony Zendejas booted a 32-yard field goal that was deemed to have been just inside the right post to knot the score 10-10.

The Dallas offense began to flounder, hampered by clogged running lanes and ill-timed penalties. There again to prevent the Cowboys from falling behind was the backbone of the entire team – the defense. With Moon beginning to work himself into a second-half groove, Thurman made a few adjustments to the Cowboys' blitz package. It paid off early in the fourth quarter when Moon, in a hurry to avoid another sack, authored a regrettable downfield pass that Ron Fellows caught in stride and returned 23 yards to the Houston 19-yard line.

Now the Cowboys were in business, positioned with a prime opportunity to re-assert their superiority. But the wheels of the Dallas attack remained grounded. Dorsett was bottled up again, and when White threw incomplete on third-and-9, Landry was forced to spin the roulette wheel one more time. Into the game came Septien, and out went the ball, bouncing off the right upright and harmlessly back into the field of play. Though it served as little comfort at the time, Septien's fourth miss of the day – a career first - was not completely his fault. Gary Hogeboom, the holder on the play, had failed to turn the laces away from his kicker, a no-no in any football manual.

Nevertheless, another scoring opportunity had been wasted, and now the Oilers had designs on claiming victory for themselves. From the 47-yard line, Moon beat the Dallas blitz by sidling to his left and finding Woolfolk in the flat near the marker. Woolfolk not only caught the ball, but then shrugged off the attempted tackle of Thurman, and rumbled down to the 21-yard line where he was pushed out of bounds by Bill Bates.

Moon's next third-down attempt, this time from the 19-yard line, was designed to hit the Cowboys where it hurt the most. But the pass into the end-zone fell incomplete, leaving Zendejas with a medium-range kick to give Houston its first lead of the game. But Zendejas, who had been traded to the Oilers by Washington after the Redskins shoved all their chips and a whole lot of money into the lap of Mark Moseley, had apparently been infected by Septien's uncommon display of errancy. His 37-yard field goal attempt from the right hash sailed wide to the right, leaving the score knotted at 10-10 with 6:04 remaining.

"There is a kickers' contagious disease flowing through the Astrodome," marveled Verne Lundquist.

After netting one first-down, the Cowboys kicked the ball back to Houston, a low, line-drive punt off the foot of Saxon that provided the Oilers with possession at their own 46-yard line with 3:20 showing on the game-clock. Hugh Campbell's team needed to gain about 25 yards to be in position for what would certainly be the former CFL head coach's most important NFL victory to date.

But the Dallas defense rose up again. On first-down, Moon was taken down in the backfield by Ed "Too Tall" Jones, who overpowered Bruce Matthews on his way to the quarterback. On second-down, Moon was hit from his blindside by a blitzing Bates to force an incompletion. On third-down,

Dallas blitzed again, allowing Dextor Clinkscale to bury Moon back at the 31-yard line, marking the eleventh Cowboy sack of the game, one short of the NFL record.

Amazingly enough, not even that muscular defensive stand could get Dallas out of the woods completely. In this game that neither team seemed inclined to seize control of, the Cowboys nearly made the fatal mistake on Lee Johnson's ensuing punt.

Against the Browns a week before, Landry had started employing two return men – Bill Bates and Leon "Speedy" Gonzalez – to field punts, instead of the usual one returner. This was in response to a series of poor judgments by Gonzalez during the first two games that buried the Cowboys deep in their own end of the field. With Bates back there also, Landry felt that the rookie would begin to develop a better feel for when to make a return, and when to signal for a fair-catch. It had worked against Cleveland because Bates and Gonzalez responded to a series of high punts by calling for a total of four fair-catches.

But that was a game that the Cowboys had control of from the start. This tussle with the Oilers had a completely different feel, as irrational energies of self-destruction emanated from both sides, turning even the simplest of mundane football exercises into wild, heart-pounding adventures.

Johnson's punt sailed high in the air-conditioned dome. As Houston's coverage unit ran down the field toward the pair of returners, Gonzalez waved his arms near the left sideline at the 28-yard line. Gonzalez had made the correct decision, one which many rookies struggle to make. He had taken the conservative course of action. By calling for a fair-catch, he was ensuring the Dallas offense one more chance to march down the field and bury the Oilers for good.

Inexplicably, Bates never saw Gonzalez signal for a fair-catch. Running over in an attempt to throw a block that would have allowed Gonzalez to begin a return, Bates barreled smack into "Speedy" just as the ball arrived. Bouncing off the backside of Bates, the ball bounded away from the boundary and toward the hashes, nearly landing in the arms of a surprised Oiler lineman. But when he couldn't handle the ricochet off his chest, the ball took another odd bounce off the artificial turf straight to

Everson Walls, who fell on it for the Cowboys at the 24-yard line.

With Tony Hill having struggled to find the ball in the Astrodome lights on several occasions, and with Newsome out of the game with a knee injury, Landry made full use of his remaining reliable speed threat – Dorsett – on that final drive. Using the block of tackle Chris Schulttz, who started in place of the injured Phil Pozderac, Dorsett broke free around the left side for a gain of 18 yards on first-down. Dorsett went left again on the very next play, but this time he only feinted in that direction, enough to allow his quarterback to author a well-timed play-fake. The defense had been tricked into forgetting all about James Jones, who was now wide-open down the left sideline. Danny White's high, arching spiral landed softly in the arms of Jones at the Houston 25-yard line. Now the Cowboys were rolling.

Landry wasted no time in going back to Dorsett, calling "31-Draw-Delay Trap," a simple run up the middle to the naked eye that revealed the manifold talents of the Cowboys' undersized workhorse. Dorsett rambled through the line, then cut outside to the left, used a block from Hill on the outside, put on the speed-burners and sprinted across patches of turf and infield dirt all the way to the 1-yard line. When he got up off the ground, Dorsett looked like someone who had just dove headfirst into Homeplate, dirt stuck up inside his helmet and all over his white and blue jersey. His face was streaked with sweat and he was gasping for breath, the toll of his 159-yard rushing performance clearly showing.

Dorsett's finest statistical effort in four years set the Cowboys up for a game-winning score, and this time they delivered. On first-down from the 1, White faked a handoff to Jones - who smashed into the center of the line - and then threw to a wide-open Fred Cornwell, the backup tight end, in the left corner of the end-zone to provide the final margin of victory, 17-10.

It was only fitting that Dorsett's long week be capped off in the jubilant visitors' locker room, where he was presented with a game-ball by his head coach.

"He kept us in the game all the time with his long runs," said an appreciative Landry.

A clearly spent Dorsett sat at his locker and attempted to quantify the satisfaction of a very long afternoon, while brushing off any notions of heroism on his part.

"Football is a game where if you can't play with pain, you're in the wrong game. I like playing football, and this is the fun part of it. If I'm walking on Sunday and the doctors are telling me I don't stand a chance of injuring it more, I'll be out there. I just feel fortunate to have been able to play 60 minutes of football."

Equally fortunate to have played a full game was Warren Moon, the Oilers quarterback who was proven to be every bit of valiant in defeat. From start to finish Moon had been treated like a despised rag-doll by the Cowboys defense, succumbing to a record-tying 12 sacks and an ungodly pounding that even had his quarterbacking counterpart shaking his head in disbelief.

"I really felt sorry for the guy," admitted Danny White afterwards.

On Monday morning, Moon awoke to a world of aches and bruises. He had trouble getting out of bed and walked but slowly, compelling him to cancel a couple of important appointments later that day. Moon never arrived at the Oilers' facility to receive his normal treatment. Nor did he dare to venture close to the dentist for some canal work.

"I chickened out," Moon admitted. "I felt I'd had enough pain for one week."

CHAPTER 19

TEST OF ENDURANCE

"Both teams made some big plays and both teams made some big mistakes. We made a few more and, more important, we made them at the wrong time."
New York Giants Head Coach Bill Parcells

"We feel good right now at 4-1 – I don't care how you win to get there."
Tom Landry

Tom Landry raised some eyebrows on Tuesday while addressing the speculation that he was prepared to call in kicking coach Ben Agajanian to fix what ailed Rafael Septien. Agajanian worked with kickers and punters during training camp, but rarely could be coaxed from his California residence during the regular season. A little chat with ol' Ben, some said, would be just the tonic that Septien needed to calm his frayed nerves.

But Landry disagreed. He refused to go along with the popular notion that Septien was going through a "crisis" period, while acknowledging the "difficult" time that his place-kicker was faced with. But it would take more than the presence of a kicking expert, Landry maintained, to help Septien move on from his debacle in Houston.

"Ben is a good coach," Landry admitted. "But this is something a player has to work through by himself."

However, Septien was rarely alone over the next few days, as Landry spent considerable time working with him at practice on the finer details of his craft. Yes, in addition to his coaching duties on the offensive and defensive sides, Tom Landry considered himself a specialist in the field of kicking as well.

First, he went to the film-room, pointing out to Septien that, due to his "dead leg" condition against Houston, he had been over-striding. The correction was a simple one. After that, it was just a matter of confidence.

"What we did was try to establish a routine," Landry said, apparently feeling that Septien's thought process had been drifting, thus affecting his rhythm. "...Kickers are different in that they are alone so much, because they think so much and have a much more difficult time keeping a groove. When I played and punted, I never thought about the punting end of it. These guys worry all the time, when they're kicking, and that's tough – the toughest part of kicking."

On Sunday at Giants Stadium, Landry spent about ten minutes of the warm-up period supervising Septien's practice kicks. It didn't take very long for Landry to nod in appreciation. Even special teams coach Alan Lowry had to admit that Septien looked once again like the player who began the season as the fourth-most accurate kicker in league history.

Septien kicked the ball well against the Giants, his two chip-shot field goals in the fourth quarter giving his team a chance to steal a win at the Meadowlands. But with just over two minutes remaining and the Cowboys trailing by two, the pressure of a potential game-winning 31-yard kick stared him in the face. Landry wasn't taking any chances on the opportunity being wasted. After all, first-place in the NFC East was at stake.

Before Septien trotted out onto the field, Landry offered a few brief instructions, reminding him to keep his head down and swing his leg through the ball in a smooth manner. As the momentary conference broke up, dozens of Cowboys players on the sideline linked arms and hands as a gesture of unity and faith in their embattled kicker.

But Landry could not bring himself to watch the play. While the football world gazed in wonder and anticipation at the figure of Rafael Septien, the only head coach the Cowboys had ever known turned his back to the players on the field and put his hands together, silently praying for what would certainly be a happy ending to what had been a most tumultuous week.

The diatribe of those lovable arm-chair quarterbacks rumbled throughout the Metroplex early in the week, discontent for what was a lackluster triumph over a far inferior Houston team causing waves of mental doubt and verbal query to begin rocking the boat of the Cowboys' fan base.

The voices had no faces, but their words had bite. Mind you, these weren't exactly the teeth-marks of higher intelligence, but they certainly left their imprint upon the airwaves of Brad Sham's sports-talk show on KRLD radio in Dallas, all the while gnawing away at the credibility rating of Tom Landry.

Caller No. 1: "Why did Landry open the Houston game with a trick play, that reverse to Tony Hill which lost six yards?"

Caller No. 2: "When is Landry going to open up the offense?"

Caller No. 3: "Why doesn't Landry ever throw long?"

Caller No. 4: "If Houston had such a sorry run defense, why did Landry even bother to pass? Why didn't he keep it on the ground?"

These sounds of restlessness from the local support group left Frank Luksa with little room but to publish the unspoken conclusion of the matter. Wrote Luksa in *Dallas Cowboys Weekly* magazine in October:

"The consensus is obvious. Landry doesn't have a clue. Behind those piercing blue eyes lies an empty attic."

Luksa was being humorous because that was the kindest option afforded him. Fans had not only forgotten that Landry's

Cowboys were tied atop the NFC East standings at 3-1, but also many of the accompanying details from their most recent victory over the Oilers. Like those long gainers of 49, 35, and 32 yards from Landry's conservative passing attack, and the bomb that Tony Hill dropped in the end-zone. And the fact that Rafael Septien left 12 points out there, which would have turned a nail-biter into a romp.

And why shouldn't Landry continue to call an early gadget play such as a reverse against defenses that tend to over-pursue? He had used it numerous times to beat Miami in Super Bowl VI, and had done so in many big games after that. Landry wasn't concerned whether the play succeeded or not, just so long as the defense was reminded to stay at home and pay special attention to the Cowboys' misdirection attack as the game progressed.

But the fans didn't particularly care for such petty details at the moment. They were still miffed that their Cowboys had struggled mightily to post 17 points against the powder-blue powder-puff Oilers from Houston.

Which only goes to prove that a body couldn't trust everyone afforded a platform on talk-radio. And, as Tex Schramm learned later that week, the same could be said for what a person happened to read in your daily newspaper.

A strong blast of arctic air had blown through north Texas over the weekend, effectively signaling the end of another hot, humid Metroplex summer. Wednesday's record-setting low temperature of 47 degrees made for an unusually chilly morning commute to the Cowboys' Expressway Towers offices for Tex Schramm. A few hours after arriving at the office building, the cold weather outside was totally forgotten, as Schramm was confronted with the hottest news story of the week.

Schramm's secretary had the object of interest waiting for him on his desk later that afternoon. Fresh from the presses of what must have been a desperate South Beach newsroom was an article that left Schramm flabbergasted, not to mention angry.

The Cowboys had suffered through their fair share of mental lapses on the field, of late. Were they even more brain-dead off of it? According to the *Miami News*, the Cowboys may have been just that. There, in 48-point type, was a headline that said it all: NFL, FBI Probing Allegations Cowboys Fixed Games For Coke.

No, kids, not coke as in soda. This kind of coke spells crime, and jail time. This kind of coke had the potential to tarnish a franchise, and leave a trail of high-ranking heads rolling.

"Shaving points for cocaine," mused Randy Galloway in the *Dallas Morning News*. "In the world of athletes, can there be a lower form of sewer rat?"

Founded on the word of a former FBI agent who had recently pled guilty to charges of bribery, conspiracy, and possession of cocaine with intent to distribute, the story was as simple as it was sickening. The agent said a convicted smuggler told him that five Cowboys players – three of whom were still on the team – had fixed games in the early 1980s in exchange for three kilos of cocaine.

The stink connected with this story only grew worse for Schramm and the Cowboys. One source said the alleged point-shaving involved only exhibition games from the 1981, 1982, and 1983 seasons. But another source claimed that both exhibition and regular season games allegedly were involved during the 1981 and 1982 seasons.

A modulated response from the office of Schramm would have been to humor a spittoon. Or maybe to simply kill the messenger. Schramm was frustrated at the report, to say the least. And for obvious reasons. As he would admit to reporters later that day, the allegations were such that they left an inevitable smear upon even a beloved organization like the Cowboys, whether actually true or not.

The Cowboys had come under the microscope of controversy more than once in the previous decade. All-Pro wide receiver Bob Hayes spent time in prison during the 1970s after being arrested on drug charges. Pro Bowl linebacker Thomas "Hollywood" Henderson was an admitted drug addict with the Cowboys, eventually costing him his career in Dallas after just five seasons. And in 1983, four Cowboy players were publicly named in an FBI and Drug Enforcement Agency investigation into cocaine trafficking in Dallas, causing some sportswriters and fans to begin referring to the football squad from Dallas as "South America's Team," or the "Cocaine Cowboys."

Schramm cursed like a sailor at the newspaper in his hand for the better part of the evening, figuring it to have been a slow news day in Miami for that tabloid to hit the front page. Schramm understood the ropes of a crowded newsroom in a major city. He knew from firsthand experience the daily pressure to deliver the big scoop that writers were faced with. But someone in the building had to show some judgment and tact, if only to avoid making libel and slander fashionable in the mainstream news market.

The lofty credibility rating of the press was predicated upon its ability to grasp every level of the affective domain process. This report from the *Miami News* meant that some credentialed pen-head in South Beach had flunked them all, or either lost his brains while surfing in the Atlantic.

The *Fort Lauderdale News* had owned first rights to the story, but plans to run it on Sunday were squashed by editors who deemed the facts to be inconclusive. What was gossip to one editor in Fort Lauderdale was front-page news to Howard Kleinberg in Miami. Eager to win the day over the rival *Miami Herald*, Kleinberg had his staff print a story so ludicrous that it should have been shredded at the receiving line, a tale with so many holes in the accusation that Schramm could fit his entire pudgy fist through it.

Was this the future of sports journalism, with writers and editors jumping at the first guy flashing a badge and promising a juicy story? Wasn't there a code of ethics involved? Schramm, at that moment, would have gladly offered himself as a code enforcement officer of good and proper journalism. He likely would have furnished his own weapon too.

Indeed, the story had more holes in it than a piece of moldy Swiss cheese, despite the fact that the *Miami News* stubbornly stood by their source. But was it true? Were the Cowboys really guilty of fixing games?

"I've been around long enough never to say something couldn't happen," said Schramm.

But it was hard to imagine an established golden boy like Danny White getting involved in a points-shaving scheme. Equally hard for Schramm to accept was the notion that Tony Dorsett, Tony Hill, and former Cowboys Butch Johnson and Ron Springs were in on the deal too.

Schramm was only shocked that Tom Landry's name wasn't dragged through the mud in connection with this gambling ring. Wouldn't that have been a courtroom scene? Schramm could just see himself on the stand as the key character witness. *Don't worry, Counsel. I know Tom. He bet on himself.*

Fixing preseason games? Really? Could anyone be that stupid? Sure, Schramm knew that he could be a bit of a tightwad toward his players during contract talks, but they weren't hurting financially enough to risk career and reputation over a penny-ante bet for a preseason game.

Come to think of it, it was difficult to believe anything about this. Little, if anything, about it made any sense. First of all, was it even possible? Randy Galloway, who had spent more than one afternoon at a Louisiana racetrack over the years, said that it was.

"Sure, an NFL game could be fixed, and if the fixer has the starting backfield and two wide receivers in his pocket, points certainly could be shaved," wrote Galloway. "…However, there's no bookmaker this side of an idiot who would handle a large wager on exhibition games. A bettor couldn't wager high enough to make a fix worthwhile."

But what if some devious mind concocted a scheme whereby smaller wagers were spread out across the country?

"You might get away with it once or twice," an unnamed gambler from Nevada told the *Dallas Morning News*, "but you couldn't hide it for long…word gets around on that kind of thing."

The claims were so outlandish that even Cowboy detractors from within the league office had no other choice but to assume the Cowboys innocent before proven guilty. Pete Rozelle, a close confidant of Schramm's, did everything but condemn the report as heresy. If it was up to only him, the league wouldn't have bothered to even check up on the story.

This invective from the *Miami News* had Schramm in full denial mode for the rest of the week, offering a clear and concise series of public rebuttals that newsmen couldn't help but find reasonable and satisfactory. Schramm even addressed the issues in a taped interview that was seen by the nation on ABC television at halftime of the Cowboys-Giants game on Sunday night.

But nothing Schramm said or did could undo the damage done to the franchise's public image. The story had been printed, a gullible public swallowing it hook, line, and sinker, invoking the reemergence – if for only a short time – of "South America's Team" onto the pro football scene.

Sunday night couldn't have come soon enough for the Dallas Cowboys, whose players only too willingly put aside the drama and speculation of the past week to focus on establishing themselves as the early-season front-runner in the NFC's Eastern division. Standing in their way was a New York Giants squad looking more muscular with each passing season.

Under third-year head coach Bill Parcells, the Giants had transformed from a division doormat into a serious contender. The defense, anchored by linebackers Lawrence Taylor, Carl Banks, and Harry Carson, was beginning to come together as a complete unit capable of dominating on a weekly basis. Phil Simms, once considered to be a bust, was now emerging as a star and a captain of New York's offense. In July, Simms signed a new five-year contract with the Giants, making him one of the league's highest-paid quarterbacks. A year after guiding New York to the postseason for only the second time in the previous 21 seasons, Simms and the Giants had their sights set on going all the way to New Orleans and Super Bowl XX.

There to allay any fears that the Cowboys, who had been whipped handily in both meetings with New York a year before, were suckers for another knockout punch from the G-Men was Dallas safety Dextor Clinkscale, who added some spice to the buildup by referring to Simms as a "myth" and the Giants as "fake." More than simply infuse his teammates with newfound confidence, Clinkscale also awoke the enemy camp, prompting Giants fans to arrive at the stadium on Sunday evening carrying "Hex on Dex" voodoo pins.

The magic from the stands was slow to affect Dextor and the Cowboys. Dallas jumped ahead early, playing a nearly flawless game for the majority of the first half, as they carved up the NFL's No. 1 ranked defensive unit with an air of superior indifference.

Tom Landry had assembled a game-plan designed to accomplish two things: Block Lawrence Taylor and get the ball in the hands of Mike Renfro. Taylor had been a one-man wrecking crew against Dallas in 1984, almost single-handedly limiting the Cowboys to just one offensive touchdown in two games. Landry spent extra time in practice during the week drilling his running backs on how to stay in front of the Giants' powerful, crazed linebacker.

If the Cowboys could block Taylor on passing downs, then Landry was sure there were yards to be had downfield for Danny White. If there was one weakness on the New York defense, it was in the secondary where Parcells and defensive coordinator Bill Belichik were working noticeably shorthanded. Elvis Patterson, a second-year undrafted cornerback out of Kansas, was starting on the left side in the place of Mark Haynes, the four-time All-Pro who was holding out in a contract dispute. During preseason play, Patterson was dubbed "Toast" by the New York media because receivers had been regularly burning him. He was the hero in New York's 16-10 overtime victory against Philadelphia a week before when he returned an interception 29 yards for a touchdown less than a minute into the extra period, but was still considered a weak-link of the Giants pass defense.

Which provided all the more reason for White to look in the direction of Renfro. Since his opening night explosion versus Washington when he caught 5 passes for 99 yards and a touchdown, Renfro had been virtually invisible in the Cowboy offense, totaling only five receptions over the next three games, as the Dallas passing attack came crashing back down to earth.

Landry vowed to change that trend against the Giants. New York's speedy half-back Joe Moriss fumbled a handoff on the second play of the game, and linebacker Mike Hegman fell on the ball for Dallas at the Giants 43-yard line. White used two completions to Renfro in a seven-play sequence that saw the Cowboys advance to the 18. Then, while scrambling to his right away from the pass-rush, White threw to a wide-open Tony Hill in the end-zone for a touchdown.

Early in the second frame, White moved the Cowboys the length of the field for another score. A methodical 14-play 83-yard march that included a bit of everything branded conservative – toss sweeps outside, quick runs inside, short passes to the boundary, even a handoff to newly-arrived fullback John L. Williams – concluded through the efforts of another third-down scramble by the Cowboys' quarterback.

The Giants' zone coverage had covered up all of his receiving options, and White had stepped up in the pocket and was running to his left. Just when it looked like he might try to outrun the defense to the pylon, White squared his shoulders and threw to Renfro, who had position in front of cornerback Perry Williams in the end-zone. The 8-yard touchdown play gave the underdog Cowboys a surprising 14-3 lead.

White continued to knife through the New York secondary, moving the Cowboys up and down the field at will. But a string of costly interceptions over the next few series prevented Dallas from extending their advantage, opening the door for a thunderous Giant rally.

Through two quarters, Simms' performance against Dextor and the Thieves was perfectly indicative of a quarterback who completed less than fifty-percent of his pass attempts during the month of September. He was hot and cold, up and down. On two separate occasions he had driven the Giants into scoring range, but was turned away at the door each time, New York settling instead for a pair of first-half Jess Atkinson field goals.

The other side of intermission proved to be an entirely different story for the Giants captain. Simms got rolling in a big way, the voodoo dolls started working their magic, and the

Thieves looked every bit of hexed during their worst quarter of the young season.

Cowboy cornerbacks had frustrated Simms at times during the first half with aggressive coverage of Giant receivers on out-breaking routes toward the sideline. Simms had exploited this strategy in the second quarter by completing big-gainers in the middle of the field to Phil McConkey and Bobby Johnson of 26 and 35 yards, respectively. But when offensive coordinator Ron Erhardt chanced sending New York's top wide-out, speedy Lionel Manuel, over the middle early in the third quarter, the dam officially burst in the Meadowlands.

After lining up on the offense's right side, Manuel had beaten Everson Walls with a sharp cut to the inside. Simms saw the route develop and was afforded a clean pocket to make a strong downfield throw between the hashes. Manuel softly cradled the pass at the 33-yard line, expecting Walls, at any moment, to drag him down from behind. Manuel turned up-field, then braced himself. Walls reached out to make the tackle. It was a process in a football game as seen in so many others, a classic case of action and reaction, of pass, catch, and tackle.

The added element of friendly fire turned this mundane sequence into an extraordinary moment for the Giants. As Walls reached out in the direction of Manuel, fellow cornerback Ron Fellows crossed over and dove at the feet of the ball-carrier. But when Fellows missed his target, Walls was unable to avoid tripping over him, leaving Lionel to play the part of a runaway train on his way into the end-zone for a 51-yard touchdown.

The miseries were only beginning for the Thieves. Another Danny White turnover gave the ball back to New York, allowing Simms to once again probe the wide-open spaces that Dallas defensive backs were leaving in the middle of the field. This time it was Johnson beating the soft zone coverage of the Cowboys for a catch-and-run of 30 yards.

Five plays later, the Giants faced a third-and-15 from the Dallas 23-yard line. With his rookie place-kicker having missed an extra-point moments before, Parcells wasn't interested in settling for a medium-range field-goal attempt. He wanted a first down, if at all possible. A touchdown would be even better.

Erhardt's play called for Simms to roll out to the left upon receiving the snap from rookie center Bart Oates, away from the towering figure of Ed "Too Tall" Jones. The design afforded Simms extra time to scan the field, but when no receiver flashed open, he was forced to hold the ball longer than expected. Simms waited, pumped once, then released the ball just before Jones caught up with him. Simms fell to the turf, his sight impaired by a flock of linemen around him, hoping that an invisible hand of luck would guide the path of a ball that he knew had been forced into a sea of bodies.

The pass appeared to be intended for Johnson, who was running across the field near the five-yard line. Johnson reached up, but Clinkscale was there to tip the pass away, a recommendable exercise on most nights. But instead of resulting in an incompletion, Clinkscale's deflection sent the ball sailing over the head of its intended target and into the waiting hands of Manuel at the goal-line. This time Atkinson's point-after try was pure, and the Giants led for the first time in the game, 19-14.

The darkest moment of the night for the Cowboys came on New York's next offensive possession. Ernie Stautner called for an all-out blitz, but someone in Cowboy blue forgot to cover George Adams. The rookie running back looped out of the backfield, and was free to turn a short pass-reception into a 70-yard touchdown play. What had once been a Dallas advantage of 11 points had inexplicably morphed into a deficit of twelve.

But the Cowboys refused to throw in the towel.

"We would have folded up last year," acknowledged Clinkscale. "We would have become dejected and probably lost by a substantial margin."

Instead, they came roaring back. White found his touch again as the Dallas quarterback, guiding the Cowboys on a five-play 65-yard touchdown drive to get back in the game, connecting with Renfro on a 24-yard touchdown play. Renfro finished the game with a career-high 10 receptions for 141 yards and two scores.

The turnaround of the defense was just as sudden for Dallas. A diving interception by Dennis Thurman and a sack and a forced fumble by "Too Tall" Jones that Jim Jeffcoat recovered combined to give the Cowboys a momentary fourth-quarter lead.

But with 2:58 remaining, Dallas punted the ball back to the Giants, trailing 29-27. All that New York needed was a pair of first downs in order to run out the clock on the Cowboys.

Up in the press-box, a sportswriter from Dallas asked, "Where is Joe Pisarcik when Dallas needs him?" Pisarcik, the former Giants quarterback of eternal infamy, was once running out the clock against Philadelphia when he bobbled a handoff and allowed an Eagles defender to return the fumble for a game-winning touchdown.

What happened next was equally lamentable for the Giants, prompting writers from New York to dub it the "Ghost of Pisarcik." On second-down from the 22-yard line, Simms fumbled the snap from center and, when Randy White used his foot to nudge the ball away from the Giants' diving quarterback, Eugene Lockhart was able to recover for the Cowboys.

"I fumbled. That's all I can say," explained a very terse Simms afterwards. "We had a pass on and I was going to roll out. I was trying to get out there real quick."

Eager to take advantage of the gift that the Giants had so unwillingly offered his team, Landry took the air out of the ball on the next three plays, forcing New York to use their remaining allotment of timeouts. On came Septien, who calmly booted the 31-yard attempt through the uprights, putting Dallas back in front 30-29.

The raucous celebration near the Dallas bench was short-lived. A healthy 2:19 still showed on the game-clock and Phil Simms, who had already piled up 394 passing yards, was coming back out. The Cowboy defense still had work to do. The aerial onslaught continued, Simms moving the Giants to midfield, courtesy in part to a completion of 17 yards to Johnson on fourth-and-10. The 720 combined passing yards between the two quarterbacks was the most ever in a game involving the Dallas Cowboys.

But with the game's next attempt, the curtain dropped on New York's comeback bid. After hesitating due to the leaping figure of a blitzing Michael Downs, Simms' sideline pass intended for Manuel was off-target. There to corral it at the 37-

yard line was Walls, who stepped nimbly out of bounds and received hearty congratulations from Leon Gonzalez, Ron Fellows, and every other enthusiastic member of the surprising first-place Cowboys.

The team plane landed back in Dallas at 4:30 a.m on Monday morning. The team that emerged onto the lonely tarmac was battle-tested and hardened, sharing a common purpose and belief that anything on any given field was possible for a group of players that stuck together and never quit. These were the benefits of a most trying week when the Cowboys overcame the Big Lie, the Big Apple, and more voodoo dolls than any one man could shake a stick at.

CHAPTER 20

SLAYING THE STEEL DRAGON

"It always feels good when you beat Pittsburgh."
Tom Landry

"They said I was too little. They said I could never take the pounding. Well, here I am. Little ol' me."
Tony Dorsett, after surpassing 10,000 career rushing yards

Thus far in the 1985 season, the Dallas Cowboys had mastered the art of victory. With sometimes ease and other times painful, heart-stopping exertion, they continued to find inventive ways in authoring weekend success stories. For beginners, it was the defense leading the charge out of the gates, intercepting six Redskin passes in a 44-14 triumph. Two weeks later, it was a boring brand of football that beat the Browns. In Houston, a record-tying twelve sacks from the defense and the miraculous efforts of their injured star running back saved the day against the Oilers. And against the Giants, it was a bit of luck and good fortune in the fourth quarter that allowed Dallas to escape as 30-29 winners.

But while sitting alone atop the NFC East standings felt good, the Cowboys couldn't afford to get comfortable with success. Not with the quality of teams chasing them in the division, and certainly not with the shadow of their next opponent looming over them. The Ghost of Pisarcik that helped Dallas to a victory over New York now gave way to the Ghost of Pittsburgh's Past.

To face Pittsburgh invoked memories of what-might-have-been for a Cowboys franchise that enjoyed so many sparkling successes during the 1970s, an era in which they participated in more Super Bowls than any other team. But it was because of the mighty Steelers that America's Team could not be crowned as the Team of the Decade.

In a four-year period, Dallas and Pittsburgh butted heads in two of the greatest championship matches that the NFL has ever seen, classic games with seemingly more storylines than television viewers. That Terry Bradshaw, Lynn Swann, and the Steel Curtain were able to best Roger Staubach, Drew Pearson, and the Doomsday defense on both occasions left a bad taste in the mouths of folks back in Dallas, who wanted so desperately to believe their Cowboys were superior to all.

Possibly even more strange than the set of circumstances that enabled Pittsburgh to walk away victorious in Super Bowls X and XIII was their stranglehold over the Cowboys during the regular season. Dating back to that memorable picture-perfect afternoon at the Orange Bowl in January, 1976, Dallas had dropped five consecutive games to the Steelers. Time and place could not affect what seemed to be an inevitable outcome. Whether on a neutral playing field at Super Bowl XIII in the evening hours, at Three Rivers Stadium during the early afternoon period, or at Texas Stadium on a Monday night as their most recent encounter in 1982 had been, the sleek, star-studded Cowboys were always a step behind the blue-collar bunch from Pittsburgh.

And though times and rosters were different – only thirteen players remained from the Dallas-Pittsburgh showdown in Super Bowl XIII from more than six years before – the north

Texas locals still harbored feelings of animosity toward the one team that had cost the Cowboys so much over the past decade.

Thus, the sellout crowd that filed into Texas Stadium on Sunday came to witness history – Tony Dorsett needed only 31 yards to become the sixth player in league history to eclipse 10,000 career rushing yards. More importantly, they had come to see the Cowboys accomplish the seemingly impossible by slaying the vaunted dragon from Pittsburgh.

The incurable Texas heat had returned just in time for Dallas' first home game in four weeks, with afternoon temperatures climbing well into the 80s, the humidity rating nearly as high. While Tom Landry and the rest of the Cowboys team enjoyed the benefits of a shaded bench area, Chuck Noll and the Steelers were baking in the sun across the way, cursing the uncomfortable conditions as well as the uneven circumstances that the hole in the Texas Stadium roof provided. *If the Steelers had to be miserable for three hours, why shouldn't the Cowboys be forced to as well?*

With the weather providing Dallas a decided home-field advantage, it was a disturbing sight for locals to see the visitors land a surprise punch in the early going. Over their first five games, Pittsburgh had failed to complete a single pass to a tight end. Lo, and behold, quarterback Mark Malone changed all of that in the first quarter with his 14-yard pass to Bennie Cunningham.

The defensive intent of the Steelers was not nearly so cunning. They were bent on swarming the backfield and postponing Dorsett's celebration until the following week. After three carries, Dorsett had all of minus-3-yards to his credit. Three more carries and his total had jumped to a grand total of 2 yards. At this pace, it would be two weeks until he broke the 10,000-yard barrier.

Adding insult to frustration was the perplexing presence of Rafael Septien. A lost cause one week, a hero the next, Septien had popped up on the Cowboys' injury report during the week. At practice, so the story goes, Septien was guilty of diving for a pass and landing awkwardly on his right shoulder. Team doctors cleared him to play, feeling that the injury would not affect his kicking abilities. Septien rewarded their confidence by missing a 48-yard field goal to cap Dallas' opening march.

Though no longer considered the behemoths of the American Football Conference, the Steelers still possessed a feisty defense and a group of talented wide receivers. Walter Abercrombie, the fourth-year running back from Baylor, was coming off a season-high rushing performance of 91 yards a week before versus Miami. The position that lacked just happened to be the most critical one.

Once upon a time, Steelers brass had high hopes that Malone could be successfully converted from a quarterback to either tailback or wide receiver. A 1981 knee operation changed all of that. Three years after going under the knife, expectations were on a much higher plane, Malone being handed the starting quarterback reins midway through the 1984 season. Suddenly, he was not just another quarterback learning the ins and outs of the position at the professional level, but the heir-apparent to Terry Bradshaw.

But much like Cowboy enthusiasts after a decade of watching Roger Staubach at work, Steelers fans had grown spoiled. Malone was competent at times, even downright heady, but he was nowhere close to being the caliber of player that Bradshaw had been.

What Malone provided the offense in athleticism he cost them in natural quarterbacking skills. Malone was at his best as a passer when the primary receiver got open on the play. But he struggled when forced to hold the ball in the pocket and go through his progressions, as evidenced by the dearth of completions to running backs and tight ends during the early portion of the season.

While Malone could not technically be considered thoroughly erratic, the evidence that he was still trying to find his way was on weekly display in the Pittsburgh backfield. He had good games, and a few poor ones mixed in. He made some nice throws, but misfired here and there as well.

After guiding the Steelers into the AFC Championship Game the year before, Malone had started the 1985 regular season on fire, accounting for six touchdowns (5 passing, 1 rushing) in an opening-day trouncing of Indianapolis. The next four games were equally forgettable, as Malone came crashing back down to earth, completing just forty-eight percent of his pass attempts while costing his team a pair of key division games.

Five games into the season he was tied with John Elway for the league lead in touchdown passes (12). But with four Super Bowl titles behind the franchise, statistics were of little consolation to a Steelers squad that limped into Texas Stadium with a record of 2-3. Were Pittsburgh to get past the Cowboys on this day, Malone needed to be at his best.

Instead of turning up the wick against Dallas, as Bradshaw had done so many times over the years, Malone lost his way in the stadium's shadows, wasting away one opportunity after another with poor, misguided passes. Wide receiver John Stallworth ran past Ron Fellows twice during the first-half and would have had a pair of touchdowns to his credit. Malone overthrew him both times. On another play, Malone was throwing toward Stallworth in the middle of the field, but could only watch helplessly as the pass fell harmlessly to the turf after being tipped at the line of scrimmage. Later, he overthrew Louis Lipps down the left sideline.

Malone's quarterbacking counterpart in Cowboy blue was not nearly so unfortunate. Like he had a week before at the Meadowlands, Danny White started fast against the Steelers, completing his first six pass attempts to four different receivers. Tom Landry knew better than to expect White's hot hand to continue for very much longer. Not if the pocket continued to collapse with such frequency. The game was barely into the second quarter, and already White had been sacked once and barely escaped from being taken down behind the line on two other occasions. So, with White clearly in a passing groove and Dorsett beginning to get frustrated from a lack of work space, Landry dialed up the perfect play call to fool Pittsburgh's aggressive defense.

Steelers linebackers had been keyed up to stop Dorsett, sticking to him like black oilcloth with yellow glue wherever he traveled. But with Pittsburgh leading 3-0 early in the second quarter, it was a big miscalculation by David Little that caused this strategy to momentarily backfire.

Little saw the snap from center Tom Rafferty go back to White and stepped up quickly, anticipating Dorsett making a move to either help with an outside block, or run into the flat. When Dorsett, instead, simply ran around Chris Schultz and sprinted down the middle of the field, Little was caught leaning the wrong way. The lumbering linebacker had no chance to run step-for-step with the world-class speed of the Dallas running back. What he had thought was an out, turned into a very noticeable up for Dorsett and the Cowboys.

White's downfield toss was picture-perfect, and Dorsett did the rest, punctuating his 57-yard touchdown reception by streaking into the end-zone and holding out both arms, as if to welcome the thunderous applause that the home crowd was only too willing to offer him.

"We were talking all week about that play," White later explained. "It's designed so Tony just clears out the middle area so Mike Renfro can come across clear. But I told him, 'If it looks like you got your man beat, try to get open.' And they had a perfect defense for us, with a blitz and man coverage – so Tony just ran by his linebacker and was wide open."

Said Dorsett: "It was a play we made some adjustments on just before the game. Coach Landry and Danny and I talked about it. Normally, I hook up on that play. They told me not to hook up, just keep on going straight...You've got to give credit not only to Danny and the offensive line for blocking, but to Coach Landry for making that change before the game."

The Steelers, revealing the stubborn heart of a champion, refused to alter their plan of defense. Though trailing for the first time in the game, they continued to aggressively clog running lanes and make life in the pocket a painful experience at times for White. Dorsett, after nine carries, had just 4 rushing yards to his credit. And White, who staked the Cowboys to a 10-3 halftime lead by completing his first 10 pass attempts for 137 yards, was sacked twice more before intermission. Pittsburgh's pugilistic approach finally paid dividends, as White was seen grimacing throughout the latter stages of the game due to bruised ribs.

There to take up the slack for the Cowboys' physically compromised quarterback was Dorsett. With his first tote of the second-half, Dorsett took a pitch from White while going left and ran around the corner for a gain of 19 yards. It was the first time he had seen a crease all afternoon, and made just enough out of it to bring the sleepy home crowd to their feet. With that run, Dorsett was only eight yards away from the record, and suddenly Texas Stadium was buzzing once again with anticipation.

The milestone moment came on Dallas' next possession, with the Cowboys facing a second-down play from their own 35-yard line. It was a classic Dorsett run that highlighted not only his quick burst, but also his exemplary vision. Dorsett followed the block by rookie guard Crawford Ker through the left side of the line. Using another block from Mike Renfro, he was able to get wide near the boundary for a few more yards before safety Donnie Shell ran him out of bounds near the Dallas bench. Needing only five yards for the record, Dorsett had gotten 19 instead, thrilling the throngs to no end.

Ker was the first player to congratulate him, but he was far from the last. With a roar of approval from the sellout crowd serving as a very noticeable backdrop to the historical occasion, rookies Robert LaVette and Jesse Penn were followed by a host of veterans – Mike Renfro, Dennis Thurman, Broderick Thompson, Eugene Lockhart, Everson Walls…seemingly everyone on that side of the field except Landry – who either shook Dorsett's hand or patted him on the back in acknowledgment of the rare accomplishment.

What was Dorsett thinking during all of this?

"My first thought was to hold onto the ball," he said. "We had a plan and the referee was going to stop the game. I knew Tom Landry wasn't going to throw this ball away, so I gave it to him."

After the stoppage, it was all business once again down on the field, the Cowboys driving for another Septien field-goal to extend their lead to 13-3. It was then that Noll pulled the plug on his young quarterback, benching Malone (7-of-17 for 83 yards) for experienced veteran David Woodley, who had led Miami to an appearance in Super Bowl XVII at the conclusion of the 1982 season.

Woodley fared little better. After three uninspiring incompletions to begin his day, Woodley forced a pass in the direction of Cunningham that instead wound up in the mitts of Eugene Lockhart at the 19-yard line. With no Steeler on that side of the field to stop him, Lockhart was able to return the interception all the way for a touchdown to give Dallas a 20-3 lead.

"They had been running that same play all day," said Lockhart, relishing his first score as a professional. "Out of a flip formation, the tight end would come down and curl in. This time I anticipated it and stepped in front of him. Then it was just a matter of my God-given running ability, as Tony Dorsett has taught me to say."

"Unfortunately," said Landry, "that's when we started letting them get back in the game."

Leon Gonzalez opened the door for a Pittsburgh comeback by fumbling on a punt-return at the Dallas 17-yard line, leading to a 34-yard field-goal off the foot of Anderson. Following a Cowboy punt, Ron Fellows allowed wide receiver Calvin Sweeney to run past him for a gain of 69 yards, leading to a short touchdown run by Abercrombie.

As they had done so often throughout the course of the young season, Thurman's Thieves showed up to save the day, staving off the advances of a suddenly confident Steelers team by making the most of another aggressive blitz package. It had been a safety-blitz by Michael Downs from defensive coordinator Ernie Stautner that beat the Giants a week before. Stautner had used that same blitz against Pittsburgh earlier in the game, resulting in a batted pass for the defense.

But with the game still in the balance in the fourth quarter, Stautner changed things up, keeping Downs in coverage and sending Dennis Thurman crashing into the backfield from the same side. Thurman reached Woodley just as he was releasing a downfield throw to Sweeney, who had gotten a step on Fellows and Dextor Clinkscale while running a deep-post pattern from the left side of the formation. But the wobbly pass hung up in the air, allowing Downs to come over from his outfield post, step in front, and make the interception.

Dorsett wrote the rest, turning a broken play on the very next snap into a 35-yard cross-country jaunt for a touchdown. He had started the play by running to the right after taking a pitch from White on a sweep. When the defense closed off that side, Dorsett stopped and started running in the opposite direction, allowing his blockers to do what little was needed to reach the corner ahead of the pack.

"My guy was back-pedaling so fast all I could do was push him a little," said White. "I went back to the sidelines and told Coach [Jim] Myers, 'I guess I just proved anybody can block for Dorsett.'"

"It's exactly the way Tom Landry draws it up," joked Dorsett, whose superlative second-half performance gave him the first 100-yard rushing day of his career versus the Steelers.

"Tony run right and if there's nothing there, run back to the left and see what your blockers can do for you."

For the first time in several weeks, the local fan base had nothing to complain about on Monday morning. The Cowboys were 5-1, blessed with a two-game advantage in the NFC East. Tony Dorsett had his place in the NFL record books. And the home team, for the first time in thirteen years, had finally slain the mighty Steel dragon. No one in Dallas could have asked for a better day's work from their Cowboys.

CHAPTER 21

WINDS OF OPPORTUNITY

"We played like we were hoping for a gift and it didn't come.
We gave the gifts."
Tom Landry, after the Cowboys' 16-14 loss to Philadelphia

Nestled in the arms of obscurity, shielded from the many spoils of success currently energizing the streets of Dallas, toiled a soldier in rusted armor who, seemingly only yesterday, had been a folk hero to so many of local origin. Though still a member of the team, he plodded along in his newfound role as an invisible component of a Cowboys squad that had taken the entire league by surprise. If not for his duties as the holder on field-goal attempts, his existence would have been completely forgotten by fans overjoyed at their team's 5-1 start.

To be a quarterback at the NFL level was universally recognized to be a tough gig. But being a quarterback in Dallas went by an entirely different name. Though just 27 years of age, Gary Hogeboom had already experienced both sides of this pressure-induced, blue-starred roller-coaster that moved along at the speed of a runaway locomotive. A year ago, he had been the toast of the town and a franchise building block. Through six games of the 1985 season, Hogeboom was firmly entrenched in his original digs as the backup to Danny White.

It was too early a date for Hogeboom to dare venture a prediction as to which football city his promising career would eventually blossom in. But of one thing he was sure. It wasn't going to be in Dallas.

Hogeboom was busy these days trying his best to stay in a positive frame of mind. He wanted to be a good teammate, and help the Cowboys accomplish their goal of getting back into the playoffs. But he also found no reason to avoid facing the reality of his situation.

Hogeboom prepared every week with the diligence of a starter, all the while knowing that the job would never be his. Barring a catastrophe, it was much too late for that to happen.

Like any self-aware athlete in a big town, Hogeboom was guilty of scanning the sports page more often than was probably good for him. As early as the previous January, he knew what sportscasters and ex-Cowboy players were saying, specifically that there was no way Tom Landry could keep both quarterbacks on the roster for the 1985 season. Hogeboom had signed a new $500,000 contract shortly afterwards intending to wage one more training camp duel with White, believing whoever lost the competition this time would be traded away to another team - if not before the start of the regular season then certainly before the recently established Week 6 trading deadline. But the deadline had come and gone, and Hogeboom was still a bench-riding Cowboy.

It was easy to understand why fans had fallen in love with the bright-eyed kid from Grand Rapids, Mich. When a star-gazing franchise such as the Cowboys is failing to meet expectations, it was an unspoken rule of thumb that the backup quarterback became the prized commodity of the fan base. And there was plenty of talent in Hogeboom's 6-foot-4-inch frame to intrigue those weary with the big-game shortcomings of White.

Hogeboom's most noticeable asset was his arm strength. Not since the days of Clint Longley had fans in Dallas seen an arm to be compared with his. But Hogeboom was not to be compared with such a wild child as Longley. For starters, Hogeboom had brains enough to not dump a bag of live rattlesnakes on the practice field, and to avoid punching out the lights of the starting quarterback. But did he have brains enough to be a winner in Dallas? That, for one summer after another, had been the million-dollar question throughout the Metroplex.

During that time, Danny White was the established goat. And the unproven Hogeboom was the angel in Cowboy armor…until he so obviously wasn't. When afforded a chance to prove himself capable at the outset of the 1984 season, the "Boomer" had mysteriously bombed, costing Hogeboom his status as an up-and-comer and allowing White to reestablish his captaincy in the locker room.

The team had found cause to rally behind White as their leader in part because Hogeboom had not given them reason enough to believe in him. It wasn't a personality conflict. Hogeboom was likable enough in the locker room. He wasn't a renegade at heart who brushed coaches and players aside. But he wasn't the on-the-field savior that so many players and members of the press had made him out to be during training camp.

Unlike White during those early days after the retirement of Roger Staubach, Hogeboom never established himself as a difference-maker in Dallas, cracks of concern showing in his armor very early in the 1984 season. He never saw the Giant blitz coming in a turnover-filled 28-7 loss at the Meadowlands in Week 2. He was the quarterback five weeks later in a dreadful loss to the Redskins at RFK Stadium.

Compounding those shortcomings was a tendency for mistakes, and Hogeboom's mistakes, mind you, were of the costly variety. Three of his 14 interceptions in 1984 were returned for defensive touchdowns.

Sitting on the bench for the final four games of the season didn't sit well with Hogeboom. He was peeved at having the job he had worked so long and hard to attain taken away from him with the Cowboys smack in the middle of the playoff race. Despite his many shortcomings, Hogeboom had put the team in position to make a deep run into January, so why was Landry punishing him for it?

After the season, Hogeboom had pondered the prospects of walking into Tex Schramm's office and demanding a trade, but when Landry promised him that he would be afforded another opportunity to win the starting quarterback job in training camp, Hogeboom decided to stick it out for one more go-around. By the time he realized that Landry was bent on avoiding a quarterback controversy in 1985, it was already too late. Hogeboom was trapped behind White on the depth chart, whether he liked it or not.

Rather than kick up a fuss as he might have done a year before when the locker room was in turmoil, Hogeboom worked at his craft during the off-season, determined to improve himself as a player and as a teammate. He patched up his relationship with White, promising to remain supportive no matter who was the starter. The two quarterbacks would never be buddies again, but at least they were now on speaking terms.

Hogeboom studied hard in the film-room, intent on learning to read defenses quicker at the line of scrimmage, especially when the Cowboys were inside the opponent's 20-yard line. Too often during the 1984 season, Hogeboom's eyes got big when the field shrunk, his rocket arm handicapped by the flickering of mental indecision. Out on the practice field. Hogeboom spent a lot of time working on feathering his short passes instead of fogging them full speed. It was a complaint of his receivers the previous season that his passes hurt them more than the opposition.

It was only inevitable, after a close competition throughout training camp, that Landry named White the Cowboys' starting quarterback for the 1985 season. But that didn't mean that Hogeboom would be sitting down during games. In addition to his duties as the holder, coaches had Hogeboom sending in offensive signals on every play. These duties were enough to keep his mind engaged with the game-plan and off of his own frustrations and disappointments.

Hogeboom was fully prepared to finish out the season in this role, until Landry came to him shortly after the Cowboys had disposed of Pittsburgh and offered him a ray of hope that he might go under center again sooner rather than later. Hogeboom's week leading up to the Week 7 divisional matchup with Philadelphia was spent on high alert. Due to the bruised ribs that White suffered against the Steelers, Landry had told Hogeboom to be ready to go on Sunday, just in case.

Hogeboom listened like a good soldier, but his heart warned him not to get his hopes up. After all, he had been down this road before, hoping for an opportunity that seemingly never was to come. By this time, it was evident to everyone in the stands and in the press that Landry wanted White to be the quarterback. And it was no secret that what Landry wanted, he got.

Hogeboom practiced with the first-team offense at practice on Wednesday and Thursday, while White sat off to the side as a wounded spectator. White suited up at practice on Friday and said he felt fine throwing a football, claiming to be about ninety-percent healthy. Coaches tried to pump the brakes on White's optimism, but Hogeboom was having none of it.

"Any time a quarterback has sore ribs like he has had, you never know when you'll get in," Hogeboom said on Friday afternoon. "The key is to wait until Sunday. I'm ready."

Then, as if he was a mind-reader who had tapped into Landry's secret thoughts, Hogeboom added, "If it goes like it has in the past, he'll be playing."

Sunday morning came, and with it a welcome surprise for young Gary Hogeboom. Cornering him in the visitors' locker room a couple of hours before kickoff, Landry advised Hogeboom to get his helmet ready, because the Eagles were out there on the field and the "Boomer" was the Dallas quarterback who would greet them.

Gary Hogeboom's afternoon proving ground was not for the faint of heart. Swelling with the pulse of that fabled northeastern city of Brotherly Love, veritable Veterans Stadium welcomed the Dallas Cowboys with a hearty – but albeit common – chorus of unpleasantness. The obscenities that greeted Hogeboom and the Cowboys as they came out of the tunnel and onto the field were loud and crude, laced with the fervor of sincerity.

No secret was more poorly kept in America than was the morbid hatred that the city of Philadelphia harbored for America's Team. Perhaps it was the sleek silver pants the Cowboys wore and the blue-bellied star crowning their helmets that provoked fans into such a frenzy. Maybe it was their stylishly dressed head coach on the sideline that pricked jealous hearts. Or maybe it was the unmatched success the Cowboys enjoyed that prompted such unspeakable metaphors from the throngs.

Whatever the reason for such behavior, one thing was a recognized fact: whenever the Cowboys came to town, the party in Philly was bound to be loud, proud, and every bit of crude. Tossing eggs at the team bus as it arrived at the stadium was tolerable fun. Throwing snowballs at Cowboy players during the wintertime was even better. But the very highest form of entertainment was witnessing a Cowboys defeat, which was what every distinguished patron inside Veterans Stadium was rabidly hoping for as Rafael Septien lined up for the opening kickoff on a mild, gray afternoon.

The setting was unique. As was the start to the game, a series of disjointed moments that witnessed the referee doing more exercise than any of the men in football armor. With temperatures in the sixties, Septien jogged forward and swung his right leg through, knocking the tee over while sending the ball sailing high and far downfield toward the waiting figure of Andre Waters near the goal-line. Waters was rendered a deft ball-handler when he made a difficult catch of the falling oblong object look easy, before turning up-field near the right sideline. He put the yards behind him with admirable fluidity. He passed the ten-yard line. Then the fifteen. Then the twenty.

All was well for this man in green, until Waters was smacked by a heat-seeking missile named Bill Bates. The collision separated Waters from the ball, allowing rookie linebacker Jesse Penn to make a recovery for Dallas at the 26-yard line. The sellout crowd began murmuring in their seats. It had been nearly five years since the Eagles had defeated the Cowboys in Philadelphia. Fumbling away the opening kickoff was a fool-proof way to continue that streak.

Out came Hogeboom and the Dallas offense, wearing their dark blue jerseys for the second time in three games. Faced with a short field and a golden opportunity to plant a seed of doubt in the minds of Eagles players, the Cowboys had every reason to make the first jump forward. But instead, they were seen making two jumps in the other direction. Jim Cooper was flagged for holding on the very first play from scrimmage, wiping out a 6-yard Hogeboom-to-Doug Cosbie completion. Negating a short Timmy Newsome plunge on the next snap was another holding penalty, this time on center Tom Rafferty.

Needing thirty yards on first-down from the Philadelphia 46-yard line, Hogeboom turned to his right, uncorked his cannon of an arm, and rifled a pass toward Mike Renfro at the 30. Renfro was reaching up to grab the ball when he was hog-tied from behind by Elbert Foules, warranting another announcement by referee Red Cashion. According to Cashion, the Eagles' cornerback was guilty of pass-interference. After seeing a video replay, Foules thought better of disputing the call. Doing so would only have created one more pause in a game already filled with them.

"The highlight reel is going to be rather short. We've had a fumble and three flags," noted Verne Lundquist on the CBS broadcast.

From there, Hogeboom moved the Cowboys inside the 10-yard line, and on second-down made a pass that had everyone on the Dallas bench pumping their fists in celebration. For a moment, anyway. Displaying patience that had been lacking on so many occasions a year before, Hogeboom waited in the pocket until he espied Cosbie running open along the backline. Sending a soft floater in his direction, Hogeboom watched as his tall, rangy tight end reached out...and dropped the pass. On third-down it was the old, impulsive version of Hogeboom that showed up, as he tried to fit a pass into Cosbie through a tight window of coverage. This time Cosbie never got his hands on the ball. This time safety Wes Hopkins made an easy interception in the end-zone.

But Hogeboom was an old-fashioned gunslinger who knew better than to waste time bemoaning bygone repercussions of misspent bullets. He had wasted away one scoring opportunity, but refused to allow that setback to ruin the rest of his day. Back he came on the Cowboys' next possession wearing the same confident look as before, guiding the offense on a slow, time-consuming 95-yard march, his 7-yard scoring pass to Tony Dorsett coming on the final play of the first quarter.

The Cowboys were now ahead 7-0 on the scoreboard, yet remained locked in what appeared to be a toe-to-toe slugfest down on the field with Eagles players. Renfro was engaged in a personal battle with Foules for the better part of the first half. Who came out the winner was probably a matter of opinion.

Having already earned a flag for hitting Renfro too early, Foules adjusted his strategy and lived to crow about it. After being beaten near the sideline for a second-quarter gain of 16 yards, Foules shoved Renfro down well after the receiver had stepped out of bounds. Two plays later, Renfro walked back to the huddle with his jersey pulled under his shoulder pad.

Hogeboom was less forgiving. Whereas Renfro walked away from confrontation, the Dallas quarterback seemed to invite it, going out of his way to prove that the Cowboys could play a tough man's game as good as the next team, or better. In the second quarter, the Cowboys were faced with a third-and-3 from the Philadelphia 45-yard line. The pocket began to close around him, and – perhaps invoking images of his days running the option while at Central Michigan - Hogeboom scrambled away to his left determined to move the chains on his own merit. But instead of meekly falling to the turf after picking up the required yardage, Hogeboom lowered his shoulder into the chest of Evan Cooper. Needing three yards, Hogeboom's efforts resulted in a pickup of nine.

The Eagles' cornerback didn't appreciate being put on his back by a lanky kid from Michigan, and tried to grab the ball away from Hogeboom after the whistle had blown. Hogeboom wasn't in a playful mood, so directed a few choice words for Cooper after brushing his arms off and while standing over him.

Hopkins, standing nearby, took exception to the Boomer's behavior, grabbing the quarterback by the shirt-front, telling him to buzz off. Hogeboom never backed down, shoving the defensive leader of the Eagles away from him with a surprising snarl.

What might have provoked little more than a yawn at a hockey game provided a moment of entertainment in the television booth for Lundquist and Terry Bradshaw, who couldn't help but chuckle at the spectacle of an unproven backup quarterback trading barbs so easily with an Eagles squad noted for having short fuses. "He's a feisty one," Lundquist said of Hogeboom.

But when it came to inciting an Eagles riot, nothing Hogeboom or any other Cowboy did that day could compare to the one ill-advised moment of taunting that Dorsett enjoyed during the latter stages of the third quarter. Dorsett's day had already been an eventful one, to say the least. He had scored a touchdown as a receiver and coughed the ball up as a runner. That fumble had proven especially costly for Dorsett. Not only did it provide the Eagles with a field-goal before the halftime break, but it also revitalized the trash-talking instincts of the Philly defense, who weren't going to let Dorsett forget about his mistake.

Linebacker Garry Cobb, a 1979 draft selection of the Cowboys, waged a verbal war with Dorsett for the remainder of the game. After a Dorsett run, Cobb could often be seen slapping the ball out of Dorsett's hands, talking loudly and proudly all the while.

Clinging to a 7-6 lead, the Cowboys were marching deep in Eagles territory yet again, a fact which disturbed Cobb not at all. He wagged his finger and wagged his tongue, his back getting pushed closer and closer to the goal-line with each play. It was after Cobb had knocked the ball from his hands on successive running plays that Dorsett finally decided he had endured enough.

On third-down from the 10-yard line, Hogeboom scanned the field from the Shotgun formation. What he saw was a defensive formation that left the center uncovered, with Hopkins and fellow safety Ray Ellis spread wide close to the line of scrimmage. To Hogeboom, it looked like the Eagles were going to send a blitz.

Said Ellis: "We were actually faking a blitz and were going to double the wide receivers..."

Hogeboom may have mis-read the defense, but it didn't matter since he still managed to make the proper audible. A pass was about to turn into a run. A run known in the Cowboys' playbook as 41 Delay Trap. "We had an option to audible off that call, and things were so wide-open in their middle I couldn't resist it," said Hogeboom.

It was as if the red sea parted in front of Dorsett, who used a trap block from Glen Titensor to break into the clear and into the end-zone. Once there, Dorsett turned around and pointed the ball at Cobb and the rest of the Eagles defense, giving them back some of the medicine they had been doling out during the game. It was all the officiating crew could do to prevent a fight from breaking out on the spot.

"I sunk to their level," said an obviously penitent Dorsett in the locker room. "I apologize to Cowboys fans for that. But they have some young kids out there who have a lot of mouth and don't know what this game is all about."

Landry was less than pleased at Dorsett's end-zone theatrics, but that was to be expected. "When you point a football at somebody, they might make you eat it," said Landry.

Which is exactly what the Eagles did. Thirty four-year old quarterback Ron Jaworski, stumped by the Dallas blitz in the first-half, came out on the other side of intermission throwing darts all over the field. Not only would Jaworski finish the game with a career-high 380 passing yards, but he also would break the Cowboys' string of thirteen consecutive games with an interception. That, of course, was what the statistical line indicated. Cowboys players, well, they had grounds to dispute that.

A 52-yard punt from Mike Saxon had just rolled out of bounds at the 1-yard line early in the third quarter. On second-down, Jaworski lofted a missile that Ron Fellows was in perfect position to snare for the Cowboys. Fellows and wide receiver Mike Quick tumbled down at the 47-yard line. The official, who was blocked from having a clear view of the play, immediately ruled that Quick had possession. Fellows couldn't believe it.

"I came down with it and hit the ground," insisted Fellows. "Quick rolled on top of me and grabbed it away."

Safety Dextor Clinkscale agreed. "I told him (the referee) that Ron was on the ground with the ball and the play's over – interception. He wouldn't listen. Why is it nobody ever overrules anybody out there? Somebody out there saw exactly what happened – and they never say a thing."

That one play jump-started the Philadelphia offense, and once it got rolling, the Cowboys were never able to stop it. A 36-yard field-goal by bare-footed place-kicker Paul McFadden drew the Eagles to within 14-9 with more than 13 minutes remaining.

The next time Jaworski got his hands on the ball, he needed only three plays to give Philadelphia their first lead of the game. On first-down from the 15, Jaworski found rookie running back Herman Hunter running free down the right sideline for a gain of 36 yards. Hunter had simply run past the coverage of linebacker Mike Hegman on the play. With Hegman intent on not getting beat a second time, Hunter looped out of the backfield on the same side, but instead of streaking down the boundary, he simply stopped. The pass from Jaworski was perfect, netting a gain of 11 yards.

From the Dallas 36-yard line came the play that broke the backs of the Cowboy defense. Ernie Stautner had been sending blitzes all afternoon, and he sent another one on first-down. Jaworski was ready for it, and immediately looked to his right where wide receiver Kenny Jackson was working one-on-one with Everson Walls.

The pass from the quarterback was good, the positioning of the cornerback even better. Though slightly off-balance, Walls reached up with his left hand to bat the pass away. The ball deflected off his fingers, but went straight back to Jackson, who strutted into the end-zone to give the Eagles a 16-14 lead.

Back came Hogeboom, who seemed destined for a Staubach-esque rally to put the naysayers to bed. He threw to Tony Hill for 16 yards. On the very next play, Hogeboom threw long and incomplete to Hill, but an interference penalty on cornerback Herman Edwards placed the ball on the Philadelphia 23-yard line.

The fourth-quarter magic that had made Staubach the world-renowned comeback wizard that he was eluded

Hogeboom that day, even if it was through no fault of his own. On second-down from the 20-yard line, Dorsett fumbled again while running left on a sweep. Hopkins, already with two interceptions to his credit, was there to make the recovery. Replays were inconclusive as to whether the arm of offensive tackle Chris Schultz had inadvertently knocked the ball out, or that Dorsett had simply dropped it.

"The bottom line is it was a fumble," said Dorsett.

Dallas got the ball back at their own 20-yard line with 4:34 remaining. Hogeboom's pass on third-and-14 was straight and true, aimed at the in-cutting figure of Mike Renfro. But before he could corral the pass to extend the drive, Renfro slipped and fell down, and could only watch as the ball went buzzing over his head. Instead of a game-winning drive in the making, the Cowboys were punting the ball away, never to get their hands on it again.

Afterwards, a writer asked Hogeboom how much responsibility he would take for the loss. The quarterback's answer came quick and crisp. "All of it," he said. "I threw two interceptions that cost us two field goals and we lose by two points."

The only way that Hogeboom could foresee getting another chance as the starting quarterback in Dallas was if Danny White turned in a stinker on the following Sunday against the 1-6 Falcons. But that didn't happen. White played well in a 26-10 victory over Atlanta at Texas Stadium, giving the Cowboys a 6-2 mark at the halfway pole, and allowing Hogeboom to fade once again into the shadows.

CHAPTER 22

THE GREAT FALLOUT

"We weren't trying to be negative or detrimental to anybody on the team. It was just our way of showing solidarity... That whole thing brought us down to a degree."
Reflections from Dennis Thurman on when Thurman's Thieves dressed up as mobsters

Tom Landry said it loud and said it clear. His football team, flawed though it was, had a 6-2 record at the halfway mark of the regular season. And he was thrilled about that. Back in August, hardly a soul existed who would dare give the Dallas Cowboys even a subliminal chance to tread water, let alone take control of the division. Even Tex Schramm, that ultimate ticket salesman, couldn't wrest himself from the clutches of preseason pessimism. No, not in his wildest football daydreams did Tex imagine Dallas being within reach of the No. 2 spot in the NFC when the calendars turned to November. Not even close.

"I can see us contending this year, but the odds aren't in that direction," Schramm admitted during the summer. "I can't remember the last time I said that."

Eight weeks into the season and Landry was wearing a big smile. Not that he was getting ahead of himself now that Dallas had the Giants and Redskins chasing them, or was actually cocky enough to crow about his team. Landry was merely glorying in the pertinent facts. These Cowboys were a surprise to all – yes, even to Landry - flexing a muscle that was said to have been far past the stages of deterioration.

Oh, sure, the flaws on the team were familiar ones. The No. 1 ranked offense in the NFL still struggled to score touchdowns from inside the opponents 20-yard line. Danny White had been a bit too loose with the ball for comfort through eight games, on pace for a career-high interception total for a single season. The offensive line still struggled in pass-blocking. Rafael Septien – bent toe, ailing back, and whatever other minor injury he may have been harboring – continued to be a source of weekly wonder for coaches. And the defense, though certainly of an opportunistic inclination, still allowed too many big plays in the passing game.

These were areas that the coaching staff had been addressing in meetings and on the practice field for the past several weeks. That the message had yet to translate into consistent results on the Sunday stage kept Landry busy in front of a chalkboard on a daily basis, but wasn't enough to keep him awake at night.

Down deep, Landry knew these were never going to be the masters of precision like so many Cowboy teams had been during the previous decade. A lack of depth and experience assured him of that. But as long as his players were engaged during meetings and stayed committed to team values, Landry felt the Cowboys would have a chance to make some hay during the stretch run.

The 1985 Cowboys were supposed to be a poor mixture of age, inexperience, and overvalued worth. And maybe they were still all of that. The jury, after all, was still out. Landry, though, was conscious of a will and a purpose in his players that, so far in the season, had managed to cover up other glaring shortcomings.

The spirit that these Cowboys played with had not been seen in Dallas since the days of Roger Staubach. This primary ingredient carrying the Cowboys higher and higher up the conference leader board, this collective energy that refused to be diminished by unfavorable circumstances, transcended the gospel of Xs and Os that Landry was renowned for, providing the Cowboys a fighters chance when they otherwise would have had none.

Playing together had kept the team from folding its tents in Houston, and prevented the Giants from running away in the second-half at the Meadowlands one week later. It inspired individuals to do more. Tony Dorsett continued to pile up touchdowns and 100-yard games even with an injured back. Ed "Too Tall" Jones continued piling up sacks, even with a pulled hamstring. It inspired the frustrated to talk less. Like Gary Hogeboom, who refused the opportunity afforded him of using the press to start a quarterback controversy in the wake of his near-comeback in Detroit. And then there was Randy White, the biggest and baddest man in the locker room who deemed it to be more profitable to say nothing than to publicly criticize the offense after a poor performance.

Landry still questioned the wisdom of teammates critiquing each other to the press, and Michael Downs' agreement with the *Dallas Morning News* to write a weekly "insiders" column during the season. But it was hard to complain when acknowledging the night-and-day difference in the locker room from what it had been only a year before. This component, prompted by the early-season success, nurtured a growing belief among teammates that, so long as everyone pulled together, the Cowboys were insuperable.

"I'm very happy to be 6-2 at this point," Landry said after the victory over Atlanta. "You give me 6-2 for the second half and I'll just go play golf now."

Alas, there was to be no early vacation for the head coach, nor a smooth road to travel moving forward. This football caravan from Dallas was humming along an unforeseen highway of prosperity, enjoying the thrill of the moment. Around the next bend loomed a misspent Monday in the Midwest that witnessed the Cowboys approaching a fork in the road, not to mention the threshold of implosion.

The birthmark of that Bloody Mary Monday was a sky of deep blue and a bright autumn sun smiling a welcome. The scar that would forever mar its memory sprouted from a common plot of ground known to all humanity, where the dark, fallow soil of boredom yields fruit of a kind.

The morning meetings were over, the primetime showdown between Dallas and St. Louis still several hours away. Sequestered in his hotel room, Dennis Thurman was tired of watching game-film for the umpteenth time. He began to twitch, and the itch to be out and doing became greater and greater. Finally, he could stand it no longer.

There was still plenty of time to kill, enough to see some sights, make a pass under the Arch, and maybe hit a few stores along the way. So he called the rest of his Thieves, and together they went out for a few hours on the town. The spoils from this joint excursion were soon broadcast to all of their loyal fans back in Dallas.

That evening, about 90 minutes before the 8 o'clock kickoff, seven members of that notorious backfield crowd known as Thurman's Thieves appeared on a live interview outside the Cowboys' locker room on WFAA-TV, wearing what they considered to be fashionable fedoras. If the Thieves' intentions had been to appear to the world as a trendy version of their head coach, they certainly failed in the attempt. These weren't the class of stately gentlemen that Tom Landry belonged to appearing on Metroplex TV sets. With longer brims, some of which were bent low in the classic "hood" style, and those sidewise glances they kept throwing at the camera lens, it was hard not to make the obvious connection. More than merely Thieves, they looked like mobsters.

Inside the locker room, a handful of on looking teammates took exception to the demonstration, curling their lips in a discontented snarl. The trio of defensive linemen Randy White, John Dutton, and Jim Jeffcoat considered it grossly imprudent to be staging an act for fans back home so soon just before a game

– and a division game, at that. Game day was a time for business, not amateur theater.

Out of view of the television cameras, off to one side of the cavernous and still nearly-empty Busch Stadium, Tex Schramm and Cardinals owner Bill Bidwell, on behalf of NFL Charities, were presenting a grant check of $25,000 to Joyce Nelopka, the president of the National Federation of Parents for Drug Free Youth.

And, just like that, a classic case of conflict of interest had arisen. Here were Cowboy players, on one hand, publicly posing in the garb of underworld leaders, while the general manager was off to the side making a demonstration and a notable financial contribution to the war on drugs.

The moment was as ironic as the game that followed. The Cowboys, not surprisingly, played like a distracted team that night, seemingly indifferent toward a far inferior foe. The Cardinals were coming off a strong 9-7 campaign in 1984, but had lost some of their coaching staff during the ensuing off-season. Rod Dodhower, who called the offensive plays the previous two seasons and was the tutor for 4,000-yard passer Neil Lomax, became the head coach of the Colts. Following Dodhower to Indianapolis was offensive line coach Tom Lovat. Also, defensive backfield coach Tom Bettis left to become the defensive coordinator in Cleveland.

This unexpected coaching turnover left Jim Hanifan's squad but a shell of their former up-and-coming selves. After a 3-1 start, St. Louis limped into their *Monday Night Football* matchup with Dallas riding a four-game losing streak in which they failed to score more than 10 points in any game, something no Cardinal team had done since 1943. When considering the fact that St. Louis would be without their top receiving threat, Roy Green, and that starting running back Ottis Anderson was playing hurt, it was all the more apparent that this was one game that Dallas had no reason to lose.

Danny White and Lomax were equally bad for their respective teams for the majority of the first two quarters, allowing both punters to get some extra work in on coffin-corner kicking on this cold night. The Cardinals' offense went three-

and-out on five of their seven first-half possessions. But the Cowboys couldn't be accused of doing much better.

"That was the dullest first half I've ever seen," said Landry. "We didn't make a first down until the second quarter. Our defense was playing well – but that may have had something to do with how (bad) St. Louis was playing."

When White orchestrated two scoring drives just before the halftime whistle, it was assumed that the Cowboys were going to parlay their 10-0 advantage into a second-half runaway. Instead, the bottom fell out.

Dead though walking for two quarters, the Cardinals awoke out of their stupor on the opening possession of the third period when a blind, dumb, lucky pigskin fell into their laps like manna from heaven. Lomax threw across the middle to wide receiver J.T. Smith. The ball deflected off his hands, continued on its downfield course, flew past the face of rookie defensive back Ricky Easmon, and landed in the arms of Cardinals wide-out Pat Tilley.

Tilley easily outdistanced Easmon down the field. Upon realizing that nobody in Cowboy blue was going to catch him, Tilley got so excited that he actually spiked the ball before he crossed the goal-line. ABC cameras caught the gaffe, but the back judge did not. The touchdown stood up on the scoreboard, and the Cowboys effectively laid down for the night. Later in the quarter, fullback Earl Ferrell scored on an 8-yard sweep around right end to give St. Louis a 14-10 lead.

Perceiving a defensive breakdown between either Jeffcoat or Jeff Rohrer, it behooved Dennis Thurman to go over and encourage defensive lineman and linebacker to be sure they understood their assignments next time. That's when the "Manster" made his voice heard, and his presence felt. Randy White, perhaps provoked by the locker room interview before the game, had been in a foul temper since the opening kickoff. When the Cowboys were either tied or in the lead, he stayed busy with an ongoing grudge match with Ottis Anderson, the two trading a chorus of legal blows and unsavory words.

Once, White hurled his 260-pound frame into Anderson's back well after the runner had stepped out of bounds, so Anderson returned the favor a few plays later by lowering his shoulder and carrying White a few yards downfield. Back and forth they went, an eye for an eye, a blow for a blow. But when Anderson limped off the field early in the third quarter with a sprained ankle, White lost his sparring partner and his escape valve. Two Cardinal touchdown drives later and White was set to blow a fuse. Maybe he was perturbed that the leader of the Thieves would choose to pick on the big men up front, even though it was a pass-interference penalty on Everson Walls that moved St. Louis into scoring position in the first place. Maybe White was spoiling for a fight. Maybe he simply misunderstood Thurman's words inside the loud stadium. Who knows.

But when he saw Thurman playing coach over near the Dallas bench, White simply lost it. He told Thurman to shut up and sit down. When Dennis gave him some lip back instead, the fight was on. Thurman cursed him. White cursed Thurman twice in return. So Thurman shoved him. It was then, just in the nick of time, that teammates intervened and separated the two combatants, with White clearly frustrated that he wasn't afforded the chance to turn the lights out on Thurman once and for all.

Reluctantly, and with much prodding from players and assistant coaches, the party broke up. Yet the strain of the moment lingered, sowing seeds of animosity while fostering a growing division in the ranks.

There was no fourth quarter rally cry heard in the blue camp that night. The feudin', fightin' Cowboys wasted away the remaining minutes of the game, and dropped a 21-10 decision to St. Louis, dragging them down into a first-place tie in the division with New York, and making a mess out of Landry's work schedule for the next few days.

Now the coach had a problem. A spat between two competitive veterans he could handle. But that the fight should be caught on television cameras and broadcast to every home in America, well, that was different. Especially in light of what the Thieves had done before the game. Especially since the local media was only too willing to stir up some locker room strife with their pens.

Landry first checked in with Schramm, to be sure he got the complete story. He shook his head upon hearing. Hats! Of all things. There were times when being a head coach wasn't all that it was cracked up to be. Shoot, being a camp counsellor was kids work compared to dealing with a locker-room full of grown men. Though it's rarely reported in mainstream publications, football players with six and seven-digit salaries tend to be more temperamental than teenagers. Nothing is ever simple.

The simplest part of the equation for Landry was in the realization that he couldn't sit around and expect the dust-up to be forgotten. There were too many pieces to this puzzle to expect a group of proud warriors to smoke the peace pipe so soon after an incident.

Had the friction centered around a handful of offensive players instead, Landry might have been able to step softly around the issue. But he couldn't afford to take a chance on the defense imploding down the stretch. If the defense fell apart, then the Cowboys might as well break camp right away and ride off into the sunset. Without the D, Dallas was dead.

Presumptions could be easily made by simply glancing at the numbers. At the midway point of the season, the Cowboys were on pace to break their franchise record of 60 sacks in one season, and were leading the league in interceptions and takeaways. Surely this was an elite unit.

Well, yes and no. How Landry was holding the defense together was a classic case of smoke and mirrors, not to mention supreme effort on the part of the players. One part of the unit could protect the other, but not necessarily complement the other. To make it all work required some ultra-aggressive tactics on the part of the Dallas head coach, and maybe a strip of duct-tape here and there.

Due in large part to poor draft classes in recent years, the Dallas defense, by 1985, was disjointed in its assembly. Though stacked with four No. 1 selections, the defensive line was getting a bit long in the tooth, and had lost a step overall in the pass-rush department. They were still solid in getting to the quarterback, but certainly no longer at an elite level. This, in turn, put pressure on a defensive backfield sorely lacking in speed. The longer the cornerbacks and safeties had to cover, the greater chance for the quarterback to find an open receiver downfield.

The linebackers complemented the front-four well in defending the run, but were often a liability in pass-coverage. More and more, Landry and defensive coordinator Ernie Stautner found cause to protect their linebackers on early downs by simply blitzing them into the backfield. Why put them in coverage and have them get burned when they could be putting a hit on the passer?

But the biggest adjustment, one which Landry had actually introduced a few years before, came on obvious passing downs when the Cowboys installed their 4-0 package. With four defensive linemen and zero linebackers on the field, it was a unit with a bit more pep in its step, able to better handle the wide-open offenses that were becoming more and more frequent in the NFL.

In the 4-0 defensive package, safety Bill Bates played in the position of the middle linebacker. Bates had the heart of a lion. He could run like a deer and hit like a truck. It was Bates, more than any other of the seven defensive backs on the field, who was responsible for corralling the runner in the event that the offense tried to catch the Cowboys unaware with a surprise run.

Stopping the run. That was always Landry's biggest concern when the 4-0 defense was in the game. If running backs ever got into the habit of slipping past Bates and into the defensive backfield with a full load of steam, Landry hated to think of the wear and tear it would take on his defensive backs. The Thieves were big when it came to taking the ball away, but actually undersized in a physical sense.

Dextor Clinkscale wasn't in the habit of laying the wood on a crossing receiver like Cliff Harris did so often for the Cowboys during the 1970s. Michael Downs wasn't the run-stuffing presence that Charlie Waters had been either. And durability was always an issue with Ron Fellows, who was known around the locker room as "Tweety," due to a pair of conspicuous stick-like legs.

Maybe he was old-fashioned, but it went against everything Landry had ever learned to be putting a defensive unit as small as the 4-0 onto the field. He preferred to have one, if not two, linebackers on the field at all times. With a linebacker in the middle, opponents were much more inclined to just drop back and pass on third-and-6 rather than try to sneak in a trap-draw against an undersized front. Dictating terms in this fashion only helped the defense anticipate the offense's next step. Like any good coach, Landry preferred that the advantage be with his team.

By 1985, Landry's version of dictating terms with the 4-0 on the field came through a relentless package of blitzes. Seven, eight, even nine men on occasion were to be sent crashing into the backfield. If the offense was going to pass against the blitz, then the quarterback had better be quick about it. If the coordinator wanted to call for a hand-off, the runner would have to break through a wall of in-rushing defenders.

It was a gambling style that could leave burn marks on a defense if they weren't careful. The Cowboys were careful, and still got burned on occasion. But it was working, not only because quarterbacks so often wilted under the pressure, but due to the savvy veterans working on the lonely island of pass defense.

Thurman and Clinkscale were like coaches on the field, their all-seeing eyes processing formations and shifts with the speed of a computer. Each had benefitted from years of sitting through Landry's detail-oriented film-sessions. They knew how to diagnose a play and anticipate a wide receiver's route before the ball was ever snapped, and were constantly preaching situational awareness during games.

This knowledge and understanding of the game helped to keep the younger members of the defense – especially in the secondary – from making critical errors in key situations. Thurman stayed on Easmon's case constantly, in order to make sure the rookie understood his job. Clinkscale stayed in the ear of Bates. But they never bothered to worry about Walls, who had led the league in interceptions in each of his first two seasons in the NFL. Walls could take care of himself.

With quarterbacks being constantly forced to release the ball quickly – or either endure the brutality of being buried alive in the backfield – the Thieves were able to spring one trap after another. Knowing they wouldn't have to cover for more than 2-3 seconds made life easy for them. The Thieves loved watching the quarterback's eyes and running to a spot the very moment they saw his arm start moving in a forward motion. It was a way of life whereby they could thrive, but they weren't the only ones.

Blitzing. It was the one routine whereby all the pieces of the defensive unit seemed to work in harmony together. The effectiveness of this high-risk formula would only last for as long as there remained harmony in the hearts of every member.

Tom Landry wasn't about to let the season waste away while players were squabbling. There was too much at stake. The Cowboys had come too far to be stopped by themselves. Landry got briefed of the situation from Schramm, and then called everyone together for a team meeting. Then he opened up the floor for testimony from the key participants. Then Landry sat back and listened in the manner of a stoic judge growing more enlightened by the moment.

Dennis Thurman didn't know what substance Randy White was under at that particular moment to jump him like that. Why, that "Manster" was a monster! Thurman and his Thieves were the victims of the whole show, innocent bystanders who were simply out for a good time. What's wrong with wearing a spiffy hat, anyway?

Not only was White mad at Thurman for the on-the-field run-in, but he was also ticked off about the gangster hats that appeared over local television waves. And, come to find out, White wasn't the only one who thought the Thieves had worn out their welcome. There were others in the locker room who had grown tired of the Thieves strutting around town and taking up so much newspaper space with snippy remarks. In the end,

White apologized for his exchange of unpleasantries with Thurman. But he refused to be budged from his stance on the hats. They were uncalled for, he believed, and completely unnecessary.

It wasn't a galvanizing moment by any stretch. Emotions were still too high for everyone to hug on the way out the door. But White's apology at least cleared the air somewhat, and allowed Landry to remind everyone once again of how important it was that everyone support each other, both during the week at practice and during games on Sunday. He reminded them of how far they had come since Buffalo. Yes, even nearly one year later, the word Buffalo still resonated with Cowboy players. Wouldn't it be a waste, Landry asked, to throw a season away over a few minor differences?

Landry broke up the meeting with that message ringing in their ears. On the following day, he called another team pow-wow to put out another grass-fire started by a newspaper article. Somebody, apparently, had been talking!

"It was a meeting-a-day kind of week for the coach," recalled Everson Walls. "There would be a new story in the papers that morning, and we'd have a meeting on it that afternoon. Coach Landry preached all week about us keeping it together and staying together."

When a reporter asked if the players held any team meetings of their own during the week, Landry answered with a stone face, "I hold the team meetings."

There was no longer any doubt about who the captain was manning the controls of the Cowboys' ship. Coach or players? The head coach had done enough in one week to diffuse that debate for a while. But as Landry boarded the team plane that Saturday for the flight to Washington, he was faced with the reality of the moment. There was more at stake against the Redskins than just first place in the NFC East. Far more. When the Cowboys walked onto the field on the morrow at RFK Stadium, the fate of the entire season would be hanging in the balance. Would the team stay the course and fight to stay on top of the leader board, or sink below the surface of relevancy to stay? Not even a studied veteran of NFL wars like Landry knew the answer to that question.

The end of Thurman's Thieves was soon to follow. Not long after the mayhem of that Monday night in St. Louis, a poster-style photo appeared in the Dallas Morning News of Thurman's Thieves dressed as steely-eyed gangsters. When Tex Schramm saw it, he knew something had to be done. This was about more than just hats. Why, Tom Landry appreciated a fashionable hat, now and again. But Landry was a noted gentleman, and certainly not to be confused with a mobster.

The Thieves had started out as football players who picked the pockets of unsuspecting quarterbacks on Sundays. They dressed like every other one of their Cowboy teammates. It was all in fun. But it was a different story when they started making the rounds on their promotional tour. Now, the Thieves had to be stopped.

Schramm had worked hard over the years to build the Cowboys' brand into something that Americans could relate to and be proud of. The Cowboys were supposed to be the good guys. They were supposed to be apple pie and vanilla ice cream all rolled into one big football flavor.

If pari-mutuel racing was still illegal in Texas, why would Schramm be comfortable with his players trying to relate to underworld leaders? It certainly wouldn't be good public relations, not with the Baptists still having a foothold in the state legislature.

The Thieves had to go. At Schramm's prodding, and with additional votes of support coming from certain corners of the locker room, Landry advised the Thieves to put an end to the tough-guy act and to stop wearing the gangster hats around the locker room. Landry faced initial resistance from Dennis Thurman and Everson Walls. They weren't about to put their hats on a shelf, not after paying $50 a piece.

Landry wasn't going to be talked out of it. An order was an order.

Reluctantly, the Thieves complied, though a tension over the issue remained among certain team members for the rest of the season.

CHAPTER 23

SHOW OF CHARACTER

"For the most part, this legendary grudge match had all the imagination of a brick...It was a good brisk scrubbing with a wire brush, to scrape away the worrisome slime that had collected of late."
Dallas Morning News **columnist Blackie Sherrod, after the Cowboys' 13-7 victory over Washington**

Brushed with the golden kiss of a fading autumn sun, RFK Stadium glistened in the manner of a royal football palace. Latecomers just passing through the gates could hear the echoes of clocks in nearby church towers striking a quarter past four, ringing out the end of another picture-perfect November Sunday in and around the District of Columbia.

Inside, brilliant rays of warm light still reached many constituents seated in the upper deck, while the soft glow of a cloudless evening added a touch of hallowed solemnity to the scene below, where stage and gallery were filled to the brim with personages from every walk of life – Cowboys, Redskins, fans and, yes, even nobility.

Seven years after Jimmy Carter became the first United States president to attend a Dallas-Washington game, Prince Charles and Princess Diana had made the trip over to see what all the fuss was about. Their shared experience – if anything else – was certainly educational.

There is no passion so pronounced, no fury so frightening as a high-stakes matchup between the Cowboys and Redskins at RFK. These weren't the laid-back lemonade-sipping gentry of Wimbledon surrounding them that Charles and Diana were accustomed to. The folks of D.C. were out of their seats from the opening kickoff, beer in hand, yelling for Cowboy blood on every play.

The aroma of payback hung thick in the air, as tangent and flavorful as the autumn breeze. America's Team was paying their annual visit to America's capitol, and sweet revenge was set in action to the tune of a gloriously-conceived opening march.

Tom Landry's greatest fear was coming to pass before his very eyes. After a week of stomping out internal grassfires back in Dallas, Landry's team had come out a step slow against their archrivals, a disconcerting fact that had nothing to do with the Giants' victory over the Rams earlier that afternoon. This wasn't about keeping pace so much as it was keeping heart.

Landry had warned his players during the week on numerous occasions of how dangerous the Redskins could be if afforded an early lead, while also acknowledging his own uncertainty about the fragile state of the Cowboys' own psyche. If Washington jumped out to a lead in the first quarter, Landry didn't know for sure if his team had enough chemistry and mutual resolve to fight back. Falling behind early on this day could very easily be the death knell of the 1985 Cowboys.

The Washington offense was driving down the field, their fans gleefully certain of the game's first blood being Cowboy blue. Joe Theismann, nine weeks after tossing five interceptions against these same Cowboys, looked a picture of calm precision, knifing his way through Landry's defense with short, quick throws and well-timed handoffs. Landry, in the midst of game

No. 400 on a Dallas sideline, gazed across the field while squinting his eyes, a customary pose of his when focusing intently. The moment of ruin was imminent. Dusk was falling in D.C., the Cowboys fading with the setting sun.

But in the game of football, fate is often guilty of having no pulse. Like a god of hidden dimensions, it simply exists, waiting to embrace and swallow its prey. It is not convenient to anticipate, but only accept.

Theismann rolled out of the pocket to his right on third-down. It was a strategy that had given the Cowboys fits over the years, wreaking havoc on the Flex's rigidly-constructed pass-rush. But Ernie Stautner was prepared for it this time, having ordered safety Michael Downs to leave his outfield post and blitz off the edge. Theismann was scrambling with the intent of gaining a step on the defense, while making himself an easy target for the crashing figure of Downs in the process.

Theismann's eyes got big when he saw Art Monk running free in the end-zone. He cocked his arm and threw the ball just as Downs leaped at him with arms outstretched.

"Just as I let the ball go," said Theismann, "I got my hand hit, and the ball didn't have as much on it as I wanted it to…"

Back into the picture frame came Ron Fellows, who had been given back his starting cornerback job opposite Everson Walls earlier in the week after Victor Scott's struggles in St. Louis. Fellows was still limping around on a bum knee suffered in the opening-night game versus Washington, pain shooting though it whenever he made a cut or attempted to slow down. But he insisted to coaches that he was up for the challenge.

Monk had outraced Fellows across the field on this play, but the efforts of Downs made it possible for him to catch up. Monk slowed and reached behind him in adjustment to the sputtering pass, but not in time to prevent Fellows from closing the gap and making the interception in the corner of the end-zone. Fellows held the ball up for all to see, before being mobbed by other members of Thurman's Thieves, ecstatic at his good fortune. Fellows had turned the Redskins away with his interception, providing the Cowboys the week's first piece of good news in the process. In that moment a great weight was lifted from the shoulders of the entire Dallas defense, mutual satisfaction in picking the pocket of the Redskins, allowing the unit to collectively distance themselves from the tumultuous days behind them.

With Theismann fuming over on the Washington bench, Danny White came out throwing bombs, connecting with Tony Hill running down the numbers for a 42-yard gain. An 11-play drive ended early in the second frame when Rafel Septien booted the Cowboys to a 3-0 lead with a 40-yard field-goal.

Septien appeared to have extended the margin later in the quarter with a successful kick from 45 yards away, but an alignment infraction on tackle Phil Pozderac wiped the points off the board and backed the offense up five yards. According to referee Pat Hagerty, the 6-foot-8-inch, 290-pound Pozderac was guilty of lining up too far off the line of scrimmage, a call that CBS commentator John Madden dared to question, albeit humorously. Said Madden, speaking of Pozderac: "He's so big he can be on the line and in the backfield at the same time."

Though Septien informed his head coach that he was feeling a tightness in his lower back and legs that he thought would prevent him from making the longer kick, Landry told him to go ahead and try anyway. In a game like this was shaping up to be, points were going to be at a premium. Septien's re-try from 50 yards was straight enough, but fell just short of the crossbar. A loud cheer went up from the RFK crowd, their hearts and hopes restored at the sight of the Cowboys' misfortune.

The two teams played on into the night, their vision brightened, their anxiety heightened by the playoff race set before them. Defense continued to dominate the occasion on the picturesque green grass, as both teams continued to shoot themselves in the foot with penalties. During the first two quarters of play, the Redskins and Cowboys combined for 11 penalties, a total that did not include the many infractions that were disallowed.

Through nine weeks of the season, the Redskins ranked second in the NFL in time-of-possession, holding the ball for over 32 minutes per game. But against the Cowboys, they couldn't stay on the field.

Fellows continued to have a field day against Monk, turning away two passes from Theismann that would have likely resulted in Redskin touchdowns. When Fellows wasn't getting his hands on the ball, his Cowboy compadres along the defensive line were. Ed "Too Tall" Jones was all of that on Washington's third possession, using his 6-foot-9-inch frame to knock down two passes.

The play on which Randy White swatted another Thiesmann heave to the sod on the following drive earned more than a few chuckles in the film-room on Tuesday. With Dallas still clinging to a 3-0 lead, the Redskins had marched across the midfield stripe. On fourth-and-3 from the 37-yard line, Washington head coach Joe Gibbs told his offense to stay on the field and try to pick up the first-down.

Linebackers Eugene Lockhart and Jeff Rohrer came off the field, as the Cowboys sent their 4-0 defensive package into the game. Over on the sideline, defensive tackle Don Smerek was unaware of the substitution.

Since coming back off the injured list a couple of weeks before, Smerek had become a critical part of the Cowboys' defensive line rotation. In his first game back, Smerek had two sacks against the Falcons, officially bumping rookie Kevin Brooks down the depth chart.

It wasn't until the Washington offense was approaching the ball that Smerek was made aware that he was supposed to be in the game. Grabbing his helmet, Smerek raced onto the field. With Theismann already barking out signals, Smerek ran smack into Victor Scott, tripping himself in the process while nearly giving his teammate a heart attack.

"It scared the living daylights out of me," smiled Scott. "I thought somebody threw something out of the stands."

Smerek got up just in time to see Randy White save the day by rejecting the fourth-down pass at the line of scrimmage. But in turning back to the Dallas sideline, Smerek realized that his own contributions had not gone unnoticed.

"Everybody was laughing at me," recalled Smerek.

Danny White ended the bitter standoff when he burned Washington's defensive backfield with a pair of third-quarter gems from his right hand. On the Cowboys' first drive after the halftime break, White found Tony Hill yet again, this time for 33 yards down the right sideline. White released the pass just before being decked in the backfield by fearless cornerback Darrell Green. The eventual payoff for this shot in the chops was a 36-yard trey from Septien.

The next time out, White was thinking big again. Walking into the huddle, he called the play out for the rest of the offense. 63 A Take Off. Tony Dorsett, the "A" receiver in the pattern, turned straight upfield with a burst of speed, as he had done so successfully a few weeks before versus Pittsburgh. Linebacker Monte Coleman turned to run with him, but came up lame with a pulled hamstring. Dorsett was all alone in the secondary when White's pass caught up to him at the 16-yard line, and was free to trot across the goal-line for touchdown No. 76 of his career, tying the franchise record held by Bob Hayes.

"We had tried the play early in the game," said Dorsett, "and I beat the guy, but I was in motion so it wouldn't have counted even if Danny had thrown to me. But Coach Landry knows when to call certain things and the time was right for it when he called it again."

Standing in the way of what would certainly have been a season-changing comeback for the Redskins was Jim Jeffcoat. Perhaps it is because players find themselves so easily bored by their profession that so many seek to add spice and meaning to their existence with a friendly little bet. Jim Jeffcoat, perhaps striving to live up to the standard set by his defensive end predecessor Harvey Martin, made just such a bet before the beginning of the 1985 regular season.

For years Ed "Too Tall" Jones had enjoyed a running bet with Martin over which one would accumulate the most quarterback sacks during the season. The wager was said to involve something small, a six-pack of adult beverages, or something like that. When Martin retired after the 1983 season, Jones went an entire season without a similar challenge to provide additional motivation on the field.

But before the Cowboys kicked off the season back in September, Jones got a surprise when Jeffcoat, a third-year player who had been steadily improving, approached him about continuing the tradition.

"Jim mentioned to me, 'Hey, we ought to make a little bet, and the loser will take the winner to the restaurant of his choice.' I said, 'Fine,'" said Jones.

If the early-season returns were any indication, Jeffcoat may have bitten off more than he could chew by challenging an established All-Pro such as Too Tall. The challenge wasn't a challenge at all. After nine weeks, Jones was leading the sack race by what appeared to be an insurmountable margin – 9 to 1 ½. By this time, the bet was all but forgotten, Jones refusing to bring it up out of fear that he would embarrass Jeffcoat. Only a record-setting performance from Jeffcoat that day in Washington could bring the wager to life again.

At this point in his young career, Jeffcoat was a good player who faced constant criticism from Cowboy fans for being something less than the Superman that Martin had been for a decade. Martin retired as the Cowboys' all-time leader in sacks and could write a novel on the subject. The only book that fans could ever envision Jeffcoat writing would tend toward the mundane.

Cowboy coaches liked Jeffcoat because he was good in run defense and his effort on Sundays was more consistent than most. Landry was of the belief that the talent was there and that, in due time, the big plays would find Jeffcoat. Meanwhile, the fans traded yarns in their seats about the bygone days of the Superman named Harvey.

On a cloudless night at RFK all of Jeffcoat's bottled-up potential came bursting out, pouring over the Redskins' comeback bid like salt on an open wound. By this point in his career, Theismann knew better than to underestimate the Thurmans and Too Talls and Walls' on the Dallas defense. Randy White was someone to be feared too, not to mention that guy named Fellows, who was proving himself especially pesky on this particular occasion. But Jeffcoat was one of the last players that Theismann would have expected to ruin his day.

Jeffcoat's first sack of the game came in the second quarter, with Jones resting on the sideline and Kevin Brooks in his spot. Jones returned a few plays later after Brooks went off the field limping with a quadriceps strain. Jeffcoat, figuratively speaking, went back into hiding.

Not until the third quarter did he resurface, falling on top of Theismann again after the quarterback had tripped over his own lineman in the backfield, ending Washington's first drive of the frame. A third-down effort the next time out ended with Jim crushing Joe again, the play ending in a takedown due to exemplary coverage by the Dallas defensive backs downfield that forced Theismann to hold the ball long enough for Jeffcoat to close in.

Washington's ensuing drive ended when Walls intercepted a deep pass for Gary Clark down the right sideline at the Dallas 36-yard line. The same bloodthirsty fans who verbally assaulted the Cowboys for three quarters then suddenly turned on Theismann, peppering the flustered veteran with a heartless shower of boos for much of the final period.

Theismann knew better than to begin doubting himself, though he certainly had cause to. Theismann was the captain and leader of a Washington attack that had underperformed from the season's outset. Only two years after setting an NFL record for most points scored in a season, the Redskins were scum-sucking bad. At the halfway mark of the 1985 season, Washington had scored 114 points, ahead of only a struggling Buffalo team. A breakout performance in a 44-10 conquest of Atlanta in Week 9 had given the team hope that they were hitting their stride in time for the stretch run.

But Dallas was putting that notion authoritatively to rest, pounding the Redskins on their own home field. Nobody felt the brunt of this pounding more acutely than did Theismann. In seven quarters this season against the Cowboys, he had tossed an equal amount of interceptions.

But this was no time for hanging heads. If the Redskins were to keep their heads above water in the NFC East race, they had to rally from 13 points down to beat Dallas. The only way that would happen was if Theismann kept flinging it downfield. When you stopped and thought about it, circumstances weren't as bad as they may have seemed for Joe. Who said fans were bastions of intelligence anyway? The hecklers could crow until midnight, but at least they couldn't sing "Happy Birthday" to him this time.

With notes of local derision burning his ears, Theismann trotted back into the huddle a few minutes later and ignited a scoring drive to close the gap. In the closing moments of the third quarter, he landed a 44-yard bomb in the arms of Monk that moved the ball to the Dallas 23. Two plays after, his touchdown pass of 11 yards to Clark moved the Redskins to within 13-7.

With less than seven minutes remaining on the game-clock, Washington gambled on a fourth-and-one from its own 20-yard line and came up with a first down that briefly provided new life. Yet another Jeffcoat sack put an end to that threat.

The Redskins got their hands on the ball for one final crack at a comeback with 39 seconds left. Theismann, still slinging it, hit Monk for a gain of 26 yards to the Dallas 48-yard line. But then Jeffcoat and his familiar No. 77 jersey came roaring around the end again, trapping Theismann all the way back at the 37 for his record-setting fifth sack of the night.

After that, it was only a matter of piling on for the Cowboys. Randy White broke through on the next play and got a sack for himself. And then, with the final desperation fling that time permitted, Theismann was intercepted by Walls yet again. Theismann trudged off the field in his grass-stained sweat-soaked jersey, looking very much like a figure of defeat, his shoulders slumped and his eyes downcast, as if in resignation to the relentless powers of the Cowboy defense.

And while Jeffcoat would certainly get plenty of praise at a later date - being named the NFC Defensive Player of the Week - the talk in the victorious Dallas locker room afterwards focused on the success of the team itself.

"Best effort, best attitude, best enthusiasm of the season," raved Randy White of the defense. "In fact, the best in several seasons."

Landry was quick during his postgame briefing to deflect questions centering on the past week's drama, instead highlighting the lessons learned during the past three hours on the football field. The Cowboys, Landry insisted, weren't dead just yet. Not in the standings, and certainly not in the locker room.

Said Landry: "If you don't have enough character to come out of adversity – any kind of adversity – then you're not the kind of team that should even consider itself capable of playing for a championship."

Then, as the final footnote to what was a critical gut-check victory in the shadow of Capitol Hill, Landry added, "We must have character."

The Cowboys had avoided the pits of self-destruction with a show of character that would be talked about on the streets of Washington during the coming months. The only discussion in Dallas pertained to the uncertain ability of Tom Landry's most confusing football team. The Cowboys were good enough to beat Washington at RFK. But were they good enough to come back home and topple over the unbeaten Bears? That was a question not only on the minds of fans in Dallas, but of those all across the sports-loving nation of America.

CHAPTER 24

THE GAME OF THE YEAR

"Big is good again."
John Madden, *CBS Sports*

"It's only one game, but it felt like a lot more."
**Defensive tackle John Dutton after the Cowboys'
blowout loss to Chicago**

It has been argued - oftentimes behind closed doors - that the very first Weight Watchers club in America originated from within the sports realm, where scouts and general managers for many decades took up the role of Goldilocks, scouring the countryside for that perfect athlete whose physique was not too thin and not too plump, but just right. Wherever your career traveled, whichever sport you happened to choose, there were some unwritten rules that seemed to apply to all. Aspirants with ribs showing were sent home. Those who were overweight rarely received even a second glance.

The increased role of weight-lifting during the 1970s helped to change some of these demographics within the pro football industry, as players slowly but surely got bigger and bigger and bigger still. So by the mid-1980s, the traditional belt restraining the fat athlete from NFL employment was set to burst. And burst it finally did.

Other leagues, it must be admitted, were still dealing with the same age-old problems at the time in the same careless fashion. Rather than marvel at the abilities of Washington Bullets rookie Manute Bol, it was all that Philadelphia 76ers general manager Pat Williams could do from laughing at the sight of the 7-foot-7-inch basketball phenom. "He looks like he went to the blood bank and forgot to say when," said Williams.

Baseball's Atlanta Braves had the opposite problem. Their pitcher, 270-pound Terry Forster, apparently didn't know what a blood bank was, prompting TV talk show host David Letterman to brand him a "fat tub of goo." Weary at being a public spectacle, Forster finished the season and immediately reported to a lifestyle center in California for two weeks of diet and fitness.

While other sports were still watching waistlines with traditional fervor, American football fans were wrapping their arms around the game's first teddy bear. William Perry was a 320-pound rookie defensive tackle out of Clemson, so big for an unbeaten Chicago team that he was referred to as "The Refrigerator," yet athletic enough to quickly morph into an unstoppable scoring machine.

This was a miracle in more ways than one. Few, if any, on the Chicago coaching staff would have given him much of a chance back in August of becoming an NFL phenomenon so quickly, if ever. An All-American while in college, Perry made a name for himself during his first summer in the NFL by allowing a holdout over contract terms to spill over into training camp. His first day back on the practice field then rendered him out of breath and out of shape, and not to mention a can't miss target for the ire of his outspoken defensive coordinator.

It had been rumored that Buddy Ryan was less than thrilled when head coach Mike Ditka selected Perry with Chicago's first-round selection during April's draft. The sight of Perry huffing and puffing through a limited portion of practice proved to be enough to provoke a highly publicized rant from Ryan, thus turning rumor into reality.

"He's a wasted draft pick, just going on what I saw...," Ryan told a group of reporters, before trying to soften his stance somewhat. "I don't know if he's a wasted draft pick or not, but he's not in any shape and can't do anything."

Perry had missed the afternoon practice that day after suffering from dehydration caused by losing 13 pounds during the morning practice. Not that "Iron Mike" was feeling any compassion towards him.

"That's what two weeks of putzing around has done," said Ditka matter-of-factly. "When a guy's not as good a football player as he can be, he can blame himself and his agent."

A diet of fish, vegetables, and soup helped Perry to slim down and get into playing shape, but still the Bears brought him along slowly to begin the regular season. By the time Perry was just starting to fit in along the defensive line, Ditka made "The Refrigerator" a can't-miss attraction by inserting him into the offensive backfield.

At Candlestick Park in Week 6, Perry carried twice for four yards, and also paved the way for a short Walter Payton touchdown run with a devastating lead-block. In his postgame comments, Ditka took exception to the notion that he was merely paying the 49ers back for using the exact same ploy to rub it in during the closing moments of January's NFC Championship Game, and made it quite clear that a backfield lummox was likely to be a regular feature of Chicago's ground-and-pound offense. To his credit, Ditka was as good as his word.

Against Green Bay the following week, Perry delighted the Soldier Field crowd by smashing his way across the goal-line with a second-quarter touchdown that put Chicago ahead to stay. Two weeks later, he surprised the Packers again, this time with a 4-yard touchdown reception in a 16-10 Bears victory.

Bears fans were predictably impressed by this show of brute force around the goal-line, and equally entertained by the sight of one so large feigning athleticism with such success. *Whoever heard of a 320-pound touchdown machine with nimble feet and soft hands?* The fact that the Bears continued to pile up one lopsided win on top of another enabled the rest of the nation to follow the fun regularly on television.

And so the "Blubber Formation" (as some members of the press dubbed it) was officially born, giving a big guy from the Windy City an unforeseen status as a superstar. Inadvertently, it also posed as one of Tom Landry's greatest coaching challenges. For, in addition to slowing down a 10-0 Bears squad on Sunday at Texas Stadium, Landry would be faced with the challenge of gearing up his Flex defense to stop the first runaway Fridge in NFL history.

The Flex or the Fridge? Somewhere in Vegas, a bookie was posing just that question.

It didn't come easy for Terry O'Neil to admit a mistake on his part. Perhaps that is the natural way of a young man who rises so quickly up the corporate ladder that his feet don't have time to catch up to the rest of his body.

By age 35, O'Neil was an established force in the sports television industry, having already been fired by the hierarchy of *ABC's Monday Night Football* for arguing with Howard Cosell, and had spent the past four seasons as executive producer of the *NFL on CBS*. One of his primary responsibilities in this capacity was determining which games would be broadcast to each part of the country. His insistence on feeding the nation a heavy dose of Cowboys games in the more attractive late-afternoon time slot had been a key reason why O'Neil's team continued to beat out rival NBC in their annual ratings wars.

"When in doubt," O'Neil said soon after joining CBS, "give them the Cowboys."

But in the summer of 1985, Terry and a handful of executives deemed it prudent to place more emphasis on the San Francisco 49ers, a team which had gone 18-1 the previous season and won the Super Bowl. The Cowboys, based upon their lackluster 9-7 record from 1984 and the numerous preseason predictions from football magazine publications of an imminent slide into mediocrity, were certainly a team in decline.

It was this philosophy which opened the door for the Peacock Network to score a couple of early-season victories. After Dallas infused their far-reaching fan base with an upset of Washington on Monday night in Week 1, NBC executives sensed an opportunity to deliver an effective counterattack. For its Week 3 broadcast of the Dallas-Cleveland game at Texas Stadium (which, to many experts, looked like a complete dud before the season began), NBC decided to send their No. 1 crew of Dick Enberg and Merlin Olsen to Irving and show it to the majority of their viewing audience from the noon slot. The 49ers-Raiders game later in the day on CBS was also a national telecast, but NBC earned the higher rating.

Three weeks later on Oct. 13, NBC's No. 1 team was back in north Texas again to call the Dallas-Pittsburgh contest at noon to seventy-five percent of the nation. Later that afternoon, CBS sent the Chicago-San Francisco game to eighty-percent of American viewers yet, once again, NBC posted the bigger ratings number.

It was this second whipping at the hands of Peacock Productions that convinced O'Neil to place less of an emphasis on 49ers games, and give the couch potatoes at home more of what they wanted: the Cowboys and the Bears. An unblemished record and the wild popularity of The Refrigerator had turned the rough-and-tumble Bears into the league's darlings in 1985.

Back-to-back matchups in early November against Green Bay and Detroit were broadcast to more than half the country, and viewers gobbled it right up. And by showing forty-five percent of Americans a seemingly lackluster Atlanta-Dallas game in Week 8, CBS was able to win the ratings battle for that weekend.

So it happened that when O'Neil sat at his desk on the morning of Monday, November 11 and pondered the slate of weekend games ahead, he found more cause to grin than debate. For sitting in his company's lap was a once-in-a-decade gift from the football gods, a high-stakes clash between conference titans that was sure to have the nation buzzing long before kickoff. 10-0 Chicago at 7-3 Dallas. The new darlings from the north versus the traditional southern sweethearts. This was as big for football fans as it was easy for television executives.

O'Neil never hesitated in making his next big decision, which was to send Pat Summerall, John Madden, and the rest of CBS' golden-armored cavalry down to famed Texas Stadium to broadcast the NFC's marquee matchup of the year to ninety-percent of the country.

O'Neil's payoff? Only the highest-rated game in the history of the network.

O'Neil's actions from a New York desk unleashed a swarm of sports writers onto Texas soil, all of whom spent the next few days beating down the door of Cowboys public relations director Doug Todd in an effort to get credentialed for Sunday's big game. Todd, who admitted near the end of the long week that the buildup to Dallas-Chicago felt like that of a playoff game, issued 730 media passes before the Friday deadline, and had to turn down several others.

Imagine the delight for so large a contingent of reporters to then discover that not only was this a meeting of NFC behemoths, but a showdown between two teams that shared a mutual dislike for the other. After a Monday night pre-season contest in late August between the Cowboys and Bears that was more akin to a brawl than a game, the NFL fined 14 different players who were involved in altercations on the field. Randy White was docked $1,500 for grabbing the helmet off the head of Chicago tackle Keith Van Horne and then whopping Mark Bortz with it. Jim Jeffcoat was fined $750 for throwing a punch, while John Dutton found himself lighter in the pocket by $400. In addition, eleven other players (six from Chicago and five from Dallas) were fined $300 each for participating in scrums. So what should we expect from a game with so much meaning attached?

"This thing could blow up in the first quarter," Cowboys linebacker Jeff Rohrer said on Wednesday.

"Thank you, Jeff," wrote Randy Galloway in the Dallas Morning News, "for not defusing the hype over Sunday's game."

Cowboy players were quick to categorize the 1985 squad as a blue-collar group that would scrap in the ditch with even the meanest of opponents, a far cry from years past when they so often meekly accepted the public verdict which labeled them a finesse team. These Cowboys, they proudly insisted, were of an old-school temperament, one prone to hit first and ask questions later, consequences notwithstanding. Or something like that.

Said Randy White: "Our attitude this season has been to go out and play good, hard football, and not to take any crap off anyone. That's what we'll do again Sunday, but this time I don't plan on getting kicked out in the first quarter."

Tom Landry, on the other hand, seemed far less concerned with what went down between the two clubs earlier in the summer, even brushing it off as a case of ironic timing. "We'd just come in (from California) after scrimmaging the Raiders two or three times,' said Landry. "Scrimmage them enough and you take on their temperament."

Landry's little press conference discussion certainly didn't encourage fisticuffs from his players during the rematch. He didn't necessarily discourage it either. But why fight at all? The irony of trying to use a bare fist to inflict punishment upon a caged face was not lost upon the media. The Cowboys may have convinced themselves they were as courageous and unforgiving as a bucket of roofing nails, but they had convinced none of the many attentive reporters milling around their new Valley Ranch training complex that they possessed anything approaching supreme intelligence.

" [A football fistfight] has about as much logic, say, as seeing how many miles you can run in shoes two sizes small," wrote Blackie Sherrod. "…These hulks are so armored, you couldn't hurt one with a softball bat. You might as well attack a tank with a broomweed."

This truth remained applicable for retaliatory gestures as well, a fact which was not lost upon Chicago's own head coach.

"If a guy hits you, you can't hurt him anyway, so why hit him back?" said Mike Ditka. "You're only going to get caught. It's kind of silly. We should be smarter than that. They should, too."

In the end, after all of the hubbub and the hype, the questions and half-answers, the kickoff for this unanimously acclaimed Game of The Year finally came and went, revealing a scene of undeniable clarity relating to the identity of the National Football Conference's supreme team. After four quarters of play, there was no longer room for even the slightest of doubts as to which was the toughest or the smartest. The kings of the conference – and likely the entire league – were not Cowboys. Indeed, they were not Bears either, but rather monsters of a rare breed, who in just three short hours enacted a one-sided beat-down that left fans and writers shaking their collective heads at such impartial thoroughness.

A soft pealing of church bells broke through the silence of a gray Sunday morning in north Texas, serving as a reminder to locals that God and game-time were finally near. Harmonizing with the echoes of past Cowboy conquests, it sounded as a comforting chorus to the hearts of provincial fans whose faith in the legacy and tradition of their beloved franchise had remained steadfast throughout a long week of intensive debate, when the surrounding nation wore the talking points to shreds. Cowboys or Bears? Landry or Ditka? The Flex or the Fridge? The 4-0 or the 46? Seemingly, it was too close to call. Even Vegas, after contemplating the many intricacies and storylines of this heavyweight matchup, couldn't choose a favorite between the Bears and Cowboys, making the game a pick 'em for bettors.

In Dallas, those familiar with the many innovative wonders of Tom Landry remained confident that the home team was up to the challenge against the unbeaten Bears. But there was more than just Bears on the minds of locals. They were also thinking Super Bowl.

Loyalists with rose-colored glasses rubbed their hands together gleefully while peering at the upcoming schedule, anticipating not only a victory over the behemoth of the league, but also a launching point going into the postseason. The noon kickoff at Texas Stadium against Chicago was the first of three consecutive home games for the Cowboys.

Alright fellas, if Dallas wins today and then takes care of business against Philadelphia next Sunday, they'll have the Cardinals on the following Thursday. Hey, Charlie, what would that make them? 10-3? You don't say. And we know how good the Cowboys are in December, don't we? How much are playoff tickets going for these days...?

Steeped in such optimistic delusion, the pom-pom waving crowd of Cowboy supporters settled into their seats. The opening stanza seduced them even further into believing their team was set to deliver a knockout blow to the big, bad bullies of the North.

On his first carry of the game, Tony Dorsett broke through a hole on the left side and scampered for 22 yards, going out of bounds at the Chicago 48-yard line. A few moments later, Danny White completed a pass to Tony Hill for a gain of 13 yards. The Cowboys were rolling.

On the very next play, White took a deep drop and dropped a deep bomb within reach of Hill at the goal-line. But Hill short-armed the ball, and the pass fell incomplete. White clapped his hands together in frustration. The drive stalled.

The Cowboys continued to peck away at the Chicago defense. White found Mike Renfro for a gain of 19 yards on the next series. Later, White beat the blitz with a nifty pass to Cosbie for 13 more. Renfro then had the ball poked out of his hands by Mike Richardson, and Chicago was there to pounce on the loose ball at the Dallas 45-yard line.

But the Cowboy defense bowed their backs once again, forcing the fourth Bears punt in as many series'. Maury Buford's high, spiraling kick that was downed at the 2-yard line drew a smattering applause from an appreciative crowd. The first quarter was winding down. The two teams were trading body blows in a scoreless tie. This was good fun, a classic chess-match between two evenly matched teams.

And then the monsters showed up, wiping the board clean of all pieces and rewriting the rules of play. Out the door went the fancy strategy and all the trimmings of traditional football etiquette. These monsters had no interest in waging that age-old tussle for field-position any longer. They wanted the ball, and they wanted blood, and didn't care how many Cowboy corpses they had to leave behind them to get it.

Having toyed with the Cowboys for nearly a full quarter, the Bears decided they needed to make up for lost time. So they swung a collective fist, and sent the hopes and dreams of what was supposed to be an upset Sunday at Texas Stadium flying back down the tunnel of fantasy. They had allowed the Cowboys to play with them this long. But the fun was over.

From his left defensive end position, Dan Hampton smelled a quick pass coming the moment he saw White begin to drop-back from under center. And like any other experienced Bear out there, Hampton had learned to trust his smeller. He tossed Cowboys' tackle Jim Cooper to the side, and then jumped as high as his 270-pound frame would allow, deflecting the ball high into the air.

Hampton initially feared that he had knocked it out of the end-zone. But when he turned around, he saw fellow Bear linemen Richard Dent and Steve McMichael near the 1-yard line preparing as if to field a punt. The ball landed in the arms of Dent, and he crashed over the goal-line to put Chicago ahead 7-0.

"We knew we had them then," said Hampton. "The Cowboys have a complex offensive scheme, and that usually worries a defense. But it was obvious that they became so worried about our defense because we were mixing some things up that they couldn't decipher."

Al Davis' Raiders were often accused of playing dirty, but they never packed the collective punch that this bunch from Chicago did. A wrecking crew defense that left opponents bruised and bludgeoned in its wake, the Bears came from all sides in a relentless pursuit of life, limb, and leather. For these Bears, toughness was not only a speaking point during the week, but a way of life on weekends. For opponents, fear was an omnipresent reality, injury but a moment away.

The Windy City's juggernaut of football judgment unleashed all its fury, enclosing White and the Cowboys in an unshakeable grip of doom. With the first play after the defensive score, White had the pocket collapse around him and was taken down by Dent for a sack. On second-down, White bobbled the snap, allowing blitzing linebacker Otis Wilson to converge for another sack. On third-down, it was all the quarterback could do to avoid being trapped in the end-zone for a safety, his short dump-off pass to Timmy Newsome setting up another Dallas punt.

White didn't know it at the time, but he had gotten off easy. But his good luck would not hold out for much longer. Wilson caught up to White in a big way on the next series, pile-driving him into the green threadbare carpet on the floor of the stadium. White was down for the count and, after laying on his back looking up through the hole in the roof for a couple of minutes, he was helped to the bench area where doctors applied a bag of ice to his neck. White was diagnosed with a minor concussion.

Into the game came Gary Hogeboom, who fared even worse than his predecessor. Hogeboom's second pass attempt, administered under the influence of the fast-closing figure of Wilson in the backfield, was intercepted by Richardson and returned 36 yards for a Chicago touchdown. His next pass, a downfield missile toward Hill, landed in the arms of cornerback Leslie Frazier.

A diversion from the ungodly beat-down came about later in the second quarter with Chicago looking to extend their 17-0 advantage. Before a first-and-goal play from the 2-yard line, William Perry made his first appearance of the game as an offensive player. With the crowd cheering the big man on, Perry came bouncing out of the huddle and got down in a stance in the backfield. Then, realizing he hadn't lined up in the correct formation, he moved to another spot. Then another. Chicago quarterback Steve Fuller had to call timeout.

"Well, the Bears got The Refrigerator delivered, but they don't seem to know which wall to put him on," said John Madden on the CBS broadcast.

Out of the timeout, Perry got aligned properly and received the ball from Fuller on a handoff. The Refrigerator trundled forward, gaining momentum, aiming to put a dent in the backside of his right guard. Mike Hegman broke through the line in time to see Perry barreling straight at him. But Hegman, a ten-year veteran at linebacker, was also a noted professor of football physics. He didn't just stand there like a blinded deer. From long study and much brutal testing of the theory, Hegman had arrived at the conclusion that the only way to tackle a runaway Refrigerator was to take the wheels out from under him. And that's what Hegman did, tripping Perry and stopping him just short of the goal-line. Perry stayed on the field for the second-down play, but was used merely as an oversized decoy. Fuller's quarterback-sneak did the trick, putting the Bears up 24-0.

Danny White re-entered the action at the beginning of the third quarter, drawing a hearty round of applause from fans weary of Hogeboom's giving ways. His comeback proved to be short-lived, thanks to another blow from the helmet of Wilson that sent White to the locker room for good with a jammed neck, joining tight end Doug Cosbie, who had taken himself out of the game earlier with a neck injury.

"We said when we left after the preseason game, that they'd better have that little cart gassed up to carry the people off," Hampton told Paul Zimmerman of *Sports Illustrated*.

"We came into the game with three keys," said safety Gary Fencik. "One, take Dorsett out of the offense early. We did it. Two, contain tight end Doug Cosbie and we did that. Three was White, and he got knocked out."

Hogeboom came back into the game, only to hear more boos from the fans and take more of the same pounding from the Bears' defense. For the quarterback and the entire team, the final whistle couldn't come soon enough.

In the locker room, after completing just 6-of-20 passes for 60 yards, Hogeboom was asked if this had been the greatest defense he had ever faced. "Let me put it this way," he said. "This is the worst I've ever been beaten in my life."

A day that started with such high hopes ended in record-setting dismay for the Cowboys, the 44-0 final marking the most lopsided loss in franchise history, and was the first time in fifteen years that Dallas had been shutout. Embarrassed, anyone?

"Sure, I'm embarrassed," said Tex Schramm. "When you've got a good football team and you lose like this before a big crowd and in a crucial game, it tests your pride.

"You don't like to have to talk about negative milestones, but that is what we have with this defeat. It's the worst defeat we've ever suffered, and that's statistically. When that happens, it's very embarrassing for a mature football team. I'd be real disappointed if the players didn't feel that way."

After 44-0, Landry didn't have time to waste on any feelings. He was already looking ahead to the next game and expected the others in the Dallas clubhouse to follow his lead.

Said Landry: "It's what we do from now on that counts."

Landry didn't have to prod his team very hard to move on from it. Because by looking ahead to the next game against Philadelphia, the bruised and battered Cowboys were able to put the beat-down at the hands of the Bears behind them. For the hosts from Dallas, the Game of the Year had become a game to forget.

CHAPTER 25

THE PERFECT REBOUND

"We need a productive Tony Hill probably more than any one guy on the team."
Everson Walls

"I don't think I've seen Danny [White] throw the ball this well since he's been our starter. His accuracy sometimes amazes me."
Tom Landry after his QB tossed four touchdowns in a Thanksgiving Day victory over St. Louis

Dallas was a happening place in those days, a dull moment hardly to be had. For twenty-five years, the Cowboys had thrived in this environment, growing right along with a town harboring a strong addiction to the national spotlight, transforming from an expansion doormat of roster re-treads into a star-studded franchise whose every move – whether on the field or off – was a noteworthy occurrence.

There had been a hope somewhere in the back of Tom Landry's mind that, by uprooting and moving their team headquarters to the suburbs of Valley Ranch in the summer of 1985, the team would get away from some of the big-city drama that followed them everywhere. Landry, you see, was an old-fashioned soul who liked a bit of peace and quiet from time to time, and could do without the daily attention the Cowboys received from reporters.

Landry needed only a short time at the Cowboys' spiffy new training facility to see that nothing had changed very much. The Cowboys were – and seemingly always would be – the coolest team and the hottest scoop in town. The spotlight had not diminished in any way. If anything, it had only grown.

It might have helped matters had the strange and unexpected stopped occurring every other week. But wherever the Cowboys were, there was always something odd going on. Like in early October, when a jet in the jumbo-sized jacuzzi malfunctioned and began spraying sand into the water, turning "Lake Landry," as players referred to it, into an unsavory mud hole.

And then there was the accident. Rookie offensive guard Crawford Ker was just minding his own business one day before practice when the plastic chair he was sitting on suddenly collapsed and dumped him onto the locker-room floor in a heap. Ker suffered a back injury due to the incident, and was placed on injured reserve.

Ker's misfortune may have invoked sympathy from followers of the team, but likely received little more than a roll of the eyes in other football towns. The Cowboys, even after all these years, still led the league in freak injuries. Offensive tackle Ralph Neely once broke his leg on a motorcycle. Drew Pearson sprained his knee while spiking the ball after scoring a touchdown. Tony Dorsett dropped a mirror on his toe. And only a year before, right tackle Jim Cooper broke his ankle after slipping on a disco floor.

In that light, Ker's injury was more of a habit for the franchise than any pill of misfortune. The Cowboys, despite the insistence of so many to the contrary, were really incredible clutzes.

Wrote Blackie Sherrod for the *Dallas Morning News:* "Can't you just hear the reaction around the league? 'Oh, did him hurt him's back in that nasty old chair?'"

Now, eleven games into the season, stunned fans were trying to make sense of the action – or inaction, depending upon the point of view – currently clouding local football airwaves. The Cowboys may have been the owners of a respectable 7-4 record, but there was nothing respectable about the production of the Dallas offense.

It went into the record books as one of the lowest times in franchise memory. No, not just Sunday's blanking at the hands of the Bears, though that certainly qualified as a noticeable portion of it. Here was something bigger to behold than even the fat 44 still lighting up the visitors side of the Texas Stadium scoreboard.

The can't miss-truth of the moment bouncing off the walls of every Metroplex home during that week centered around a Cowboy offense leaking oil at an historic rate. No matter which way you spun the numbers, the high-flying unit that soared to the top of the league rankings in early October was a thing of the past. Proof positive could be personally obtained with a strong stomach and a general understanding of how to operate a calculator.

Dating back to that ugly night in St. Louis, the Cowboys had scored less than 14 points in three games running, an ignominious mark not seen around Dallas since the expansion days of 1960. If only the number-crunching could have stopped there. But no. The news reaching as far as five weeks back was no better. Since Gary Hogeboom's Week 7 spot-start in Philadelphia, the Cowboys ranked at the very bottom of the league in scoring, averaging 12 points-per-game.

What in the name of holy pay-dirt was going on in Dallas? According to Landry, nothing much of a productive nature. But that, he reminded a group of reporters just minutes after watching team doctors unload the body-bags following three destructive hours with the Bears, could change at any moment.

"It obviously couldn't be any worse than today," Landry said. But then he quickly added, "This is this week, and every game is a new game in this business."

"Meaning, of course," wrote Randy Galloway, "the Cowboys now go back to playing the Eagles, Cardinals and so on. Against that type of team, the regular game plan – have the offense scratch up a few points and let the defense make them stand up – has a workable chance."

So who was to blame for the offense falling off the side of a cliff? Which underachieving Cowboy was dragging the entire unit down to his level?

It was easy in this situation for writers to tag the starting quarterback. Danny White, in all fairness, had been less than stellar three games before against the Cardinals. And he was frequently guilty of tossing up freebies for the defense like candy at a carnival.

But it was hard to make White the No. 1 whipping boy when considering the many injuries he had been dealing with since the middle of August. Or maybe it was that the entire theme had grown stale. Yeah, that was it. Quarterback-bashing had become boring in Dallas. Almost as boring as the current Cowboy offense.

So instead of White, the ball of criticism was tossed in the lap of Tony Hill. In his eighth season out of Stanford, Hill had compiled an impressive resume to his name. But he also had a problem. Hill was a sucker for a left-hook of local criticism, whether from fans, writers, coaches or teammates.

It wasn't enough that Hill was a certifiable All-Pro talent or that he was currently leading the entire NFL in receptions. There was always something more that the success-crazed town of Dallas wanted from him.

"Thrill" Hill's troubles began with Butch Johnson's theory in the aftermath of Dallas' loss to Philadelphia in the 1980 NFC Championship Game. "He's afraid to go over the middle," Johnson said of Hill.

Hill was unable to shake himself free from Johnson's barb. In the following years, whispers would float around the locker-room about how Hill was a half-hearted blocker, how he cut off routes on occasion, how he moseys through pass patterns when he's not the primary target on a play, and those occasional displays of butter-fingers in the end-zone.

Fans read about this in the paper during the week and then showed up to the game on Sundays seeking proof. A few plays of focusing on Hill was usually all anyone needed to come to the conclusion that his teammates were spot-on. Hill really was a prima-donna.

There was a West Coast grace about Hill's playing-style that made everything he did on a football field look incredibly easy. He was so smooth that he easily came across to fans as being debonair. He wasn't like other receivers. Hill didn't fly down the field like a sprinter. He loped with the grace of a long-striding panther.

Was all of this criticism warranted? Well, that depended upon whom one asked. Drew Pearson had his opinion on the matter, but that didn't necessarily mean that it agreed with the player next to him.

"Tony," said Pearson, "is living in the shadow of Butch because Butch always said Tony couldn't go over the middle. That's where all that stuff got going. Butch did a lot of talking and a lot of people believed him. What people didn't realize, though, is that Butch was talking because Tony was keeping him on the bench."

Everson Walls had another theory. "Tony is living in the shadow of Drew Pearson," Walls said. "Drew was the hardest working receiver I've ever seen. On top of that, Drew got a great block on every long run Tony Dorsett ever had. Now, everyone wants our receivers to be just like Drew...."

"I think everyone's problem with Tony is that in expecting so much from him we tend to magnify his shortcomings," Walls continued. "What it comes down to is that Tony is going to be Tony. He's California through and through. Laid-back, I guess you'd call it. And he's not going to change. You can say anything you want to him or about him, but it's obvious by now he's still going to go out and do the same thing he's been doing. Which is not so bad. Look at the numbers this year."

"If we concentrate more on what Tony does do, instead of what he doesn't do, then we'll all be better off. Coach Landry has always done that with Tony. Tom really likes the guy, you can tell that. Tom is the one who stood up for him and defended him last year when a lot of teammates were down on him."

Hill's 1985 campaign had proven to be much like every other. He made big plays for the Cowboys, but all anyone could remember were those handful of occasions when he didn't. Based on the talk, you'd think "Thrill" was over the hill.

It all started in July at training camp. The coaching staff had recommended that Hill report to camp at a maximum of 204 pounds. Hill instead showed up at a beefy 220.

"How could you be 16-pounds overweight?" a reporter asked him.

"Really, I'm about 204," Hill said in all seriousness, "but I ate a big meal last night and I haven't had a chance to run it off."

Not long after running it off, Hill drew some criticism from some Cowboy offensive players for what they deemed to be a lackadaisical effort against the Oilers in Week 4. Hill smoothed things over in that regard with an eight-catch, 100-yard outing in New York a week later. But Hill still struggled to get down to his prescribed regular season playing-weight of 197 pounds, hovering constantly at or just slightly above 200.

Of late, Hill had been a punching bag for the bleacher bums, even earning criticism from Cowboys' radio play-by-play analyst Brad Sham. From a distance, it was unfathomable that Hill could drop a second-quarter rainbow from White that would have given Dallas a 10-0 lead at RFK Stadium. It was equally perplexing that he followed it up one week later by dropping another pass at the goal-line against Chicago on the opening drive.

If Hill had caught that pass, things might have been very different. The Cowboys, in fact, might have been able to run away from the Bears, instead of the other way around. One touchdown might have made all the difference. What do you think, Dennis Thurman?

"I don't know about that," said Thurman, "because one may have been all we got."

It was a joyous moment indeed, more than 24 hours after the Bears left the Cowboys bloodied and bruised in their own backyard, when the Redskins – minus starting quarterback Joe Theismann, who suffered a gruesomely broken leg – surprised the football world by upsetting the Giants on Monday Night

Football, drawing Dallas once again into a first-place tie with New York atop the NFC East leader board.

It would have been no less surprising to Cowboy fans had they known what to expect from their team the following week; specifically, that over a four-day period the Cowboys would win a pair of games on the strength of superlative offensive outings, in which Hill was not only a contributor, but a conspicuously blameless one.

The gathering on that Sunday afternoon in Irving, Texas was noticeably subdued at the outset, doubts and concerns provoked by the unforgettable devastation of a week before hanging like a low, ominous cloud throughout Texas Stadium. Tom Landry had called this bi-annual meeting with Philadelphia a "must-win." So soon after 44-0, nobody was quite sure if it was proper etiquette for the Cowboys to even be dreaming about winning. It was all that many in the near-sellout crowd could do to hope that Dallas simply kept it close versus the Eagles.

The bad vibes only intensified after the opening kickoff, as Ron Jaworski moved Philadelphia easily down the field with the same precision passing that had beaten the Cowboys five weeks before. A pass-interference penalty on Everson Walls put the Eagles in scoring range. But Dallas held at the 9-yard line, forcing a short Paul McFadden field-goal that limited the damage to just three-points.

The offense that took to the field a few moments later for the Cowboys was unlike any that the home faithful had seen all season long. Aided by a game-plan that used an array of formations and a new emphasis on utilizing the fullback, Danny White enjoyed his finest game in two years, keeping the Eagles off-balance and frustrated at every turn. After Robert LaVette returned the kickoff to the 39-yard line, Tony Dorsett burst through the line for 14 yards. Then, with the Eagles double-covering Hill on the outside, White threw short to Newsome for gains of 7 and 23 yards. On third-and-2 from the Philadelphia 3-yard line, Landry threw a curveball at his opponent. Rather than line-up in the Shotgun formation as was the custom for the Cowboys in short-yardage situations, Landry sent in some extra beef along the front-line. Instead of finesse, Landry was relying on pure American muscle. Dorsett took the handoff going left, and walked into the end-zone past a group of reeling Eagles on the ground. The show of strength had worked rather well, providing Dallas with their first opening-drive touchdown since Week 5.

Everything was working for Dallas, until Landry got too cute for his own good. With the Cowboys marching again, seeking to extend their 7-3 lead, Landry took the ball out of his quarterback's hands, allowing James Jones to attempt a halfback-pass. Jones threw it up for Dorsett down the left sideline, but Wes Hopkins was there waiting on the interception.

On the very next play, Herman Hunter ran 74 yards untouched to give Philadelphia a very sudden 10-7 advantage. Landry put away his trickery and got back to the simple brand of football that had been working so well. Not surprisingly, he and the Cowboys were rewarded for it. The Eagles continued to slide a safety over to Tony Hill's side of the field to prevent the big play, but White still managed to find his big target on several underneath patterns. Hill finished the day with 5 receptions for 49 yards.

With Hill garnering so much attention, White was able to spread the ball around to other targets. He found Doug Cosbie open twice for touchdowns in the second quarter, and later connected with Mike Renfro on a 19-yard scoring play during the fourth quarter. A week after being beaten to a pulp, White completed 20-of-28 passes for 243 yards and a trio of touchdowns, allowing the Cowboys to coast home with a 34-17 victory.

There was life after Chicago.

Forty-degree temperatures greeted fans as they filed into Texas Stadium on Thanksgiving Day to watch Dallas complete a rare three-game home stand versus the St. Louis Cardinals. The conditions were cold enough to warrant bringing a coat along to the game, but were no match against the smokin' hot offense of the Cowboys. Not even those pesky Cardinals, a team that had embarrassed Dallas in early November up in St. Louis under similar conditions, could slow down Danny White & Co. They were not to be turkeys on this day.

The field was a green stage in the first-half, brightly-lit by red, white, and blue fireworks, both quarterbacks dazzling the audience with one big pass after another. Yards came in stacks, points came in bunches. Fortunately for the Cowboys, they didn't stop stacking and bunching at halftime, keeping right on going past Neil Lomax and the rest of the Cardinals for their ninth victory of the season.

Working with a short-field to begin the game after Eugene Lockhart recovered a Stump Mitchell fumble, White looked left and threw quick to Renfro at the 6-yard line. Running on an artificial surface still damp from earlier rains, Renfro maintained his footing while turning up-field, shrugged off the defender, and jogged in for a touchdown.

With 6:30 remaining in the second quarter White tossed his second scoring pass of the game, completing a soft rainbow of 19 yards to Doug Cosbie in the back right corner of the end-zone. The pass was pretty but, according to White, the call from the sidelines was even prettier.

"Coach Landry had almost a Super Bowl game plan," White said. "I didn't think he could come up with that much detail in a couple of days, but he was adding or changing formations an hour or so before kickoff. One of the things he noticed is they dropped their strong safety in some formations and put a linebacker on Doug. That was one of those times."

The score put Dallas ahead 14-10. Back came Lomax again, shredding the Dallas defense while working from a clean pocket. He found Pat Tilley running free in the secondary for gains of 16 and 22 yards. Then, from the five-yard line, Lomax spotted Roy Green – bad ankle and all – working one-on-one against Ron Fellows. The mismatch was too tempting for the quarterback to pass up. Lomax threw it wide, and Green made a simple cut to the outside before grabbing it out of the air with both hands. The easy pitch-and-catch put St. Louis back on top of this see-saw battle 17-14 with 1:51 left in the half.

In response, White moved Dallas 78 yards in just four plays to reclaim the lead. First, Timmy Newsome ran around the end for nine yards. Tony Dorsett caught a pass for eight yards. Following a St. Louis penalty, White went back to Renfro for 30 more. St. Louis tried to stem the tide by blitzing on first-down, but instead opened up a passing lane to Hill who made a routine catch from 16 yards out to move the Cowboys back in front 21-17.

"I knew if I made a quick move out and then came in there was a good chance that Danny would see me and get the ball to me," said Hill of that play. "He was obviously looking for a blitz because he looked my way as we broke the huddle and told me to be alert. When he says something like that you want to be alert because he's expecting something of you."

His first touchdown reception in nearly a month seemed to inspire Hill. He not only showed up for the second-half, but went out of his way to take it over. Hill walked into the huddle before a third quarter play from the Dallas 47-yard line and told his quarterback that he would be open on the next play. White heard him, but didn't necessarily pay special attention to the message. After all, in Hill's world, he was open on every play, and was often guilty of letting his teammates know about it on the way back to the huddle.

But when White began barking out the signals while under center and looked over to his right, he saw that Hill was going to be battling man-to-man with third-year cornerback Cedric Mack. It was worth a shot.

So White threw one up for Hill down the sideline. Mack appeared to be in good position, but when he inexplicably hesitated when turning around to look for the ball, Hill was left by himself when the high, arching pass finally came down. Hill bobbled it just for a moment, recent memories of other critical drops perhaps flashing before his eyes. But he did manage to get his hands around this particular pass, and was able to finish the 53-yard scoring play with a cool California smile.

White's fourth touchdown toss of the game was a season-high, helping him earn NFC Offensive Player of the Week honors a few days later. More imperative for a team trying to keep pace in a playoff race, the Cowboys had scored touchdowns on all eight trips inside the opponents 20-yard line in the two games since losing to Chicago. The offense appeared to be hitting its stride at the right time.

Leading 28-17 and with Lomax having been knocked out of the game on a hit by Lockhart, the Cowboys were seeking to deliver the knockout blow later in the quarter. Landry didn't think twice about putting the ball in the hands of Hill to accomplish it.

After the game, reporters asked Landry if it was wise to call an end-around pass while owning an eleven-point lead in a critical game with the Cowboys moving the ball well. Don't you think that's a bit risky, Coach?

"If you (reporter) didn't think it was going to work at the time, the Cardinals certainly didn't think it was going to work," Landry said. "So they weren't expecting it."

White handed the ball off to Hill on what appeared to be a simple reverse play. The defense was out of position, and Hill had an open field in front of him, an easy 15-20 yards if he so wanted it. But his job on this play was to be a distributor. Once upon a time, Hill was a quarterback in college at Stanford, so he knew a little something about chunking the ball downfield. Or that's what he liked his friends to believe.

When Hill took the handoff and continued curling around in the backfield, he looked downfield and nearly froze. The play's design and timing were perfect. Cosbie was running wide-open far beyond the entire defense. He was so wide-open it made Hill a wee-bit cautious. The last thing he wanted to do was to overthrow a 6-foot-6-inch target who had no defender within fifteen-yards. So instead of showing off his strong throwing arm, Hill authored an auspiciously suspicious floater that hung in the air far too long for comfort.

"I thought the ball would never come down," said Landry, with a smile.

"If he'd thrown one like that in practice," said Cosbie, "I would have signaled for a fair-catch."

With all the eagerness of a wind-blown feather, the ball finally landed in the arms of Cosbie at the 10-yard line. What probably should have been a walk-in touchdown for the Cowboys' rangy tight-end wound up in the record books as a 42-yard pass play that died on the five-yard line. That Dorsett scored from three yards out a moment later afforded everyone in Cowboy blue the chance to smile afterwards.

"Today," said Hill, "anyone is entitled to one turkey."

Tex Schramm sat back in his reclining chair at home, a man sick at heart. The last few hours of the long Thanksgiving weekend were slipping away, and Schramm had that sense of sinking deep within him when watching a golden opportunity slip past his team.

Only five minutes before, Schramm would have declared it to have been a perfect week. The Cowboys had stuck out their neck in admirable fashion, winning two home games in four days. The out-of-town scoreboard indicated that Philadelphia had just choked on a 20-point lead at home to fall to 6-7 on the season, while New Orleans had pulled the rug over the favored Rams 29-3, giving Dallas the inside track to the No. 2 seed in the conference. (In the late-afternoon time slot, Washington would fall to San Francisco at home, dropping them a full two games back in the division race.)

And, most importantly to Schramm, the Cleveland Browns appeared to be on their way to an upset of the New York Giants. After trailing by twelve-points early in the fourth quarter, Cleveland had rallied to take a 35-33 lead with 1:52 remaining. But Phil Simms, even with his conscience pricked by a pair of earlier interceptions, moved the Giants inside the Browns' 20-yard line with the ease of long practice. Eric Schubert trotted out in the final seconds for what Schramm anticipated would be a game-winning field-goal of 34 yards. And why should he expect anything different? Schubert had already connected from 35 and 40 yards earlier.

Schramm just couldn't believe it. The Cowboys had been that close to putting some distance between themselves and their closest pursuer in the division. Now, it appeared the Giants were going to tie things up in the Eastern division again. But then Schramm sat up, his eyes wide and staring at the television screen, his fist pumping at nobody in particular. The snap from rookie center Bart Oates had been low, shattering Schubert's fragile sense of timing, causing the kick to sail low and wide left of the upright. The impossible dream had become an improbably reality.

Schramm was as happy in that moment as he had been for several months. December was now here, and the Cowboys – someway and somehow – owned a one-game lead in the division. The end was in sight, the title there for the taking.

CHAPTER 26

THE NO-SHOWS

"They embarrassed us, and we embarrassed ourselves."
Everson Walls, after the Cowboys allowed 50 points in a
blowout loss to Cincinnati

"Just another example, of course, why America's Team needs to
be examined by America's shrinks."
Dallas Morning News columnist Randy Galloway

A wind with the cunning sharpness of a probing icicle greeted Cowboy players as they walked onto the field, nicking unprotected cheeks like a blade of cold, well-tempered steel. A din of contagious excitement from the gallery left ears a shade of comparable red, as a sellout crowd of nearly 60,000 inside Riverfront Stadium bellowed out their long-awaited welcome to America's Team.

It was 38-degrees on the banks of the Ohio River, and comforts were few for the outlanders from Dallas. The AstroTurf was frozen hard, promising to be as unforgiving to exposed flesh as a cheese grater. Footballs, noted for being supple and pleasing to the touch, felt more like dense bricks in the hand.

And there as an ever-present companion was the breeze blowing in off the river, so soft to the touch, yet so very, very cold. This was a very different world than the silver and blue strangers were accustomed to. The pale light of a winter's sun attempted in vain to peek through a dull gray cloudbank above, casting an odd hue of yellow and purple on the setting below, making this highly-anticipated inaugural visit by the Dallas Cowboys to the city of Cincinnati appear to be straight out of a Star Trek novel. Was this Ohio or Tarsus IV?

Even the patrons looked suspicious. Peculiar creatures bundled up in coats and scarves (and, yes, even sunglasses) were in abundance. Whether they were actually humans or merely humanoids shivering underneath all those layers of clothing nobody ventured to guess. A few elegant tigers swayed drunkenly in their seats. And down near the railing, a pair of baboons shared a few jokes with the front-row rowdies. Had Commander Spock been misfortunate enough to gaze upon the scene, he would have raised an eyebrow, no doubt.

A game that had been talked about all week around the football world held intrigue on multiple levels. For once in their lives, Cincinnatians were anxious to witness the world-famous Cowboys at work. They wanted to see what all the fuss had been about for the past twenty years.

Sportswriters from Dallas were interested to watch a pair of stubborn franchise trends go head-to-head against the Bengals. Which would prevail? The Cowboys' 16-1 all-time record in games immediately following Thanksgiving, or their penchant for going belly-up in cold weather?

Dallas Morning News reporter David Casstevens recalled the moment when Tom Landry was asked earlier in the week why the Cowboys weren't a good cold-weather team.

"The question appeared to catch Landry off-guard," wrote Casstevens. "Judging by his blank look, it was as if someone had asked how he felt about the Cowboys not being a good practice team on Wednesday or not being a good team against clubs from the AFC who have one or more players named Theotis... It was obvious the coach had never heard the premise, or if he had, he hadn't given it any thought."

Blinking back at his questioner, Landry answered, "I didn't know we weren't."

But come on, Tom. It's no secret. Haven't you heard the talk? Everybody else has.

Perhaps this testimony from the pen of Randy Galloway puts it best: "You know the NFL whispers about the Cowboys – put them on the road in a cold weather town, let the weather conditions get nasty and they'll freeze up faster than cheap plumbing."

Landry clearly wasn't interested in whispers or high-handed theories at this juncture of the season. His team had everything to play for on Sunday. Beating the Bengals, if coupled with a New England victory over Detroit, would secure a playoff spot for the Cowboys. Even if the Patriots didn't hold up their end of the bargain, a Dallas victory would make it nearly impossible for them to miss out on the postseason. Without question, this was a big game. But not only for the Cowboys. Though just 6-7 on the season, Cincinnati was trying to make up a one-game deficit to division-leading Cleveland in the watered-down AFC Central.

The excitement of a December playoff race, combined with the presence of the royal Cowboys, had the crowd at Riverfront Stadium worked up into a frenzy not seen in those parts since the heyday of the "Big Red Machine." As Jim Breech booted the ball up and into a sad sky to mark the beginning of the game, fans present cheered with all the energy commonly associated with a conference championship game, their roars increasing even more when James Jones was tackled at the 32-yard line.

It was assumed that the 11 men trotting out onto the playing surface from the Dallas bench constituted the Cowboy offense, but it was never confirmed. Other than the names on the backs of their jerseys, there was no evidence remaining on that day in Cincinnati of the Cowboy team that had so handily beaten Philadelphia and St. Louis during Thanksgiving week. Gone was the surgeon-like offensive unit and the hot-handed quarterback. Gone was an opportunistic defense that wreaked havoc in the offensive backfield.

If the Cowboys didn't feel misplaced in such a frigid electrically-charged setting, they certainly played that way. Tony Dorsett fumbled on the game's second play. The ball, rather than lay on the ground and play dead as so many other fumbles do, was inadvertently kicked deep into the Dallas backfield, and it was all Danny White could do to fall on it at the 5-yard line. Needing 37 yards on third-down, White dropped back to pass in the end-zone. He failed to find an open receiver, just like he failed to get rid of the ball before defensive end Ross Browner swallowed him up for a safety, the first two-point play recorded against Dallas in more than fifteen years.

Over on the sideline, wide receivers coach Drew Pearson clapped his hands, exhorting the offense to stay calm and do better the next time out. Pearson had been in this kind of atmosphere several times during his playing career, and knew that patience and persistence were the keys to survival.

"Tom used to tell us," said Pearson, "that every time we come into a foreign stadium, where we hadn't been before or been there in a long time, people would want us so bad that we would just have to weather the storm and see where we were when the sun came out."

Too bad for Dallas that the sun was so long in showing against the Bengals. Cincinnati jumped all over the Cowboys in the first quarter, burying them in a relentless wave of football fervor. Second-year quarterback Boomer Esiason, when not throwing bullets all over the yard to an array of open Bengals receivers, watched running backs Larry Kinnebrew, a 255-pound bruiser, and James Brooks run wild through the Dallas front. It was the speedy Brooks who burst around the right end for a pickup of 33 yards on the first Bengal march, part of a seven-play drive that concluded with a pile-driving touchdown run of 3 yards by Kinnebrew.

It was a bad day for Dallas pass-catchers. Tony Hill looked noticeably uncomfortable in the cold weather, short-arming a couple of passes during the first-half. Doug Cosbie, a fellow Stanford alum, appeared to be just as miserable, fumbling away Dallas' second drive of the game near midfield.

Two plays later, the same Eddie Brown who the Cowboys could not get their hands on during April's NFL draft, outran Everson Walls across the field and hauled in a strike from Esiason for a 45-yard touchdown. The game wasn't even six minutes old, and the fans were already tossing confetti and beach balls around in the stands, thoroughly ecstatic about the Bengals' 16-0 lead.

Brown continued to run laps around Cowboy cornerbacks, beating Ron Fellows for a gain of 22 yards on Cincinnati's next possession. Brown was open along the right sideline against Walls on the next play, but Esiason threw wide. On third-and-10, he caught a short pass, made Michael Downs miss, and dove for an 11-yard pickup, extending the drive.

Moments later, the Bengals reached into their bag of tricks to pull a fast one on the Cowboys' 4-0 defense. On third-and-5 from the 27-yard line, Dallas crowded the line, showing their customary blitz look for Esiason, who was busy barking out the signals under center. Brooks stepped up alongside Esiason, and acted as if he was going to be blocking on the play.

"I got Clinkscale," Brooks said, pointing at the Dallas safety who was lined-up over center Dave Remington.

When Esiason said "Okay," Remington snapped the ball and the quarterback authored a quick handoff to Brooks, who burst up the middle and was gone for a third Cincinnati touchdown. The rout was on.

The 22 points scored by the Bengals were the most ever allowed by the Cowboys in the opening frame of a game. But the bad news didn't stop there for the Dallas defense. Though afforded a brief reprieve from the onslaught when Esiason left the game early in the second quarter with a minor knee ailment, the third period would prove to be a resounding continuation of that first-quarter beat-down.

With Esiason back in the huddle, the Bengals marched 70 yards in seven plays to begin the second half. Steve Kreider's 29-yard scoring reception made it 29-3. But Victor Scott fumbled the ensuing kickoff return, giving Cincinnati the ball back at the 18-yard line. Brooks ran it in from there to put the Bengals up 36-3, squelching any far-fetched hopes the Cowboys may have been entertaining of staging a comeback.

Up in the press box, Tex Schramm wore a glowering expression in his seat, looking like a man growing increasingly frustrated and burdened by doubts of his team. He wanted so badly to believe the Cowboys were good enough to get into the playoffs and do some damage. Occasionally, over the past three months, he had seen glimpses of a really good team. But for the second time in three weeks, he was an embarrassed spectator at a Cowboy blowout.

As the Bengals continued to pull away into the second half, it became clear that Schramm was mad not only at the players, but that he also had a beef with the coaching as well. When Landry, with the Cowboys trailing 43-10, called two consecutive running plays in which Dorsett netted three yards, reporters overheard Schramm say, "That's right. Let's establish our [!@#$%!] running game *now*."

Schramm would curse again later in the game when Tony Hill came up gimpy after landing on his head while attempting to make a reception at the Cincinnati 5-yard line. Only in Dallas can a player land on his head and manage to pull his hamstring in the same motion.

Like Dorsett was to the running game, Hill was the heartbeat of the Dallas passing attack. If he went down, the whole unit might very well come crashing down with him. As Hill limped off the field with the attendance of team doctors, Pearson walked over to personnel director Gil Brandt on the sideline and said, "Check and see how long it would take to get me activated."

If only that were possible.

Hill's hamstring strain was severe enough to put his availability for the remaining games in doubt, relegating him to the bench for the remaining few minutes against the Bengals, and allowing the Cowboys to trudge to the finish line in Cincinnati cold in body and meek in spirit. There was nothing from this day with which to hold onto with pride. Not the 50-24 score, and certainly not the franchise-worst mark of 570 yards allowed by the Dallas defense.

Even weeks later, defensive coordinator Ernie Stautner was pulling no punches on the effort of his unit that day. "That game against Cincinnati is one of the worst games I've seen as a coach," said Stautner.

The head coach couldn't help but concur with his assistant during his postgame briefing. "I can't reason anything out of today. This was by far our worst game of the year," said Landry.

"It was much different than the Bears game, because this time we had no defense. You could analyze the Chicago game, but there's nothing to analyze here. Any game you lose hurts you, but losing this way is more than that."

Mike Renfro was one of only a handful of Cowboy players that stuck around in the locker room long enough to do a postgame interview. He was quick to diffuse the negative tones of the questions being directed his way, focusing instead on the prize at hand the following week.

"The Giants game is just as big as it was before the opening kickoff," said Renfro. "Winning or losing didn't change that."

Just who were these crazy Cowboys of uncertain habits? Their 9-5 record suggested they were contenders. Recent film suggested otherwise. Ever since they had flown into St. Louis to begin the second half of the season, the Cowboys had been riding a roller-coaster usually marked for pretenders. They were embarrassed by the Cardinals, yet rebounded at RFK to beat Washington. They got steamrolled by Chicago, only to bounce back with two division wins. The latest episode of this soap-opera had a .500 Bengals squad pasting a big, fat 50-spot on Cowboy backsides that should have been ready to play.

Just how low could the Cowboys go? More pertinent to the situation; were the Cowboys capable of rebounding from such a debacle as this? Or, as one striving humorist posed to his audience in a crowded, smoke-filled barroom that week: "Could South America's Team get high one more time?"

When asked by a reporter if a real playoff-caliber team loses games by a 50-24 margin in December, Landry smiled and said, "I haven't seen many." Then he quickly added, "But this team might be. This team is real unusual."

"No," wrote Randy Galloway, "this team is nuts."

The Tex Schramm that reporters witnessed on Sunday in Cincinnati was in stark contrast to the one that greeted the press on Tuesday back in Dallas. Speaking at Tom Landry's weekly press luncheon, Schramm not only put away the foul language and pointed sarcasm, but actually dared to make light of the Cowboys' newfound propensity for being blown out. Said Schramm: "We've lost five games by a total of only 88 points! America's Team doesn't do anything halfway."

By Saturday afternoon, Schramm was back to his former ornery self. The police report on his desk said it all. Linebacker Jeff Rohrer, demonstrating the higher benefits of a Yale education, had been booked in a local jail overnight for being intoxicated while behind the wheel.

Schramm shook his head, a habit he had become accustomed to in recent weeks. *So much for the renewed focus the Cowboys were going to show on Sunday! So much for intelligence!*

Rohrer, who had sat out the game against the Bengals due to a sprained ankle, had been slotted to start against the Giants. And, after conferring with Schramm, Landry decided to stick with his original plan. He would allow Rohrer to start against the Giants, but had no such intentions of doing so on the following week against the 49ers.

In effect, Rohrer's moment of indiscretion had cost him his starting job. Schramm could only hope that Rohrer wouldn't be a conspicuous cause for defeat in a game the Cowboys needed so desperately to win.

CHAPTER 27

THE UNEXPLAINABLE

"I saw the ball come off of Ed's hands. I thought I would have a perfect chance to take it all the way. This is the kind of play that you dream about at night."
Jim Jeffcoat, on his miraculous runback of a tipped pass for a Dallas touchdown late in the second quarter

It was early on a Sunday never to forget at Texas Stadium. Dextor Clinkscale looked over to the sideline to receive the defensive signals from Ernie Stautner, while the gathering of players surrounding him on the field near the 40-yard line chirped with the uncouth bravado of desperate men. Randy White bemoaned a missed tackle in the backfield, and Michael Downs verbally patted himself on the back for being there to clean up White's mistake. Then, as if in accordance with some invisible signal seen by all, the chatter stopped, allowing Clinkscale to bark out the call for the benefit of every nearby Cowboy.

The huddle broke, and Everson Walls trotted out wide to the defensive left side. Honest to a fault, Walls normally carried himself with the brash confidence of an undrafted free-agent who fought his way up the ranks to achieve NFL stardom. He was often guilty of talking a big talk between the lines and had obtained respect around the league for being able to back it up.

But on this Sunday, unlike any other in franchise history, it was a more composed version of Walls that lined up on an island at cornerback, eyeing the New York wide receiver across from him as a big-game hunter does his prey; cautiously, warily. This was it. Second-down and nearly a complete football game to go still. The first-quarter clock had just dipped below 11 minutes, leaving 56 more to decide the champion of the NFC's Eastern Division for 1985.

Walls would have been the first to inform you that his season to that point had been a sparkling success. Through 14 games, he led the league in interceptions and was a lock to represent the NFC in February's Pro Bowl in Hawaii. To many in the Cowboys locker-room, Walls had been the MVP of the Dallas defense.

But there was an age-old saying in sports that Walls found especially applicable to football players. If Walls truly was only as good as his last game, then he had a lot to improve on against the Giants. Gaudy numbers and future accolades aside, Walls had earned the same report card that every other member of the Cowboy defense did for their work against Cincinnati; "A" as in Awful.

Walls, in his fifth season out of Grambling State, had been made to look silly by that kid from Miami, Eddie Brown. Whatever pass-route Brown wanted to run – whether short, deep, cross-country, or somewhere in between – was there for the taking. From beginning to end, the rookie had owned the vet's number.

In the days since, Walls had publicly stressed the importance of the team putting the past (especially the recent past) behind them, and of focusing on the momentous challenge facing them. It didn't matter that the Cowboys had lost their last two regular season games in each of the 1983 and 1984 campaigns.

A sixteen-game season had boiled down to a mere one for the Cowboys. A victory over New York would not only give

Dallas the NFC East crown but would also prevent them from having to travel out west to San Francisco in the finale with a must-win situation hanging over their heads. They had seen the black magic of Candlestick Park work against them too many times in recent years to believe they were going to be able to upset the defending champion 49ers.

Privately, Walls focused not so much on winning as simply playing better. It wasn't exactly a secret around town that, were the Cowboys to accomplish any of the goals they had laid out for themselves during the summer, the defensive unit needed to show marked improvement, beginning when the Giants came to town.

Over the past four weeks, the Dallas defense had yielded an average of 428 yards-per-game. It was enough to make a proud competitor like Walls sick to his stomach, enough to make him take a long, hard look at the man in the mirror over the next few days. Walls watched extra film of himself, noting particular fundamental flaws that had crept into his game. He spent extra time with secondary coach Gene Stallings on breaking down some of the latest tendencies of a New York offense dealing with the loss of top receiver Lionel Manuel to injury. He did anything to make himself better-prepared to do his job on Sunday.

The Walls that stared into the face of Phil McConkey on that second-down play against the Giants had something to prove. He needed to show Tom Landry, Stallings, Stautner, and everybody else in a silver helmet that last week was only a cruel aberration, a nightmare best forgotten. On this day, more than ever, he needed to be the All-Pro cornerback that had made so many big plays for the Cowboys over the years, someone trustworthy and dependable.

The signals from the sideline that Clinkscale had relayed in verbal form to the rest of the defense called for all three Cowboy linebackers to blitz on the play, leaving Walls in man-to-man coverage with McConkey. It wasn't going to be the straight-line speed of an Eddie Brown that McConkey would attack Walls with. Much like Mike Renfro for Dallas, McConkey was a short, undersized tactician whose reliance on quickness and cunning made him a headache to defend. Walls, even though affording himself a few yards of cushion, would have to be alert.

McConkey came off the line and ran straight at Walls, before cutting sharply to the post. Walls, with fresh legs under him, was there to cover the spot. McConkey then turned back upfield, angling toward the corner. It was the old post-corner route, and Walls had fallen for it like a blind rookie. Now the veteran cornerback was behind, but he could still make up a step on a moderate stepper such as McConkey.

But just as Walls began to pedal hard, thinking he was about to cover up for his misstep, McConkey did the unthinkable by cutting back to the post. Walls was now out of position and out of answers, his body language expressing utter disbelief as he half-heartedly chased the small Giant receiver across the field. *Who runs a post-corner-post anyway?*

A collective groan of dismay arose from the sellout crowd, telling Walls everything that his eyes could not. The blitz had failed in its intent, and Phil Simms had launched an arrow from a clean pocket straight at the heart of the Cowboys' fragile psyche. Before the ball ever reached the mitts of McConkey at the 24-yard line, Verne Lundquist told television viewers on CBS everything they needed to know. "McConkey's going to score!" exclaimed Lundquist.

A picture-perfect spiral turned its trajectory downward, its aim as sweet and true as the receiver's effort had been to obtain separation from his defensive shadow. McConkey reached out his gloved hands to make the catch.

Trailing by a healthy five yards, Walls jogged in the distance as one stricken by an overwhelming sense of helplessness. This was not the beginning to the game that he had envisioned. Not for the Cowboys, and certainly not for himself. The nightmare was supposed to have been buried in the past. But in that moment, it was a very present reality in Dallas, engulfing Walls and the Cowboys in a cloud of impending, inescapable doom.

Long after the final verse has been written, when the pigskin resides on a dusty museum shelf as a relic of a bygone age, it will come. Down the corridors of time, echoing in the earnestness of acknowledged distance, riding the wings of the wind of secret yesterdays, a vision will dance upon the walls of human memory, replaying the story of that December afternoon underneath a blue sky and a half-finished roof.

Ears faint of hearing, hearts long for longing, spirits wistful in the struggle for an honest remembrance of a day ever elusive, will blush with the innocence of youth at the recollection of so many hopes, cares and dreams long, long forgotten. Echoes distant, shadows near, the mind afforded a small taste of a unique moment in time, when an aging dynasty was gifted one final hurrah from the heavens.

A sun most bright in a backdrop of purest blue shone down upon the children of Destiny wearing silver star-splashed helmets, while the strong arm of Fortune and Fate pushed, prodded, and sometimes even dragged them along toward the finish line. This invisible force worked on behalf of the Cowboys, and worked with the cunning hands of an Executioner against the Giants. It worked, after three hours of steady labor, a football miracle most astounding.

A game steeped in the unexpected had a pulse that pounded with the sincere thrill of the moment, leaving a hearty, cheery gathering with no other alternative but to wipe sweaty palms and clap glad hands. The celebration, when it was all said and done, spilled over into the streets. They sang loudly that day in Dallas, of Tom, of the Thieves, and of a group of fresh-faced kids who knew no better than to do no wrong.

A moment's wonder and then, just as mysteriously as they came, the shadows fade, the echoes die. A moment of calm and then it all returns, this time more vividly than before, with all of the many sights, sounds, and smells present even as they were then, from the beginning, in their correct order. The ball on its flight, McConkey to the race, and Walls for the chase. The faces in the crowd frozen into shock, the feet of Walls that slowed in disbelief, the hands of McConkey that reached out. The ball that landed, the fingers that fumbled, the touchdown that never was. To see it was to believe the unbelievable.

No matter the strenuous, superior efforts of the Giants, this sweet fragrance of improbability could not be extinguished, buoying the home team with hope and opportunity at every bend in the road, carrying them to a title they would otherwise have not obtained.

Were a philosopher of eloquent speech to gaze long enough at such shapely shadows of past events, he would have blessed the day in the regal manner of a poet kissing a rose, jotting it down as an historical event unlike any other. December 15, 1985. Many days have shone fair upon the Cowboys, but thou exceedest them all.

The first-quarter rolled on under the banner of a scoreless truce, both teams trying to regain their equilibrium from the emotional trauma accompanying Phil McConkey's impossible mishandling of a sure-thing touchdown gift from Phil Simms. The New York offense was floundering, and the Cowboys were falling faster than dominoes on a ship deck.

It had already been a markedly different Dallas team starting the game than the one which had last played at home on Thanksgiving Day versus St. Louis. Robert LaVette and Leon Gonzalez had since been placed on injured reserve, forcing Gil Brandt to make a quick search through list of available free agents to find a replacement. Wide receiver Kenny Duckett, who had started with New Orleans earlier in the season, was now working alongside James Jones on kickoff returns, while defensive back Gordon Banks, a USFL convert, replaced Bill Bates as the Cowboys' returner on punts.

But an epidemic appeared to have broken out along the Dallas sideline during their most important game of the season. One by one, veterans the Cowboys relied upon came up lame. Tony Hill, who had been cleared to start by team doctors, managed to make a token reception of 9 yards on the Cowboys' first possession to break Drew Pearson's franchise-record for most consecutive games with a catch, before coming up lame with a sore hamstring. He would be in and out of the lineup for the remainder of the game.

Jim Cooper didn't last very long against the Giants before a pinched nerve in his shoulder flared up again. Cooper was replaced at offensive right tackle by Phil Pozderac. Doug Cosbie was soldiering on with a bad back and a sore knee, suffered earlier in the week at practice when Mike Hegman fell against his leg.

Not until Danny White walked off the field and back to the locker-room with a bruised shoulder early in the first quarter did fans begin to look around on the Dallas bench with concern. Two starters had gone down, and two more were at least halfway there. Just how many players did the Cowboys have remaining?

New York was punting again, and Banks was waiting downfield to receive it. Banks had been something of a star as a return-man in the USFL, his speed allowing him to break open numerous sizeable returns. Tom Landry had thought enough of him from watching on film to give Banks the opportunity to author a quick turnaround of the NFL's worst punt-return unit.

At the time, Landry figured it to be a no-risk decision on his part. What could it hurt to let the new guy have a shot. He couldn't possibly do any worse. Or could he? Banks fielded the punt from Sean Landeta cleanly and raced up-field toward the midfield stripe. A crowd engulfed him for a brief instant, before the ball popped loose and was seen rolling away from him, allowing a Giant to make a recovery in Dallas territory. The new guy picked himself up off the turf with that age-old expression of gullibility embedded on his countenance.

No doubt about it. Banks had bungled it. But wait! The referee was suddenly signaling an illegal block against New York, nullifying the turnover and forcing Landeta to punt all over again. This time, Banks authored a simple fair-catch at the Giants 42-yard line, figuring it was a safer bet at that moment to allow the offense to try to gain some yardage. For the second time in just a handful of minutes, the Cowboys had managed to skirt the cliff of disaster.

But the hits just kept on coming for the Cowboys. This time it was Gary Hogeboom slow to rise after being whacked by blitzing safety Terry Kinard on what was recorded as a 23-yard sack. Hogeboom stayed in the game, and everyone was glad that he did.

On third-and-27, the Boomer unleashed a bomb that, at first glance from the stands, looked like another one of his misguided missiles. The Giants were playing soft zone coverage, specifically guarding against the deep pass. Surely the pass from Hogeboom would either be intercepted or – by the grace of God – be allowed to fall harmlessly to the turf as an incompletion.

These expectations were gladly relinquished in the light of a much brighter reality awaiting downfield. Running down the right sideline beyond the coverage of cornerback Ted Watts was Mike Renfro, who was open on the merits of another trademark out-and-up move against Watts. It had worked to perfection against Washington in the opener, and it worked like a charm against New York in the home finale. Renfro put his hands out and the sizzling ball from Hogeboom stuck there.

"We were in a third-and-long situation and the play from the sideline was for Renfro to run his corner route," recalled Hogeboom. "We had a play in the game-plan where you can run a corner and then go into a streak and I signaled back to [the coaches on the sideline] that I wanted to run the up route and they said fine, go ahead. Mike made an excellent move on the route."

All that remained was a race. Watts and New York safety Herb Welch caught up with Renfro, but not before it was too late. Needing 27 yards when the play began, Renfro provided a gain of 58 instead, the Dallas receiver falling across the goal line to provide the game's first points.

Boom! Cowboys, 7. Giants, 0. And the afternoon was young yet.

An even 2:00 showed on the second-quarter clock. Head down, hands on hips, Ed "Too Tall" Jones made the most of the customary stoppage by sucking some wind and taking stock of things. As the dean of the Dallas defense, Jones had learned to recognize a critical moment in a game when confronted by one. Now was unquestionably one of those times.

The 7-0 lead that Dallas had owned late in the first quarter seemed like an eternity ago. Since then, New York had settled down and seized control of the game. As they had in their earlier meeting at the Meadowlands, Giant receivers found gaping holes in the middle of the Dallas secondary. Phil McConkey's catch-and-run of 48 yards set up Bobby Johnson's 7-yard game-tying score during the early stages of the second frame. A defensive interception by cornerback Elvis Patterson then gave New York the ball on the Dallas 6-yard line, allowing the Giants to take a 14-7 lead moments later with a short scoring toss from Simms to Tony Galbreath.

Now, with the first-half winding down, Phil Simms had the offense on the move again. Mixing an array of short, effective throws from Simms around strong runs by NFL touchdown leader Joe Morriss, the Giants placed their foot on the neck of the Cowboys, giving every inclination they were about to begin squeezing the lifeblood out of them.

"We were a little down," admitted Jones. "I could sense it on the sideline and on the field."

With the ball on the 22-yard line of the Cowboys, the two-minute warning came at an opportune time for Jones and the Dallas defense, affording them a chance to catch their breath and regroup. The weather was brisk, Christmas only ten days away. But right then, Jones was a sweaty and frustrated man. What he would have given at that moment for his hamstring to be fully healed!

Lost amidst the wild roller-coaster ride that the Cowboys had been on for the past month was the running bet between Too Tall and Jim Jeffcoat. After Jeffcoat pulled even on the tally sheet against Chicago, Jones had stretched out his lead again, recording a sack in each of the next three games.

But nobody in the Dallas locker-room cared about who had more sacks when the team was being blown out every other week. The wager, if not conceded to Jones by this point, had definitely been pushed to the back-burner by both players. New York was marching down the field, attempting to go ahead by two touchdowns on the scoreboard. This was no time to be thinking of any penny-ante bet. This was about survival. This was about saving a season.

There was an unspoken acknowledgment among all eleven defensive players that, once back on the field, someone in blue-and-white needed to make a play to stem the tide threatening to wipe the Cowboys off the NFC East map. Someone. Anyone. Why not Jones? Why not Jeffcoat? Why not both?

It had been suggested in more than one local newsroom over the past month that Too Tall was enjoying the finest season of his career in 1985. These rave reviews were, of course, founded primarily upon the liberal sack totals he was piling up. But Jones had been having trouble getting anywhere close to Simms on this day, convincing the 6-foot-9-inch giant that the time had come for a new plan of attack. Actually, in his case, it was something quite old.

When Tom Landry made Too Tall and Harvey Martin switch sides before the 1975 season, it wasn't because he thought Jones would develop into a sack artist on the defensive left side. If anything, the move was designed to unleash Martin's speed around the right end, which it did. Jones' first and greatest value to the Dallas defense on passing downs was his height and abnormally large wingspan.

The move was really easy for Landry to make. Since the majority of NFL quarterbacks were right-handed and statistically proven to favor receivers on the side of their strong-arm, it only made sense to put a giant such as Too Tall on that side to obstruct their view.

It was difficult for even the tallest of quarterbacks to see over Jones' hulking figure, and even harder to sneak a pass on that side past his long arms. Of the many things that Jones did so well on a football field, he will be most remembered for the many passes he deflected throughout his career near the line of scrimmage. Jones really was Too Tall for quarterbacks to miss, often serving the Cowboys in the manner of an extra defensive back, wiping away one possible downfield completion after another.

Jones had logged 16 batted passes during the 1984 season. Due in part to the hamstring that he pulled near the end of training camp, reaching up and jumping had come harder for him than usual in 1985. Through fourteen games, he had only 6 batted passes to his credit. But if New York offensive tackle Karl Nelsen was going to continue to throw up a roadblock in his path, then Jones would have to start reaching again and hope that the ball would find him.

On first-down from the 22, Simms dropped back to pass again. Jones charged off the line, but when Nelsen was there to prevent him from turning the corner, Jones cut back inside. Nelsen was there to cut off that advance too. Simms was looking to his right, in the direction of Everson Walls, who had been struggling for most of the game. The quarterback saw another receiver running free on that side, cocked his arm, and fired away.

Jones saw Simms' throwing-motion as a blur, and simply stuck his right arm out. Maybe – just maybe - he would get lucky this time. The ball caromed suddenly and violently off of Jones' taped-up hand, and was sent flying into the backfield. And just as suddenly and no less surprisingly, the ball was in Jeffcoat's hands and the big defensive end was lumbering away from everybody in the opposite direction.

Batted pass No. 7 of the season for Jones was lucky indeed. Jeffcoat's 65-yard run-back for a touchdown had tied the game 14-14 and put a jolt of energy back into the Cowboy bench. Players were jumping up and down, waving their towels at the fans, high-fiving each other, slapping Jeffcoat on the back, and talking trash once again to the Giants, who were still trying to process the turn of events in their own minds.

What *Dallas Morning News* columnist Blackie Sherrod referred to as a "ricochet romance" between Jones and Jeffcoat was actually long overdue, in Too Tall's opinion. For years, he had seen linemen of other teams score touchdowns off deflections, and wondered if he would ever be a part of such a play with the Cowboys.

"I see them all the time on TV and I say, 'Wait a minute, that guy doesn't hit as many passes as I do. When am I going to get one?' It couldn't have happened at a better time. This play just took all the air out of [the Giants]. It turned the game around."

On the next play from scrimmage, Jeffcoat tracked Simms down in the backfield for the first Cowboy sack of the game. On third-down, Jones busted through to get a sack of his own. The Cowboys were rolling, and the Giants obviously reeling. And it didn't stop there.

The fourth-down snap took Sean Landeta a step to his right, into the path of Everson Walls, who was rushing off the edge. Fearful of having his kick blocked, Landeta hesitated, bobbled the ball and, just before he was swallowed up by the defense, tossed it ahead for an incompletion.

From the New York 12-yard line, Danny White, who had returned to the game after Mike Renfro's long scoring play, needed only one play to find Renfro in the corner of the end-zone for another touchdown. And when Jeffcoat added a second sack to his total on the ensuing play, the crowd at Texas Stadium knew no end to jubilation.

It had been a sequence of events that would be talked about in Dallas for months. In the final 6:28 of the second quarter, New York ran off 17 offensive plays to the Cowboys' 1 – yet were outscored 14-0 in the process.

Theatrically and miraculously, the home team found themselves riding on a high wave of emotion going into the halftime locker-room, and Jeffcoat was taking a bite out of Too Tall's lead, while helping to stake the Cowboys to an unlikely lead of their very own.

CHAPTER 28

HEROES

"I don't ever remember using three quarterbacks, except in the early years where it was quite common to get them knocked out."
Tom Landry

"It's an unbelievable feeling."
Third-string QB Steve Pelluer, whose passing prowess on a fourth-quarter touchdown drive proved crucial in the Cowboys' playoff-clinching victory over New York

In light of the debacle in Cincinnati, and perhaps taking advantage of a devilish inner-delight in cunning sportsmanship, Tom Landry had chosen to play a coy game of Guess Who with the media during the week, creating a sense of uncertainty as to who would start at quarterback for the Cowboys on Sunday versus New York. Danny White? Gary Hogeboom? Santa Claus? Landry would commit to neither.

Not until the day before the game, when meeting with Verne Lundquist and Terry Bradshaw of CBS, did Landry finally divulge that White would start against the Giants. But he quickly asked for them to keep that news to themselves. Landry preferred that the advantage of surprise – however slight – be with his team for as long as possible.

Landry's little mind-game – for that was all it really was – had little effect upon a Giant defense still smoldering from their poor showing against Dallas in Week 5. No matter which quarterback was under center for the Cowboys, the goal from the New York perspective remained the same – hit him hard, hit him early, and hit him often.

White felt the brunt of this formula first, leaving the game during Dallas' second possession with a shoulder injury. He returned, but suffered another shot to his rib area on the same play that he gave the Cowboys a lead with his 12-yard touchdown toss to Mike Renfro. This time White would be on the bench for good.

Hogeboom fared no better. A blitzing Perry Williams landed a perfectly-placed helmet-to-chin punch in the third quarter, leaving Hogeboom staggering in the end-zone. And when defensive tackle Jim Burt piled on a few plays later with a sack of his own, Hogeboom was out of the game, bells ringing in his head from a concussion.

The ultimate game of Guess Who? would follow.

Many a campfire discussion had broken out over the years on the merits of Tom Landry being a perfect man. Here was Landry, a unique someone who dressed impeccably, went to church on Sunday mornings, worked magic with a piece of chalk on a blackboard, and was part of a dying breed of men who remained married to one woman. The subject was certainly intriguing.

Landry's players never bothered to get involved very much in this hero-worship. They knew too much. They knew Landry's fatal flaw, the one defect in his armor that made him certifiably – and somewhat humorously - human.

No matter how hard he tried to fix it, or how hard he tried to remember, Landry possessed a special way of butchering the names of his own players. Gary Hogeboom could testify to this probably better than any of the current Cowboys. Now in his sixth season with the team, Hogeboom had been referred to as everything from Hogenbloom to Pozderac, before Landry finally settled upon a suitable compromise and just started calling him Gary.

Landry's nickname for Mike Renfro provided players another reason to chuckle among themselves. Landry occasionally referred to Renfro as "Pro," a title of respect that the head coach had heard – or thought he heard - many teammates refer to the hard-nosed wide receiver as during practice, when actually those cries of "Pro" were players saying "Fro," short for Renfro.

Karl Powe's was another name that Landry had trouble with. During training camp, Landry had walked around the meeting rooms calling the rookie wide receiver from Alabama State "Pow." A few assistant coaches attempted to correct him, providing Landry with the correct pronunciation and the inherent grammar reminder attached. *You know, Coach. Remember that rule we all learned in school? Long O, silent E...*

A light went on in Landry's head. Now he had it! In preparing for the crucial showdown with the Giants, Landry realized that, with Tony Hill limping around on one good hamstring, Powe could very easily be called upon to make a handful of catches. So at practice one day, the head coach held up a play-card with the rookie's name on it for the offense to run. It read: "Poe."

Ahh, names. They were all the rage of that unforgettable fourth-quarter versus New York, when Pows and Poes and Scotts and Steves were running all over the Texas Stadium field, carrying the Cowboys to an ending too wildly improbable to suit the fancy of anticipation.

The Dallas defense sat on the bench, tired and thoroughly winded. For the second time after intermission, the Giants had just penetrated deep into Dallas territory only to be turned away without scoring a single point.

In the third-quarter, it had been Michael Downs jumping in front of a Phil Simms pass from the 18-yard line and snuffing out a threat with an interception. And just moments before, as the fourth-quarter moved along toward its midway point, Downs had come through again for the Cowboys, snuffing out a fake field-goal attempt and tackling Jeff Rutledge behind the line of scrimmage.

The 21-14 Cowboy advantage had been preserved, but was far from secure. The quarterback that walked into the Dallas huddle had yet to attempt a single pass as a professional. On the back of his jersey, emblazoned in bold blue lettering was his last name: Pelluer. According to the game-program, his christened name was Steve. But Terry Bradshaw, up in the television booth, continued to refer to him as Scott. Either way, Pelluer's correct name (Steve) wasn't nearly as important at that moment as his ability to accurately chunk a football around the yard. A second-year standout from Washington where he led the Huskies to a runaway victory in the Rose Bowl as a sophomore, Pelluer was a fifth-round draft selection of the Cowboys in 1984 who had been steadily improving and gaining in confidence while working in the shadows of Danny White and Gary Hogeboom.

He had earned high praise from Tom Landry for his work during preseason, but that had been against third-team scrubs. Lawrence Taylor and the rest of the Giants starting defense were of a different quality altogether.

The pressure of the moment was altogether different as well. The Cowboy defense had been getting pushed around for the majority of the second-half. That they had managed to keep New York off the scoreboard in the process was more luck or simply poor execution on the part of the Giants than any special cunning on the part of the Cowboys. The Flex defense was bending…bending…bending. When would it break? Just how many more times could the Giants be expected to threaten before actually pushing the ball across?

The mutually-appointed hour had come. Both the fans and Landry knew that the time was now for Pelluer to take the ball and help the Cowboys run away and hide for good. It was time to get a few first downs. It was time to burn some clock. It was time to score.

Could young Steve Pelluer complete a pass in a meaningful game with the season in the balance? Ready or not, all of America was about to find out.

Since Danny White's departure from the lineup at halftime, the Dallas offense had come to a complete standstill, accumulating fewer than 20 total yards. To get his unit moving forward again, Landry decided to put all of his eggs in the basket of his best player – Tony Dorsett. It was Dorsett who caught Pelluer's first pass attempt as an NFL quarterback, snaring it in the right flat and putting a quick juke move on Taylor before running out of bounds. The little flare pass had gained four yards.

Pelluer was slow in calling out the next play in the huddle. Landry and quarterbacks coach Jim Shofner were yelling at him to hurry up. The last thing the Cowboys needed right then was a delay-of-game penalty.

Pelluer got everyone on offense set in time to avoid a five-yard walk-off, received the snap from Tom Rafferty and stuffed the ball in the gut of Dorsett, who used the block of left tackle Chris Schultz to gain six more yards. First-down.

Once again, Pelluer had trouble processing and delivering information in the huddle. Landry was beside himself. Once again, the quarterback managed to get the play off in the nick of time and Dorsett worked his magic to an even better result, bursting through the middle of the defense for 14 yards.

On first-down from the 47-yard line, Pelluer approached the line of scrimmage and saw a defensive formation he didn't like. He looked up at the play-clock, and realized there was no other alternative left to him. Pelluer signaled for a timeout and, while walking toward the sideline, cast a discreet glance at the game-clock. 7:09 remained.

When Steve Pelluer trotted out into the huddle to begin the drive, he harbored no dreams of becoming a hero. In fact, it was determined in his heart to do everything in his power to avoid becoming a goat.

"All I was worried about was not turning the ball over and hurting the team," Pelluer said.

It suited Pelluer just fine that his first handful of passes as a pro were of a conservative nature. A flare pass to Dorsett, four yards. A swing pass to Dorsett, dropped. A short toss to Mike Renfro, incomplete.

But now the fun was over. To convert a third-and-15, Pelluer's kid gloves were going to have to come off. The kid on the block was going to have to make a man's effort to keep this Dallas march going.

Pelluer lined-up in the Shotgun and scanned the defense. In the backfield on the quarterback's right side was Dorsett, while flanking Pelluer on the opposite side was Timmy Newsome. But Pelluer wasn't thinking about another dump-off to a running back. He needed fifteen yards, and that called for the services of one of the three Dallas wide receivers currently on the field.

Tony Hill was positioned in the left slot. Normally a go-to guy in these situations, Hill was merely a silver-and-blue-legged decoration for this play, his hamstring allowing him to do little more than limp through a pass-route. But he had drawn the coverage of New York's top cornerback, Elvis Patterson, for the third-down play, so Hill's presence on the field wasn't without some value.

To Hill's outside was Mike Renfro, a quick, darty receiver who had given the Giant defense fits all afternoon, catching 4 passes for 123 yards and a pair of touchdowns. But on a play the Cowboys needed so desperately to convert, there remained two conspicuous marks against Renfro. 1: He was short, which could easily be a problem for a cold-armed quarterback making a downfield throw. 2: Renfro, as a starting wide receiver, had not practiced long enough with the No. 3 quarterback to develop even a remote sense of chemistry.

So it happened that when Pelluer scanned the field from his Shotgun perch, he knew exactly where, and to whom, he would be going with his next pass. Karl Powe was tall, with long arms, and had caught many a pass from Pelluer over the summer. He was also isolated on the right side against cornerback Ted Watts.

"When he first came into the huddle," said Powe, "I told him, 'You're new at this game, but if you throw it to me, I promise you I'll catch it.'"

The NFC East was on the line. A quarterback with all of three pass attempts to his credit would be relying on a rookie wide receiver with only five career catches in his past. This was a storyline nobody could have predicted three hours earlier.

But Pelluer also knew something else. The Giant defense, crowding the line of scrimmage, had every intention of blitzing on the play. Not that it took a football wizard to discern that.

"Everybody in the stadium knew they were blitzing," he said.

"I saw their 'storm blitz,'" said Powe, "because we had practiced against it and what to do. I just hoped Pelluer saw it too. He did."

The snap from Rafferty back to Pelluer hit the quarterback in the hands, and here came the New York pass-rush, aiming to hit Pelluer where it hurt. Turning his hips, Pelluer had just enough time to set his feet and make the throw before he was belted to the turf by Lawrence Taylor. Did he wince while on the ground? "I was too numb to feel it," Pelluer said afterwards.

If anything, Pelluer's first pressure-packed test in the NFL had the Giants wincing in disbelief. Powe had beaten Watts to the inside on a slant and caught the pass from Pelluer in stride. In the manner of a wily veteran like Drew Pearson, the rookie named Powe then shrugged off the tackle attempt by Watts and turned up-field for even more yardage. Not until he was at the New York 24-yard line was Powe finally wrestled to the ground.

He had gained 28 yards on the play, and more than 60,000 new fans inside a suddenly raucous Texas Stadium.

"Pelluer to Powe – yes, it had come down to that for the Cowboys, and both came through," marveled Randy Galloway in the *Dallas Morning News*.

"That was probably the biggest play of the game," admitted Dorsett. "That enabled us to go down and score our last touchdown."

Dorsett certainly did his part on the final leg of what turned out to be a 72-yard march, getting the Cowboys close with a 10-yard run around end on third-and-1. From there, the rest was left up to Newsome, who walked in untouched off left tackle from 1-yard out to give Dallas a 28-14 lead.

As Newsome celebrated his touchdown run by spiking the ball in the end-zone, Danny White, injured shoulder and all, came out onto the field and gave Pelluer a hug of pure joy. Nobody, not even Roger Staubach, could have led a better or more timelier march than the one that Pelluer had just led.

"I've never been involved in a game when so many people contributed – especially guys who you didn't expect to," said White. "We got some big plays by guys like Mike Renfro and Jim Jeffcoat, who are starters. And then guys like Karl Powe, who came in and make a couple of real crucial plays. Not only did [Powe] read the blitz, but he read the right blitz, because if one guy blitzes he runs one route and if two guys blitz he runs a different route."

"And I was prouder of Steve Pelluer than anybody. I know how tough it is to prepare for a game when you're on the second-string. But I don't think anybody knows how tough it is to prepare as a third-stringer."

But the Giants weren't dead yet. Despite a fourteen-point deficit with less than five minutes remaining, they still had enough energy to make one more push down the stretch, providing the Cowboys and their fans with every reason to pray, and almost as many reasons to expect an ending written with the blood of broken hearts.

Victor Scott knew a little bit about expectations. As a 1984 second-round draft selection of the world-renowned Dallas Cowboys, he was expected to develop into a defensive playmaker for a team that prided itself on being a perennial Super Bowl contender. He practiced alongside Dennis Thurman and Everson Walls every day, listening to them swap tales about one big play or another they had made over the years, wondering all the while if his time in the spotlight would ever come.

Thus far in his young career, Scott had walked a fine line between being a young underachiever and a certifiable disappointment. It was Scott more than any other player who fans blamed for the Cowboys missing out on the playoffs during his rookie season, hearkening back to that dark night at the Orange Bowl during the season finale when Scott allowed Dan Marino to complete one big pass after another against him in the fourth quarter, paving the way for a comeback Dolphins victory in a game Dallas had to win.

Coaches had tried to soften the blows of criticism being aimed at Scott by insisting that he had been playing out of position that night. Scott's lack of speed, Landry and secondary coach Gene Stallings maintained, really made him a better fit at safety, instead of cornerback.

But, due to a logjam at the safety position, Scott continued as a cornerback in 1985. He had started the season on a high note, intercepting a Joe Theismann pass in Dallas' Week 1 blowout of the Redskins. His luck, however, would not hold out. Scott was given a starting job opposite of Everson Walls early in the season when Ron Fellows was coping with a knee injury.

But Scott continued to struggle. After Ron Jaworski shredded him at Veterans Stadium in Week 7, Landry decided he had seen enough, and placed Fellows back in the starting lineup, bad knee or not.

With the Cowboys clinging to a 28-21 lead over the Giants, Scott was on the field as a nickel cornerback, lining up across from New York wide receiver Byron Williams. The Giants had two timeouts and 1:37 in which to navigate 62 yards and tie the game. Scott's job in this situation was simple: Don't allow a big play. Keep the receiver in front, and make a quick, sure-handed tackle in-bounds, to keep the clock running.

Williams was positioned out wide to the right side of the formation, and Scott had positioned himself in a manner to directly cut off any advances that the receiver made toward the middle of the field. If Williams was going to get anything on this play, it would be short and toward the boundary.

The ball was snapped, and Williams charged off the line. After about ten yards, Williams feinted to the outside, as if he was only too willing to accept the small gainer that Scott's coverage was affording him. Scott took the bait, eagerly stepping forward toward the sideline. But Williams was ready for the move, and cut back toward the middle of the field, catching a bullet from Phil Simms and then streaking away downfield.

Though beaten badly on the double-move, Scott never gave up on the play. He ran after the runaway ball-carrier, hurdled a blocker, until Scott finally dragged Williams down at the Dallas 16-yard line. The gain of 46 yards had put the Giants in grand position to complete their comeback bid, while placing Victor Scott once again squarely in the crossfire of public criticism.

It had been a long day for Everson Walls. From the opening series when Phil McConkey left his legs in knots, Walls had been giving chase to runaway Giant wide receivers. It didn't matter whether he was in bump-and-run coverage or was playing a soft-zone. Walls was getting toasted, early and more often than he cared for.

His best coverage technique of the day was something he called "positive mental attitude," and was the very reason he had gone nearly all four quarters without yielding a back-breaking play. Even when beaten and an accurate pass was on the way far in front of him, Walls believed this technique allowed everything to turn out all right.

"You keep thinking, 'drop it, drop it, drop it,'" Walls said, smiling.

Which is exactly what McConkey did. And when Byron Williams got behind Walls early in the fourth quarter down the right sideline, Walls was left alone with his thoughts again. *Drop it, drop it, drop it.* Williams lunged, but he couldn't quite get a hold on the ball. The power of positive thinking had saved Walls for a second time. At least, that's what he'd have the world believe.

Now the Giants were scrambling, the offense running down the field to catch up with Williams, who had just run past Victor Scott for 46 yards. The eyes of Texas Stadium cast a glance upwards, nervous hearts beating out a slow, rhythmic pulse in time with the tick-tick-ticking of the game-clock. Eighty-seconds. Then seventy-seconds remained. The ball was snapped, and the Giants were going again. Phil Simms was rolling out to his right and had his eye fixed on the figure of Williams, who had gotten away from Walls and was standing in the front corner of the end-zone.

Simms' pass sailed through the crisp, cold air, straight toward its intended target. Walls, out of position yet again, turned to his magical mental chant as a last resort. *Drop it, drop it, drop it.* Williams jumped, and this time he managed to hold onto the ball with both hands. But he had landed with one foot out-of-bounds. What initially was thought to be a catch was actually an incompletion, of equal value to a drop. Walls clapped his hands together in relief.

Second-down from the Dallas 16-yard line. The clock showed 59 seconds. Dextor Clinkscale blitzed into the backfield, forcing a quick, errant throw from the Giant quarterback. 55 ticks still to go.

The same Randy White who had incurred a 15-yard penalty against Dallas for a personal-foul on the previous New York possession then rumbled around the end and delivered a withering blow to the backside of an unsuspecting Simms. The sack moved the Giants back to the 24-yard line, and brought up fourth-down.

Over on the New York sideline, Bill Parcells signaled for a timeout, and called Simms over to talk about the next play. Head coach and quarterback soon agreed on a plan. More than just pick up a first-down, the Giants were going to try to score a touchdown on fourth-down.

Parcells and Simms were expecting the Cowboys to bring a full-house blitz into the backfield. But when Simms walked to the line of scrimmage and saw both safeties, Clinkscale and Michael Downs, parked in the outfield, he knew their original plan wasn't going to work. It was time for Plan B.

Simms stepped out from under center with the ball and rolled out once more to the right side. Ed "Too Tall" Jones had dropped out in zone coverage, affording the quarterback an easy path to the edge. But before he could get his feet comfortably set, Downs came flying at him from out of nowhere in almost the same manner as he had on the final play of Dallas' Week 5 victory in New York.

With Downs in his face, Simms was forced to deliver the pass toward Williams in a side-arm motion. The ball that sailed toward Williams along the boundary and near the marker looked for a moment as if it would provide the Giants with a first-down near the 6-yard line. But as Williams reached out, Victor Scott reached in and plucked the ball away, tapping his toes while falling out of bounds to author the game-saving division-clinching interception.

And the celebration began with all the earnestness of a bursting dam. Scott, when he sprinted back onto the field while holding the ball aloft, was mobbed by each and every one of Thurman's Thieves. Dennis Thurman. Walls. Downs. Clinkscale. Bill Bates. Ron Fellows. Even Vince Albritton, a safety/linebacker added to the roster from the injured list at mid-season, came over to offer congratulations.

The procession continued over on the sideline. Ernie Stautner gave Scott a hug and an atta-boy, as did Gene Stallings. Randy White patted him on the back.

Yes, Victor Scott was a hero. As were all the Cowboys on this day.

Only Tom Landry, it seemed, was too busy to get caught up in the moment. While the party had begun off to one side of the Dallas sideline, Landry was on the other side explaining to Pelluer the proper rudiments of taking a knee. The old ball coach was taking nothing for granted. And how could he, after the game and the season he had just endured?

Pelluer apparently listened well. He kneeled down twice without fumbling the ball, allowing the final 46 seconds to run off the game-clock. At long last, it was official. The Dallas Cowboys were the champions of the NFC's Eastern Division for the 1985 season. Landry could finally afford to smile.

"This has to rank up there as one of the most important wins for us," said Landry. "You can't measure it in terms of games that you won to get to the Super Bowl, but to win this after the disappointment of the last few years, it's a big one. "…Our offense couldn't have gotten the job done today, when you know going in that the Giants were going to score 21 points – and we were running out of offensive players… So the kicking game had to help, the defense had to help, and just about everybody had to help on our last touchdown drive."

In the victorious locker room, players celebrated as if they had just won the Super Bowl. Champagne bottles were opened and sprayed all over the room. Walls, unable to get his hands on a bottle, had to settle for a few cans of diet Coke before joining in the fun.

"There was lots of emotion with a lot of our guys," said Danny White, recalling the wild party scene in the locker-room. "I think this team has re-discovered the emotion and togetherness we had earlier this year. I, personally, have never felt it like this. I was all choked up and hugging guys. I never felt like kissing a 270-pound guy like Jeffcoat before. "When you're picked to finish fourth or fifth in the division and get blown out a couple of times like we did, it's especially sweet to win the division like this."

Trying to avoid the spray as best he could, Tom Landry walked from locker to locker, shaking hands with his players. In some corners it was too loud for Landry to voice just how proud he was of each and every one of them. But they didn't need to hear it. His smile said it all.

The head coach was dutifully making his rounds, as was his custom after a big victory, until he was stopped by Dennis Thurman, who signaled for Landry to hold up his hand.

"Higher," said Thurman. The two then slapped palms, as roars of delight erupted from behind them.

It was believed to have been the first high-five in the storied and stoic career of Tom Landry. Many tears have been shed since in acknowledgment of it being his last.

PART III

THE
TAKEOVER

CHAPTER 29

A SHIFT IN TACTICS

"[Tex] Schramm actually seemed to end up with more power when [Bum] Bright took over controlling interest of the club."
Bob St. John

    Tom Landry was many things to many people. A coach to fear. A gentleman to admire. A Christian to respect. A role model to look up to. But never in more than 35 years of touring an NFL sideline was he ever accused of being a fool.
    When Bum Bright bought the Dallas Cowboys from Clint Murchison Jr. in March, 1984, Landry knew better than to believe that the old business model had survived the changing of ownership. No longer would Landry be able to bank on the lifetime contract that Murchison had given him and construct a winning roster through slow, painstaking efforts. Bright was a hard-nosed businessman who demanded results. He expected the Cowboys to win, just like they always had. Job security, as Landry had known it for so long in Dallas, had become a thing of the past.

Though certainly innovative, Landry was no idealistic dreamer. He had sat through too many weekday meetings over the years to think of pro football as just a mere game. It was a business, inside and out. Landry had no doubt that if Bright at any time became frustrated with the product on the field and gave the word, then Tex Schramm would have no other choice but to fire the only head coach in franchise history.

But Landry wasn't exactly a sitting duck in this situation. He had options, and he meant to use them. Landry knew that his greatest enemy in this battle against perception was the monumental burden of expectations saddled upon the Cowboys. More than any other franchise in the league, the Cowboys went out of their way every July at the outset of training camp to highlight the fact that they expected to be playing in the Super Bowl on an annual basis. Anything less was an acknowledged disappointment.

Having just watched a boatload of veterans depart from the team, Landry spent Bright's first summer as owner promoting the theory that Dallas would be doing good to merely make the playoffs in 1984. Too many key contributors, Landry insisted, had been lost to expect the Cowboys to make another deep playoff push into January. According to Landry, a Cowboy team which had owned a league-best 12-2 mark the previous December going into a critical showdown with Washington was now a team in a transitional phase.

By hinting that these weren't the same old Cowboys, Landry was signaling to the owner's box for a little patience and understanding. But Schramm's attempt to alter his coaching staff after the 1984 campaign gave Landry all the indication he needed that Bright had not gotten the memo. 9-7 wasn't good enough for the owner. He wanted more.

Landry's stance for the 1985 season had been little different than the previous one. The first and primary goal for the Cowboys was to rebound and make the playoffs. Their "outstanding" goal was to win the division. Landry wouldn't even entertain the notion that the Cowboys would be competing for a Super Bowl.

He didn't want to say that the Cowboys were in full-fledged rebuilding mode. Not with guys like Tony Dorsett,

Randy White, Tony Hill, and Everson Walls still on the roster and performing at a high level. But Landry did make sure the outside world understood that the Cowboys were definitely regrouping.

With an emotional December victory over New York now in the rearview mirror, Landry and the Cowboys had achieved the near impossible by winning the NFC East in 1985. Their "outstanding" goal had become a reality. Was that going to be enough to preserve the integrity of Landry's sacred domain? Had the Cowboys shown enough for Schramm to call off the hunt for another season?

As it turned out, Landry wouldn't have to wait very long to find out.

It was no mirage of the mind. Tex Schramm was a different man walking around team headquarters in 1985 than in years past. For so long a brash promoter of organizational optimism, Schramm had caught numerous members of the sports media off-guard over the course of the season with multiple displays of moroseness. More than just a promoter, Schramm was now a man on the prod.

He butted heads with Tom Landry before the second game when 18 players were allowed to testify in court for a former teammate rather than attend practice. He subtly questioned the motivation of the team after the Cowboys had taken a turn through the meat-grinder that was the Chicago Bears. As if losing 44-0 wasn't bad enough, Schramm found it especially embarrassing for it to happen at Texas Stadium and on national television.

A few weeks later, Schramm was openly cursing Landry and his play-calling during the Cowboys' 50-24 loss in Cincinnati. During the ensuing week of preparation to play the Giants, he then attempted to add a spark of energy to what he believed was a lifeless Dallas locker-room.

"This is a really key game for the Cowboys," Schramm said of the showdown with New York, "because if we win, we can be regarded perhaps as a Cinderella team. If we lose, this current Cowboy team could be regarded as the worst in the last 20 years."

It was with Schramm's new behavioral patterns very much in mind that *St. Petersburg Times* columnist Howard Mizell made the following observation after the 1985 season.

"Seems to me," wrote Mizell, "I notice a little more panic in the [Cowboys] organization than I did 15 years ago."

What appeared to be panic from afar was actually something quite different. Schramm wasn't the same man as in former years because he was no longer in the same leadership role. Longtime *Dallas Morning News* columnist Bob St. John perceived this fact, writing in his 1989 book *The Landry Legend*,

"Schramm actually seemed to end up with more power when [Bum] Bright took over controlling interest of the club." Schramm did exercise more power during Bright's tenure. Not by design, but out of necessity.

It has been presumed by historians ever since that the impact of Clint Murchison Jr. upon the Cowboys disappeared when he sold the team in 1984. But nothing could be farther from the truth. You see, Schramm's pledge to Murchison wasn't finished when Bright agreed to become the new owner. Rather, it was only beginning.

When Murchison made his final request as the team owner - asking that Schramm find another owner who would allow the Cowboys' superstructure to remain in place - the team, per se, wasn't at the forefront of his concerns. The people were. It's why, prior to selling the team, the owner raised Schramm's salary to $400,000 and gave him a $2.5 million bonus, and why Landry was awarded a $2 million bonus and Gil Brandt a bonus of $500,000.

But it was more than just money weighing on Murchison's mind. Murchison, more than anything else, wanted to ensure that these three figureheads who had been so loyal to the franchise over the years were taken care of when he wasn't around. It was up to Schramm to make sure that happened. Schramm knew exactly what he was getting into by luring Bright into the owner's chair. Bright was up front about his motives. He expected the Cowboys to make money and open up other business opportunities for him. Bright was honest. He promised to give Schramm and Landry a free hand to run the show as they always had. And Schramm had no doubt that Bright would do just that…as long as things were rolling along smoothly on the football field.

Such had been Bright's mode of operation all the way up the long corporate ladder. Bright never hesitated to shake things up in the face of unfulfilled expectations. Whereas Murchison would remain committed to an associate even past the point of no return, Bright was quick to sever business ties, remaining committed steadfastly to the stolid demands of the bottom-line.

In Dallas, the only bottom-line that mattered was winning football games, and Schramm didn't have to guess who Bright would be inclined to blame in the event that the Cowboys began to struggle to meet these demands. Schramm, for whatever reason, was in Bright's good graces, the new owner often referring to him as "the best general manager in football." If the Cowboys started losing more than was their norm and Schramm – the front-office czar of the organization - was beyond the reach of reproach, that left Landry – the field general - in an exposed position.

How could Schramm serve to protect Landry from the wrath of Bright? Once again, the shadow of Murchison edges its way back into the picture.

For the majority of his twenty-four-year partnership with Murchison, Tex Schramm had worked without a contract. Mutual trust and a free-flowing line of communication between the two made a contract unnecessary.

Bum Bright didn't learn about this until late in the negotiating process to buy the team, when he suggested to Schramm that he have his lawyers draw up the papers to define the working parameters for the new owner and his general manager. Bright thought it odd that an orderly office stooge like Schramm would reject such an arrangement so flatly. A contract, he reminded Schramm, would offer protection for both individuals.

But Schramm wasn't after any legal protection. As long as he had an understanding with Bright, a handshake would suffice. This was about a partnership between two individuals. This was about two men and their given word.

Bright didn't push the issue. He had already given Murchison and Schramm everything else they had asked for, so why argue over one more petty detail? He shook hands with Schramm, and that was that.

What may seem like a minor issue now was actually a major victory for Schramm at the time, one that paid dividends for him and the franchise down the road. The absence of a contract allowed Schramm to continue acting as the de-facto owner of the franchise, and even put him in a position to override the wishes of Bright at certain times. And what could Bright do about it? His hands were tied. He had already given his word that Schramm could run the team as he saw fit.

Nevertheless, Schramm recognized that Bright was just the type of man to go behind the general manager's back and fire the head coach on his own, if he deemed it fitting and proper. It was Schramm's job, therefore, to pacify the owner in subtle ways, and be proactive toward change in the face of on-the-field failings. He had to keep Bright in the owner's box and off the sidelines.

Schramm realized that there were far more days in Dallas behind Landry than ahead of him. The "Man in the Funny Hat" wasn't going to coach forever. Several discussions pertaining to Landry's longevity had taken place between general manager and head coach in recent years, merely as an acknowledgment that Landry's career was, in fact, winding down.

But Schramm wasn't trying to push him out the door. Retirement was a decision for Landry to make, and him only. It was the way Murchison would have wanted it and was therefore part of Schramm's final pact with the founding owner of the Cowboys. Landry's lifetime contract may have been dissolved with the arrival of Bright upon the scene, but it still existed in the heart of Schramm, who became Landry's protectorate over the next handful of turbulent seasons.

CHAPTER 30

THE END

"In my opinion, [injuries] is what prevented us from going any farther than we did."
Tom Landry, after the Cowboys were eliminated from the playoffs by Los Angeles

Maybe the situation would have been different in Dallas had the Cowboys outlasted Dan Marino and the Miami Dolphins on the final day of the 1984 regular season to qualify for the playoffs. Or maybe not. It's hard to tell concerning a franchise that prided itself on being more than mere participants in the NFL postseason.

The only thing Tex Schramm knew for certain was that Bum Bright wasn't going to sit back in the shadows for very long if his football team continued to flounder near the middle of the pack, making 1985 a critical campaign for Tom Landry. Yes, the clock was ticking on Tom in 1985. Tom knew it. More importantly, Tex knew it too.

Schramm had done the only thing he knew to do. He had opened his big mouth and promised Clint Murchison Jr. that he would take care of Landry in future seasons, and Schramm was a man of his word. Nothing Bright could ever say or do would persuade Schramm to personally pull the plug on his head coach, so the general manager had to give the owner every reason to refrain from such an inclination.

The simplest method of keeping Bright at bay was for the Cowboys to go on a regular season rampage in 1985, lock up the top seed in the conference and win one or two playoff games. Winning the Super Bowl in New Orleans would be even better.

In the more-than-likely event that the Cowboys underperformed on the field, Schramm's flair for theatrics would come in handy. Bright needed to be shown that the Cowboys weren't content with mediocrity, leaving Schramm with no other alternative than to put on an act that Bright could relate to.

Bright wasn't the kind of owner to be content with his team merely qualifying for the postseason. Bright wasn't an owner who cared for excuses or multi-layered reasons why failure was unavoidable. He didn't want to hear about injuries or a roster changeover.

There waiting in the gap was Schramm, who provided a tough brand of leadership that Bright could see, hear and understand. Normally a boastful cheerleader of his squad, Schramm seemed to go out of his way to dwell on the Cowboys' shortcomings, relying predominantly on a blunt, cranky demeanor to get his point across.

He questioned the effort and heart of the players after Chicago steamrolled Dallas at Texas Stadium in Week 11. Then he dared to criticize the coaching in Cincinnati. As if that wasn't enough, Schramm publicly stated a few hours later that the Cowboys were one loss to the New York Giants away from being "one of the worst" teams in franchise annals from the past twenty years. Would Schramm ever let up?

Schramm celebrated with the rest of the team after Dallas outlasted New York to claim the division title, even calling it "one of the biggest wins" in recent memory. But he still wanted more, his mind going automatically to the Cowboys' next opponent on the schedule - the San Francisco 49ers.

The regular season finale at Candlestick Park was filled with meaning for Dallas. Beating the 49ers would assure the Cowboys of the No. 2 seed in the NFC playoffs, a first-round bye, and a home date with Los Angeles in the Divisional round. A Cowboy victory would also prevent San Francisco from claiming the final wild-card playoff spot, a sweet thought indeed when considering all of the agony the 49ers had inflicted upon the Cowboys during the decade.

But there was another reason that Schramm wanted so desperately for the Cowboys to end the regular season on a high note. Bum Bright's beloved Texas A&M Aggies had won the Southwestern Conference in 1985 and were scheduled to be in Dallas for the Cotton Bowl on New Year's Day. What could be better than for the Cowboys to host a playoff game later that week? Not only would it serve to validate the efforts of the entire team for that season, but would also go a long way toward pacifying the owner, whose financial investment toward the brand-new "Crown Suites" inside Texas Stadium had yet to yield anticipated returns.

Which explains some of Schramm's frustration at the 31-16 loss to San Francisco that Dallas suffered on the following Sunday. Even with Danny White on the bench nursing a shoulder injury, the Cowboys started fast by the Bay and were looking to build upon a 13-0 lead in the second quarter when Tony Dorsett lost a fumble deep in 49er territory. The turnover turned the game around, leading to a 49-yard scoring pass from Joe Montana to Dwight Clark that jump-started the stagnant Niners' offense. The Cowboys led 16-10 at halftime but were thoroughly outplayed after the break.

Afterwards, Schramm blew his top when a few players attempted to downplay the defeat by saying the only thing that mattered was for the team to play well in the playoffs. "If you don't want to go out there and win, then why play the [!@#$%!] game?" Schramm said off the air.

In front of a live microphone, Schramm was much more diplomatic. "It looked like we had a team that said, 'Don't get too concerned with this one – wait for the big one,'" said

Schramm. "Then you get to the big game and rely on the stakes to be the motivator, rather than being concerned about losing or being fearful of becoming embarrassed. [In past years] we slipped into a certain syndrome – when we had to turn it on, we could. That attitude didn't always work. We have to get back to basics, that competitive athletes play for the sake of winning."

Two weeks later, the Cowboys turned in a most disheartening postseason effort at Anaheim Stadium against the Rams. Danny White looked rusty after the long layoff. Tony Hill was still limping around on one good hamstring. Kurt Petersen left the game and was replaced at guard by Broderick Thompson. Then Mike Renfro and Rafael Septien went down with injuries.

"When we got into the LA game, we got hit where we didn't have anybody – kickers, receivers, offensive guard. Every injury came in that ballgame where we couldn't replace people," recalled Landry.

Everson Walls did his part to stall the Los Angeles passing attack, intercepting two Dieter Brock passes. But he was no hand at slowing down Eric Dickerson. The Rams' superstar running back ran over, through, and around the Dallas defense, accumulating a playoff-record 248 yards and two touchdowns.

The events down on the field thoroughly rankled Schramm, who ranted and raved, swilled booze and shouted profanity in the press box for the majority of the game. After the final whistle had been blown, Schramm paced the Cowboys' locker room carrying what *Dallas Times Herald* columnist Frank Luksa referred to as "a full boiler of steam." Schramm was embarrassed and furious, and not necessarily in that order. The NFC East champion Cowboys had bowed out with a 20-0 whimper of a defeat.

"We're not going with the same deck again," Schramm bellowed.

Schramm, once again, was as good as his word. He was about to shuffle the coaching deck in Dallas and insert a shiny new ace into the stack while he was at it. Landry would have expected nothing less.

The Cowboys had come far in 1985, but not far enough. The clock had struck zero in Dallas. A newcomer named Paul

Hackett was stepping in. Landry was stepping back. America's Team would never be the same.

Tom Landry found himself standing at one of life's crossroads. It was only a matter of days until Tex Schramm would hire some bright young assistant to inject a new spark and new life into an increasingly unpredictable Dallas offense. There was no way for Landry to stall the wheels of change for another year this time. Schramm had spoken, and that was that. Youth. It was the lack thereof that Schramm continually used against Landry's current staff. Offensive line coach Jim Myers was 64. Quality control coach Neil Armstrong was 60. Defensive coordinator Ernie Stautner was 59. Wide receivers coach Dick Nolan was 54. Linebackers coach Jerry Tubbs was 51, while both special teams coach Gene Stallings and quarterbacks coach Jim Shofner were 50.

Schramm wanted younger blood in the mix, someone with new ideas and a better ability to relate to the modern football player. Schramm was worried that the Cowboys were growing increasingly stale.

For 26 years, Landry's coaching staff had been a sacred establishment founded on the bedrock of solidarity. In many ways, his assistants were no different than his players. Cowboy staff members weren't allowed much room for free-lancing in the classroom or on the practice field. They either toed the line and reinforced the fundamentals of his system, or they were sent packing.

But things were going to be different in Dallas moving forward. Landry would still be the head coach, but no longer would his voice and formula be autonomous at meetings. The door had been opened and a chalk-wielding stranger was about to step into the room.

Landry mulled over retirement in the days following his team's playoff loss to Los Angeles. But he didn't want to step down with the Cowboys on a downward trend. So Landry eventually settled on a compromise, informing Schramm that he planned on coaching for one or maybe two more years, before calling it a career.

Looking back upon it, Landry wished he could have a re-do of that decision. "The end of that '85 season would have been a logical time to retire," Landry wrote in his autobiography.

Landry stayed, and was there to welcome Paul Hackett into the building as the Cowboys' new passing game coordinator. Hackett came over from Bill Walsh's staff in San Francisco, where he had tutored 49er quarterbacks and receivers for the past three seasons. He wore a Super Bowl ring on his finger and was heralded by the local media as an up-and-coming genius. A few writers even dared to tab Hackett as the heir-apparent to Landry's head coaching throne.

The signing of Hackett signaled the end of Shofner's three-year stint as the Cowboys' quarterbacks coach. Schramm still held Shofner largely responsible for the rift between Danny White and Gary Hogeboom that caused so many problems for the Cowboys in 1984. And despite the fact that Dallas led the NFL in passing yards for the 1985 season, Schramm was still disappointed that the offense failed in so many key situations.

Shofner didn't take kindly to the coaching staff shake-up after the season, feeling as if Landry was attempting to force him into semi-retirement. He defended his work, pointing out that the Dallas offense had improved in nearly every area from the previous season, statistically speaking. But, as one local scribe pointed out, "that's like saying Phyllis Diller is getting prettier." Though he was offered a job in the Cowboys' front office, Shofner quit and joined new Cardinals head coach Gene Stallings in St. Louis.

Schramm attempted to make one more alteration to the offensive staff, but when negotiations with Rams' offensive line coach Hudson Houck broke down at the last minute, he was forced to allow Jim Myers to coach the line by himself for his final go-around on an NFL sideline. Not that Schramm was overly put out by Houck's sudden change of heart. There was still plenty of other moves being made to keep his attention.

Bob Ackles was brought in from the Canadian Football League to be the Cowboys' pro personnel agent. Joe Bailey was promoted to the title of vice president of administration and would oversee all contract negotiations with players. Both of these moves were designed to allow Gil Brandt to focus primarily upon his area of greatest expertise - college scouting. Just like he was doing with Landry, Schramm was taking care of Brandt also.

The influx of new faces invoked a spirit of optimism around the city of Dallas. For the first time since the team played its games at the Cotton Bowl, the Cowboys were being promoted as young and exciting. That excitement centered around the resident genius now working at team headquarters.

Hackett's title in Dallas was only a poor disguise for what was so apparent to everyone else in town. Hackett wasn't there to merely coordinate the Cowboys passing attack. He was supposed to right the entire ship. Hackett was the mastermind on the block expected to fix everything that ailed the Dallas offense, from passers and catchers on down to runners and blockers. He was, in fact, the unofficial offensive coordinator.

Landry turned the play-book over to Hackett, allowing him to re-write the entire Cowboy offense to suit his own liking. Landry, meanwhile, shifted his focus to the defensive side of the ball, where he would call all of the signals for what turned out to be a topsy-turvy 1986 season.

Hackett's offense came out of the gates on fire, scoring more than 30 points in six of the first eight games, as Dallas soared to the top of the division with a mark of 6-2. With 1985 draftee Herschel Walker having joined Tony Dorsett in the backfield, the Cowboys were a trendy pick to go all the way to Pasadena for Super Bowl XXI.

But, during a Week 9 showdown with the Giants at the Meadowlands, the fatal flaw in Hackett's scheme came back to bite the Cowboys in a big way. Hackett's formula on passing plays was similar to a lot of the West Coast gurus infiltrating the NFL ranks at the time. He preferred to have four, or even five, receiving options for his quarterback to look for. With Walker, Dorsett, Doug Cosbie, Tony Hill, and new rookie wide receiving sensation Mike Sherrard in the lineup, it sounded like a good idea. But it didn't do much for the Cowboys' pass-protection.

Defenses were blitzing Dallas in earnest. Danny White was experienced enough at quarterback to know where to go with the ball, and he made some big plays against the blitz early in the season. White managed to withstand these weekly Sunday beatings for a while, but it was a crunching blow he received from a teammate during practice while – of all things – running downfield on a punt drill that prevented him from playing against Denver in Week 5, a game that Dallas handily lost. He returned two weeks later but was having trouble playing a complete game without suffering one ailment or another.

Nevertheless, the Cowboys continued winning. Then came New York. During the second quarter of a crucial matchup with the Giants, the pocket collapsed in the face of White again, leaving him with a broken wrist. He was placed on injured reserve.

With Gary Hogeboom having been shipped to Indianapolis during the off-season, it was left up to Steve Pelluer to step in and not only save the day, as he had done the previous December versus New York, but save the entire season.

Unfortunately, this wasn't the same Pelluer that fans had showered bouquets upon in 1985. Pelluer, after having grown accustomed to Landry's play-book, had yet to grow comfortable with Hackett's offense. The ripple effect was visually and statistically disturbing.

Not only was Pelluer's natural release of his passes slower than that of White's, he was often hesitant as to which receiver to throw the ball to, compounding the Cowboys' problems in pass-protection and inviting a backfield bludgeoning not seen in Dallas since the dog days of the early 1960s. Pelluer was sacked at least four times in six of the final eight regular season games, including an 11-sack nightmare at San Diego in Week 10, the only game, ironically, that Dallas managed to win down the stretch.

Landry felt handcuffed during the season's second half. On numerous occasions, he went to key the radio during games to offer a helpful suggestion to Hackett up in the coaches booth, only to catch himself. Not only had he promised Hackett a free hand to run the offense, but Landry found it nigh impossible to suggest technical alterations to an offense that he wasn't familiar with. For Landry, the terminology attached to Hackett's scheme was like an altogether different language, making the head coach a virtual outsider where the offense was concerned. Landry's input was severely limited.

In early December, Landry decided he had seen enough. With the Cowboys' playoff hopes hanging in the balance, the head coach made his presence felt on the offensive side for the first time all season, eliminating an allotment of Hackett's plays from the game-plan and inserting a handful of his own. But the power move was too little and far too late to save the Cowboys.

Shortly after Dallas finished 7-9 for their first losing season since 1964, Landry began to experience a change of heart. A lot had changed in one year, providing Landry much food for thought.

Danny White's age was beginning to show. The Cowboys, undoubtedly, were in need of a franchise quarterback.

Hackett obviously had a lot to learn about making adjustments as an NFL coordinator. Surely Schramm didn't plan on making him the next head coach in Dallas.

And Bum Bright's empire was suddenly facing a financial crisis. 1986 had been the worst year since the Great Depression for America's banking system. A total of 138 U.S. banks went under, the majority of them centered in the oil and agricultural states of the Midwest, Rocky Mountains, and Southwest. Texas was hit particularly hard with 26 bank failures being recorded. A collapse of the real estate industry was on the horizon. Maybe, just maybe, Bright had too much on his plate in the corporate world to get too involved with his football team.

After thinking it all over, Landry told Schramm that he wanted to coach past the 1987 season and asked for a new three-year contract with a $1 million annual salary, just like Chuck Noll (Pittsburgh), Don Shula (Miami), Joe Gibbs (Washington) and Walsh in San Francisco each had. Schramm said he would see what could be done and went to confer with the owner.

Bright balked at Landry's request, telling Schramm to instead give him three separate one-year contracts with salaries of $800,000, $900,000, and $1 million. Under that agreement,

Landry's contract could be terminated any time that Bright chose to.

When Landry insisted that he wanted a three-year deal with fully-guaranteed money, Schramm relented. Going behind Bright's back, he gave Landry the brand-new three-year pact and broke the story to the press.

Hackett saw the headlines in the morning paper and was very disturbed. When Hackett had come to Dallas, he had been led to believe that Landry was on the way out. Now, it appeared as if Landry was preparing to be on the Dallas sideline into the 1990s.

When Hackett confronted Schramm, he got little more than a shrug in response. "It was out of my hands," Schramm said.

Schramm had surreptitiously bought Landry some much-needed security as the head coach. But it couldn't save the Cowboys from the trouble awaiting them.

Landry began to assert his position more frequently at offensive meetings, causing Hackett to become frustrated. Rather than the virtual free hand he had been allowed the year before, Hackett was definitely collaborating with Landry on everything pertaining to the weekly game-plan. Elsewhere in the office, a few tenured assistants were irked that Landry seemed to be listening less to them and more to new offensive line coach Jim Erkenbeck.

On the field things were changing too, and not necessarily for the better. Tony Hill retired. Sherrard suffered a season-ending leg injury during a training camp scrimmage. Tony Dorsett appeared to have lost a half-step after off-season knee surgery. Throw a tumultuous players-strike in September on top of all that, and you have the basic outline of a very disappointing 7-8 campaign for the Cowboys in 1987.

Bright met with Schramm after the season and voiced his desire to fire Landry. It was then that he learned of the three-year fully-guaranteed contract. It would cost Bright and the Cowboys $2 million cash to be rid of Landry. With Bright's financial belt already tightened beyond discomfort, he swallowed his pride and allowed Landry to remain for a twenty-ninth season in Dallas.

With Bright's empire on the rocks, rumors had surfaced during the season that the Cowboys were on the market again. The owner's misfortune proved to be a grand opportunity for the head coach. In the aftermath of the 1987 season, Landry took back the reins of the Dallas offense, demoting Hackett to the role of quarterbacks coach. Landry was beginning to reestablish himself as the unquestionable king of the Cowboys.

But Bright wasn't about to let Schramm handpick another owner who suited his own purposes. He had some unfinished business that needed to be done before he officially bowed out, a special brand of payback that, from his perspective, was long overdue. And Bright meant to have his way this time.

During the Cowboys' long and dreary 3-13 season in 1988, Bright stayed busy courting prospective owners. Cash on the barrel-head was important, but the criteria most dear to Bright's heart centered around the head coach. Any group of investors that wanted to keep Landry around would be automatically dismissed. Bright meant to have Landry fired, even if it was his last act as owner.

Behind Schramm's back, Bright began to dicker with Arkansas wheeler-and-dealer Jerry Jones. By late February of 1989, the two businessmen had come to an agreement. Jones would buy the team, dismiss Landry, and bring in Jimmy Johnson from the University of Miami to become the head coach in Dallas.

Bright was satisfied. His vengeance was complete.

EPILOGUE

A FINAL WORD

(Note from the Author)

As you have undoubtedly gleaned from the previous pages, the 1985 season was a momentous hour in the history of the Dallas Cowboys. Not only did it mark the twentieth consecutive winning season for the franchise and Tom Landry's final playoff team in Dallas, it also marked the final year that Landry had complete control over his coaching staff.

It is my hope that, by reading this book, you have obtained a more complete knowledge, understanding, and appreciation for the front-office figures who made the star-spangled franchise from Dallas into the one and only "America's Team."

Landry's Last Stand is the story of the far-reaching impact of a promise well-kept, of Tex Schramm's struggle to serve two masters, and how Landry and his team became winners one last time.

It truly is a story unique in its time.

And for all of the fans out there who have requested that I write a book about the 1980s Cowboys, I hope that the in-depth look into the 1985 season satisfies your appetite and brings back many precious memories. In the event that you're still yearning for more, a few notes and quotes about the 1985 season have been compiled below...

1: The 1985 season afforded Danny White the worst beating of his pro football career. He suffered (1) a sprained right hand, (2) fractured ribs, (3) bruised ribs, (4) concussion, (5) neck sprain, (6) bruised left shoulder, (7) separated left rib cartilage, and (8) a sprained left ankle.

2: The Dallas defense set a franchise record in 1985 for net yards allowed, yielding 5,608 over the 16-game slate.

3: In 1985 the Cowboys had three different players (Tony Hill, Mike Renfro & Doug Cosbie) record 60 or more pass receptions. Before the season, the Cowboys had never had more than one player with 60 or more pass receptions in a single season.

4: The 1985 Cowboys notched 62 defensive sacks, breaking the old franchise record of 60 set back in 1966.

5: *"This has been the strangest season...because the valleys have been so low. I've never gone through the tremendous ups and downs we went through this season."*
Tex Schramm

6: *"I don't think this team has as much talent as teams in the past. It's the most unusual team I've been associated with, because they've had so many highs and lows. This team has to be pretty competitive to bounce back after the catastrophes we've had."*
Offensive line coach Jim Myers, after the conclusion of the regular season

7: *"I'm proud of our team. We had a long way to come... I'd be the first to say we were on the verge of disaster many times, but it didn't happen."*
Tom Landry, after the conclusion of the regular season

8: *"Some of the most embarrassing moments in club history came in 1985."*
Mike Rabun, *Dallas Cowboys Weekly*

9: *"That [the Cowboys] managed to win a divisional title in a season they were widely picked to finish fourth showed how good of a coach Tom Landry is."*
Tom Weir, *USA Today*

10: *"For that team to win the NFC East was one of the all-time great upsets in the history of sports. People just couldn't see it because it happened over several games instead of in just one."*
New Dallas offensive coordinator Paul Hackett in the spring of 1986, after reviewing the tapes from the previous season

11: *"The team I enjoyed the most was the '85 team that won the East. It was so outmanned. There was no reason why New York or Washington shouldn't have won the division that year. We won it because of guys like Mike Renfro. And Steve Pelluer coming in and throwing to Karl Powe. I enjoyed coaching them and seeing them perform."*
Tom Landry

Bibliography

An Autobiography: Tom Landry by Tom Landry with Gregg Lewis (Zondervan/Harper Collins, 1990)

Tex! by Bob St. John (Prentice Hall, 1988)

The Murchisons by Jane Wolfe (St. Martin's Press, 1989)

The Landry Legend by Bob St. John (Word Publishing, 1989)

The Man Inside...Landry by Bob St. John (Word Publishing, 1979)

The Catch by Gary Myers (Crown Publishers, 2009)

One Knee Equals Two Feet by John Madden with Dave Anderson (Villard Books, 1986)

God's Coach by Skip Bayless (Simon & Schuster, 1990)

The Redskins Encyclopedia by Michael Richman (Temple University Press, 2008)

The Great Texas Banking Crash by Joseph M. Grant (University of Texas Press, 1996)

Dallas Cowboys Weekly/Star Magazine

Dave Campbell's Texas Football Magazine

Texas Monthly Magazine

People Magazine

Sports Illustrated

Sporting News

Street & Smith

Pro Football Illustrated

Petersen's Pro Football Annual

Inside Sports

Forbes

Pro Football Weekly

Dallas Morning News

Dallas Times Herald

USA Today

Los Angeles Times

New York Times

Associated Press

Detroit Free Press

Miami News

Fort Lauderdale News

St. Petersburg Times

ABOUT THE AUTHOR

At the age of 18, Ryan Bush began writing a weekly column about the Dallas Cowboys for several small-town newspapers across Texas. His talent was initially recognized by H. Leon Smith, then Owner of *The Clifton Record*, a multi-award-winning newspaper in central Texas. After three years, his literary pursuit and passion for the Cowboys led him to write **Decade of Futility**, his first book. Ryan published his second book in 2016, **The Dirty Dozen.** He is currently working on additional projects about the Dallas Cowboys to be published in the future.

You may follow Ryan and his Dallas Cowboys' work online at:

Web Site - Dallas Cowboys Vault at RyanBush.biz
Facebook Pages:
    Dallas Cowboys Vault
    Decade of Futility
    Dallas Cowboys Dirty Dozen
    Dallas Cowboys Landry's Last Stand
Twitter - @rcbushCowboys

Landry's Last Stand

www.ingramcontent.com/pod-product-compliance
Lightning Source LLC
LaVergne TN
LVHW051513070426
835507LV00023B/3091